GOD AND HUMANITY

T&T Clark Explorations in Reformed Theology

Series Editors
Paul T. Nimmo
Paul Dafydd Jones

Editorial Board
Christophe Chalamet
David A. S. Fergusson
Angela Dienhart Hancock
Leanne Van Dyk
Matthias D Wüthrich

GOD AND HUMANITY

Herman Bavinck and Theological Anthropology

N. Gray Sutanto

LONDON • NEW YORK • OXFORD • NEW DELHI • SYDNEY

T&T CLARK

Bloomsbury Publishing Plc, 50 Bedford Square, London, WC1B 3DP, UK
Bloomsbury Publishing Inc, 1359 Broadway, New York, NY 10018, USA
Bloomsbury Publishing Ireland, 29 Earlsfort Terrace, Dublin 2, D02 AY28, Ireland

BLOOMSBURY, T&T CLARK and the T&T Clark logo are trademarks
of Bloomsbury Publishing Plc

First published in Great Britain 2024
Paperback edition published 2026

Copyright © N. Gray Sutanto, 2024

N. Gray Sutanto has asserted his right under the Copyright,
Designs and Patents Act, 1988, to be identified as Author of this work.

For legal purposes the Acknowledgments on pp. vi–vii constitute
an extension of this copyright page.

All rights reserved. No part of this publication may be: i) reproduced or transmitted in any form, electronic or mechanical, including photocopying, recording or by means of any information storage or retrieval system without prior permission in writing from the publishers; or ii) used or reproduced in any way for the training, development or operation of artificial intelligence (AI) technologies, including generative AI technologies. The rights holders expressly reserve this publication from the text and data mining exception as per Article 4(3) of the Digital Single Market Directive (EU) 2019/790.

Bloomsbury Publishing Plc does not have any control over, or responsibility for, any third-party websites referred to or in this book. All internet addresses given in this book were correct at the time of going to press. The author and publisher regret any inconvenience caused if addresses have changed or sites have ceased to exist, but can accept no responsibility for any such changes.

A catalogue record for this book is available from the British Library.

Library of Congress Cataloging-in-Publication Data
Names: Sutanto, Nathaniel Gray, 1991- author.
Title: God and humanity : Herman Bavinck and theological anthropology / N. Gray Sutanto.
Description: London ; New York : T&T Clark, 2024. | Series: T&T Clark explorations in reformed theology ; vol. 5 | Includes bibliographical references and index.
Identifiers: LCCN 2023058389 (print) | LCCN 2023058390 (ebook) |
ISBN 9780567709011 (hb) | ISBN 9780567709066 (paperback) |
ISBN 9780567709028 (epdf) | ISBN 9780567709059 (epub)
Subjects: LCSH: Bavinck, Herman, 1854–1921. | Theological anthropology–Reformed Church. | Reformed Church–Doctrines.
Classification: LCC BX9479.B35 S87 2024 (print) | LCC BX9479.B35 (ebook) |
DDC 233.088/2842492–dc23/eng/20240224
LC record available at https://lccn.loc.gov/2023058389
LC ebook record available at https://lccn.loc.gov/2023058390

ISBN:	HB:	978-0-5677-0901-1
	PB:	978-0-5677-0906-6
	ePDF:	978-0-5677-0902-8
	ePUB:	978-0-5677-0905-9

Series: T&T Clark Explorations in Reformed Theology

Typeset by Integra Software Services Pvt. Ltd.

For product safety related questions contact productsafety@bloomsbury.com.

To find out more about our authors and books visit www.bloomsbury.com
and sign up for our newsletters.

CONTENTS

Acknowledgments	vi
List of Abbreviations	viii

Chapter 1
BAVINCK AND THEOLOGICAL ANTHROPOLOGY   1

Chapter 2
PERSONALITY AND THE UNCONSCIOUS: CHARTING BAVINCK
ON THE UNITY OF BODY AND SOUL   17

Chapter 3
RELIGIOUS CREATURES: REVELATION, AFFECT THEORY,
AND THE COGNITIVE SCIENCE OF RELIGION   43

Chapter 4
KNOWING GOD AND INTRANSIGENT SIN   73

Chapter 5
ORGANIC HUMANITY AND SIN   103

Chapter 6
RACE AND HISTORY   123

Chapter 7
RACE AND RELIGION   147

Chapter 8
CONSUMMATION ANYWAY   169

Chapter 9
BEATIFIC VISION   185

CONCLUSION   201

Bibliography	205
Index	216

ACKNOWLEDGMENTS

I began thinking about this book as soon as I finished a final draft of my first monograph (*God and Knowledge: Herman Bavinck's Theological Epistemology* [London: Bloomsbury T&T Clark, 2020]). As I was writing about Bavinck's epistemology for that first work, I was struck by the way in which such questions were untreatable without asking questions about the human knower, the subject, and thus of human nature. What I found in Bavinck was a particularly humane, Reformed, yet romantic account of the human self. We exist as embodied and religious creatures, exposed to the divine, and embedded in relations. In Bavinck I found resources that developed my own reflections on the intellectual task, and, more deeply, on what it means to be human. Theological anthropology was thus always in the background even as I wrote on those epistemological matters.

I am indebted to many for the writing of this book. Michael Allen, Daniel Treier, Gayle Doornbos, Cameron Clausing, and Gregory Parker Jr. read an earlier draft in full and provided generative feedback. Kelly Kapic, Murray Smith, Skyler Flowers, Stephanie DiMaria, James T. Turner, Suzanne McDonald, and Steven J. Duby read sections of the work and gave valuable encouragement. Thanks are also due, of course, to Marinus de Jong, James Eglinton, and Cory C. Brock, for weekly conversations that have helped shape my own thinking on some of the topics broached in this work (along with checking some of my Dutch readings). Thanks as well to Vincent Bacote, George Harinck, Timothy Keller, Joanna Leidenhag, Henk van den Belt, Jessica Joustra, Simeon Zahl, D. Blair Smith, William Ross, Scott Swain, Harrison Perkins, and Mark McDowell, for help and conversations at different stages of this project. I led a seminar on theological anthropology for a stellar group of students in the Spring of 2023: thanks to Victoria Turner, Isaac Whitney, Joshua Putrasahan, and Jennifer Ilchishin for their engagement with the project there. Steven Preston, my research assistant during the summer of 2023, also helped with some last minute editorial work. Joshua Putrasahan helped with proofreading and with forming the index.

My thanks, as well, to the editors of the T&T Clark *Explorations in Reformed Theology* series, Paul Dafydd Jones and Paul Nimmo, for their comments and encouragement along the way. Their meticulous attention to detail pushed me toward greater clarity, precision, and rigor. This monograph is a much better work due to their editorial oversight, and I count it a privilege for this work to be included within this series. I am grateful, too, to Anna Turton and Jack Curtin at Bloomsbury T&T Clark for their editorial help, as ever. I take responsibility, of course, for any shortcomings that remain.

I was able to test out material for this work in different occasions, including a presentation of earlier chapter drafts in the 2019 Bavinck Ethics conference, and the 2021 Bavinck Centennial Congress, both of which took place at Kampen, the Netherlands. I am grateful for the Neo-Calvinism Research Institute for their hospitality for those conferences. Earlier versions of chapters were also published as N. Gray Sutanto, 'Egocentricity, Organism, and Metaphysics, Sin and Renewal in Bavinck's *Ethics*,' *Studies in Christian Ethics* 34 (2021): 223–40; 'Consummation Anyway: A Reformed Proposal,' *Journal of Analytic Theology* 9 (2021): 223–37, and 'Herman Bavinck on the Beatific Vision,' *International Journal of Systematic Theology* 26 (2024): 25–42. All of these were revised substantially for inclusion in this volume. My thanks as well to Baker Academic, a division of Baker publishing group for permission to include excerpts from *Essays on Religion, Science, and Society* by Herman Bavinck and John Bolt, copyright © 2008, and *Reformed Ethics Volume 1* by Herman Bavinck and John Bolt, copyright © 2019.

I wrote this book as I transitioned from ministry at Covenant City Church in Jakarta, Indonesia, to Reformed Theological Seminary (RTS), Washington DC, between 2019 and 2023. A two-year immigration delay, while frustrating, helped propel my writing forward. At Covenant City Church, we were constantly benefitting from the hospitality and kindness from our dear friends, Tezar and Tatiana Putra, Elius Pribadi and Ayrin Bellina, and too many others to count. I am grateful to my colleagues at RTS for providing such an idyllic work environment, so that projects like this can be completed: Scott Redd, Paul Jeon, Jennifer Patterson, Thomas Keene, and Peter Lee make ideal colleagues.

My wife, Indita Probosutedjo, above all, deserves all of the recognition. She has been patient, bright, and encouraging through our transition here, even giving birth to our first daughter, Kiandara, just a little over a month after we landed. She has allowed me many early mornings so that I could put the finishing touches on this work. Thanks especially to Scott and Jennifer Redd, and Retno Sulistiowati, as they helped us with our transition to the United States, and cared for Kiandara when we needed the help. This book could not have been completed without them.

N. Gray Sutanto
Fairfax, VA
2023

Abbreviations

BT	Martin Heidegger's *Being and Time*
FP	Foundations of Psychology
KGHG	The Kingdom of God, the Highest Good
PoR	*Philosophy of Revelation: A New Annotated Edition*
RD	*Reformed Dogmatics*
RE	*Reformed Ethics*

Chapter 1

BAVINCK AND THEOLOGICAL ANTHROPOLOGY

The human being and the child of God, the human being and the Christian, cannot be in conflict. The best Christian is also the best human.[1]

What does it mean to be human? Who am I in relation to God? What does it mean to be made in his image? What constitutes the self, and how is the individual related to his or her neighbor, given the diversity of nations, ethnicities, and races? These remain perennial questions, and theologians have not offered a unified voice in response to them. When surveying the contemporary dogmatic literature, one sees, for example, competing visions of each dimension of theological anthropology. On the issue of the *imago Dei*, there are models that center on the structure (and faculties) unique to human beings, our relational character, or our vocation as that which constitutes the image. On the body–soul relation, there are physicalist accounts that offer a purely materialist account of the soul, or a dualist model that prioritizes the soul over the body, and debates linger concerning the faculties of the soul and how they relate to the body. On humanity's destiny, two pressing debates have arisen: one on whether the incarnation is the means by which one is united to God *absent* the fall, and the other on the weight and place of the beatific vision. How is the body involved in the beatific vision? And is the end of humanity more other-worldly or this-worldly, and will humanity be uniform, or will the end include the diversity that has developed among the nations over human history?

On original sin, debates continue on whether human beings are guilty of Adam's (or the first human community's) sin, or are merely polluted by it, and there are further questions on *how*, precisely, Adam's sin is transmitted to us. Two answers have been offered to that question of the transmission of Adam's sin. Federalism argues that Adam's sin is transmitted to us because God has determined that Adam represents humanity as its federal head, and so counts Adam's sin as our sin. On the other hand, realism argues that Adam's sin is ours because we were somehow *in* Adam, participating in his human nature, or are in his loins, as it were. When it

---

1. Herman Bavinck, *Christelijke wetenschap* (Kampen: Kok, 1904), pp. 107–8. ET: Herman Bavinck, *Christianity and Science*, N. Gray Sutanto, James Eglinton, and Cory C. Brock (trans. and eds) (Wheaton: Crossway, 2023), p. 203.

comes to Christian ethics, then, differing accounts of sin are offered on the basis of these prior theological answers on offer – is guilt something corporate or merely individual? Are my responsibilities to pursue my own virtuous character and piety before God, or is there a primarily social direction that should norm my actions? And if humanity has developed into a diversity of ethnicities and nationalities, how should we characterize the fundamental unity of humanity?

This study offers an exploration of the answers of Herman Bavinck (1854–1921) to some of these perennial questions. It seeks to show that Bavinck's theological anthropology offers a holistic vision that cuts across binaries that one often sees in the current literature on theological anthropology. More specifically, it seeks to show that Bavinck's account cuts across the debates between affective and cognitive accounts of the self and the self's relation toward God in creation, between federalism and realism, and between structuralist and relational accounts of the human being; and it offers fresh answers to questions around the body–soul relation, federalism and original sin, the unity and diversity of humanity, consummation, and the beatific vision. As such, the subtitle of this work is chosen intentionally. This work is not merely an exposition of Bavinck's theological anthropology; it is also an *application* of his insights into contemporary conversations. What emerges is an account of the human being that is religious through and through, which informs Bavinck's understanding of the self, the self-in-relation to others, and the self's telos in fellowship with God.

The rest of this introduction moves as follows. First, I locate this book within two contemporary and momentous trajectories in Bavinck studies. It follows on the heels of the current flourishing in Bavinck studies and the recent scholarship that is more cognizant of the overall unity of Bavinck's work. Furthermore, while there are studies that focus on specific details on Bavinck's account of humanity, this work is the first scholarly monograph on Bavinck's theological anthropology taken as a systematic whole and as applied to contemporary conversations. Second, I provide a chapter outline that canvasses the argument of the whole book, which covers the human individual as a religious creature and corporate humanity as image of God. Third, I finish this introduction by offering a summary of Bavinck's account of the image of God that has been established in the literature, which forms the backdrop for the argument to come.

Herman Bavinck and Theological Anthropology: Current Trajectories

Bavinck studies is enjoying a renaissance. Completed in 2008, the translation of his four-volume magnum opus, the *Reformed Dogmatics*, has stimulated newer studies on Bavinck's thought that reckon with its systematic character and prompt further efforts to introduce some of his lesser-known works to Anglophone readers. Indeed, the recent translation and digitization efforts related to the University of Edinburgh and the Neo-Calvinism Research Institute in Holland have created greater access to the whole of Bavinck's corpus than ever before. One result of these newer resources is that scholars are now coming to grips with the overall unity and coherence of his dogmatic project. Whereas past Anglophone interpreters have argued that Bavinck was an indecisive thinker who struggled to maintain Reformed orthodoxy in face of the demands of modernity, producing the so-called two-Bavinck thesis, scholars are now recognizing that Bavinck's thought formed a coherent whole that sought to model an eclecticism that drew on classical and modern ideas alike. In the attempt to free Bavinck scholarship from this past binary – which produced an inconsistent picture of a Reformed theologian who oscillated between retrieving classical confessionalism, on the one hand, and capitulation to the intellectual movements of the modern age, on the other – new categories and trajectories have been mapped to locate and understand his oeuvre.

This greater awareness of the entire scope of Bavinck's work has prompted, in turn, a more granular description of his theological development and interests. This involves recognizing that the *Reformed Dogmatics*, written relatively early in his theological career, is just one (albeit large) piece of his larger dogmatic project, and that his lesser known, more occasional writings, are no less important to grasp his concerns and insights. One must reckon with his earlier essays prior to the *Dogmatics*, and also his later works that discussed matters of Christian worldview, scholarship, philosophy, and the soul in greater detail.

Recent Bavinck scholarship, moreover, has begun writing more constructively, in an attempt to describe and apply Bavinck's project in positive terms in contemporary dogmatic thought. However, much of this scholarship is still caught up with the necessary work of clearing the way forward from the past interpretive debates. My earlier monograph on Bavinck's theological epistemology reflected this twofold task.[2] On the one hand, I attempted to apply and rearticulate Bavinck's thought in a way that was conversant with recent work in analytic theology and phenomenology, and with current debates concerning illumination. However, the first half of the work had to undertake the spade work of disentangling Bavinck from the older scholarship that tended to provide one-sided accounts of his epistemology. The recent monographs of Cory Brock and Bruce Pass, too, evidence this twofold task.[3] While both of their works explored the constructive yields of Bavinck's use of Schleiermacher or certain patterns of reasoning within German idealism, respectively, much of their argumentation is directed toward resolving this modern-orthodox binary.

Brock's study, in some ways, closely anticipates this one, as he shows that human beings are formed and epistemically conditioned by pre-theoretical feelings, prompted by their dependent relation on the world and absolute dependence on God. Brock demonstrates that Bavinck was influenced by Berlin romanticism on this point, and that he enfolds a nineteenth-century sense of the

---

2. Nathaniel Gray Sutanto, *God and Knowledge: Herman Bavinck's Theological Epistemology* (London: Bloomsbury T&T Clark, 2020).

3. Cory Brock, *Orthodox yet Modern: Herman Bavinck's Use of Schleiermacher* (Bellingham: Lexham Press, 2020); Bruce Pass, *The Heart of Dogmatics: Christology and Christocentricism in Herman Bavinck* (Göttingen: Vandenhoek & Ruprecht, 2020).

importance of feeling and the unconscious into a Reformed dogmatic outlook. These studies, along with James Eglinton's recent groundbreaking biography of Bavinck, have paved the way for more explorative and constructive research on Bavinck's thought.[4] No longer constrained by the burdens of throat-clearing that was necessary to clear the way from the former debates, scholars are now freed to provide studies that are of a more explorative, dogmatic, and constructive character. This study seeks to embody this new openness and offers an exposition of Bavinck's anthropology that is precisely that: explorative, dogmatic, and applied constructively to contemporary theological discussion.[5]

Second, this study follows on the recent explorations of Bavinck's theological anthropology in particular and offers the first monograph on the topic taken as a systematic whole. Though some exciting interpretive trajectories of research have emerged, this area of Bavinck scholarship remains relatively sparse.

The most significant study on Bavinck's theological anthropology is Brian Mattson's *Restored to Our Destiny*. Mattson's monograph was pivotal (along with James Eglinton's *Trinity and Organism*) in reshaping Bavinck scholarship to focus on the unity of Bavinck's thought, as it resisted identifying Bavinck's use of organicism with its contemporary counterparts.[6] It also succeeded in expounding the teleological dimensions of Bavinck's theological anthropology. Considering humanity as a single organism means that human beings were created with an embedded 'destiny' – a destiny of glory that could be obtained through the obedience of a federal representative within a covenant between God and humanity. Thus, Mattson unfolded the relationship between theological anthropology and eschatology in particular, and located Bavinck within the broader Reformed tradition with its emphasis on the covenants of works and grace.

The present work, however, builds on and goes beyond Mattson's work in three ways. On one level, much of Mattson's work was burdened by the sort of throat-clearing that was necessary to disentangle Bavinck from the debates of the past scholarship. This work, by contrast, dives into an exposition and application of Bavinck's thought unhindered by such concerns, and is able to do so in part because of the success of his work. On another level, this study uses a broader array of Bavinck's texts, both translated and untranslated, as the scope of this

---

4. James Eglinton, *Bavinck: A Critical Biography* (Grand Rapids: Baker Academic, 2020).

5. This fresh reading of Bavinck's work has coincided with a lively re-discovery of neo-Calvinism as a theological movement. See Nathaniel Gray Sutanto and Cory Brock, eds, *T&T Clark Handbook of Neo-Calvinism* (London: Bloomsbury T&T Clark, 2024); Cory Brock and N. Gray Sutanto, *Neo-Calvinism: A Theological Introduction* (Bellingham: Lexham Press, 2023).

6. Brian Mattson, *Restored to Our Destiny: Eschatology and the Image of God in Herman Bavinck's Reformed Dogmatics* (Leiden: Brill, 2012). For a summative presentation, see Richard Brash, 'Anthropology', in *T&T Clark Handbook of Neo-Calvinism*, Nathaniel Gray Sutanto and Cory Brock (eds) (London: Bloomsbury T&T Clark, 2024), pp. 73–84.

work is also more far-ranging, concerning itself not merely with human destiny and covenant but also with other dogmatic and metaphysical subjects, such as personality and the body–soul relation, the religiosity of human beings, faculty psychology, race, the necessity of incarnation, and the beatific vision. As such, it presents a more systematic and broader overview of the content and significance of Bavinck's project in theological anthropology. Finally, while Mattson's work focused almost exclusively on exposition, this work applies Bavinck's work to contemporary debates on a variety of theological-anthropological topics.

My argument also involves exploring the importance of the body for Bavinck's account of humanity's relation to God. More recently, Jessica Joustra and Philip Ziegler have both written on the body in relation to Bavinck's conception of the image of God.[7] In their judgment, Bavinck's emphasis on the body means that a focus on the image of God offers an invitation to reflect on the value of human diversity (Joustra), and that what we do with our bodies is a properly theological concern, not merely ethically adiaphorous (Ziegler). Indeed, Ziegler writes that Bavinck characteristically typifies a kind of 'holism' that represents the best of the Reformed tradition – a holism that includes the body–soul relation as constitutive of what it means to be made in God's image.[8] This holistic view of the *imago Dei* in Bavinck's anthropology is well documented in the secondary literature. Bavinck's account of the image is distinctly anti-dualistic, holistic, and embodied, grounded in his conviction that a human being does not merely have or bear, but rather '*is*

---

7. Jessica Joustra, 'An Embodied Imago Dei: How Herman Bavinck's Understanding of the Image of God Can Help Inform Conversations on Race', *Journal of Reformed Theology* 11 (2017): pp. 9–23; Philip Ziegler, '"Those He Also Glorified"': Some Reformed Perspectives on Human Nature and Destiny', *Studies in Christian Ethics* 32 (2019): pp. 165–76. Interestingly, though Joustra contrasts Bavinck's inclusion of the body within the image with the positions of Augustine and Calvin ('An Embodied Imago Dei', pp. 14–15), Ziegler includes Calvin as a forerunner to Bavinck's own position ('Some Reformed Perspectives', p. 168). There is diversity in the Reformed orthodox in respect of the body–soul relation, depending on whether Plato's substance dualism or Aristotle's hylomorphism is the preferred model that informs one's theological anthropology. See, e.g., Turretin (*Institutes of Elenctic Theology*, 3 vols, James Dennison Jr. [ed.], George Giger [trans.] [Philipsburg: P&R, 1997], 1: p. 465), and Van Mastricht (*Theoretical-Practical Theology*, vol. 3, *The Works of God and the Fall of Man*, Todd Rester [trans.], Joel Beeke [ed.] [Grand Rapids: Reformation Heritage Books, 2022], pp. 255, 285). See also, the discussion on Calvin and Vermigli in Paul Helm, *Human Nature from Calvin to Edwards* (Grand Rapids: Reformation Heritage Books, 2018), pp. 27–54.

8. Ziegler, 'Some Reformed Perspectives on Human Nature and Destiny', p. 169. Likewise, Helm, in his cursory appendix on Bavinck's psychology: 'Bavinck commits himself to a very integrated form of soul-body interactionism' and is 'against various kinds of reductionism', Helm, *Human Nature*, pp. 246, 253.

the image of God'.⁹ Indeed, Bavinck's view of the image is strongly non-partitive, as he refuses to isolate one particular capacity or aspect of humanity as the 'proper seat' of the image, but rather points concretely to humanity as such as image-bearers. The articles of Joustra and Ziegler have identified a proper emphasis on this holism and the body, and yet, as we shall see in Chapter 2, several questions remain. What exactly unifies the body and soul, and how are they related? What role does the category of personality play in Bavinck's theological psychology? What are the implications of these to contemporary studies on the cognitive science of religion and bodily phenomenology? As I will show, *that* Bavinck emphasized the importance of body and soul as included in the image is well observed, but the precise *workings* of their unity and relationship within the locus of the unconscious and personality, and *how* those insights might intersect with contemporary conversations on cognitive science of religion and affective psychology, have not yet been fully investigated – precisely because Bavinck's account of the embodied self has not been sufficiently explored.

In Bavinck's hands, the physicality of the self also reflects the religious nature of who we are. A neglected passage in Bavinck's *Dogmatics* is Bavinck's argument that essential to the image is one's 'habitation in paradise'.¹⁰ What this means is that because humans are image-bearers, human action represents and marks their environment, and the environment, in turn, forms and situates human beings: 'there is a connection between virtue and happiness, the ethical dimension and the physical dimension … spirit and matter – they may not be opposites.'¹¹ Virtue is correlated with paradise, and vice with the notion of a cursed and fallen world. This emphasis on physical embeddedness in Bavinck's anthropology will be significant for this book's exploration of bodily affect, phenomenology, sin, and corporate humanity. Indeed, the inclusion of the body within the image indicates that humanity's physicality cannot be ignored for Bavinck, and that human religiosity is situated, embedded within an environment, and representative of that embeddedness.

Another issue broached by Joustra's article is that of race. She gestures toward the usefulness of Bavinck's theological anthropology for understanding the diversity of human existence especially because of Bavinck's emphasis on embodiment. I seek to develop this claim in particular relation to Bavinck's account of the corporate image of God, and to situate Bavinck's argument for the unity-in-diversity of the human being in the context of the early twentieth century. Bavinck anticipated the rise of German nationalism and pointed to the grounding of morality on immanent history, concomitant as it was with a rejection of the

---

9. Herman Bavinck, *Reformed Dogmatics*, vol. 2, *God and Creation* (Grand Rapids: Baker Academic, 2004), p. 554. Hereafter, *RD*. Nathaniel Gray Sutanto, 'Herman Bavinck on the Image of God and Original Sin', *International Journal of Systematic Theology* 18 (2016): pp. 174–90.
10. Bavinck, *RD* 2: p. 561.
11. Bavinck, *RD* 2: p. 561.

older theology's emphasis on the transcendent as a moral ground. Identifying this aspect of Bavinck's work is necessary precisely because, while much work had been done to situate Kuyper within current discourse on race, little scholarly attention has been paid to Bavinck's most developed theological arguments and his potential contributions, beyond James Eglinton's biography that details Bavinck's negative reactions to racism in America and the Dutch colonial project in the East Indies, and popular-level works that have noted the fruitfulness of Bavinck's position on race and diversity for contemporary American conversations.[12] I thus explore Bavinck's account of corporate humanity and race in some detail within the latter chapters of this book. I detail Bavinck's critique of the racialization of Christianity in particular German and Dutch philosophical projects and the implications of a Christian and Trinitarian account of the human being for the subject of human diversity.

Other than these works, my own earlier writings have anticipated this study of Bavinck's anthropology. In a series of essays, I have shown that Bavinck's theological anthropology is multi-layered, as he considers the image of God as properly identifying not merely the organism of human individuals but also the human race as a whole, while showing the implications of these for particular debates in original sin, actual sin, consummation, and Christian social ethics.[13] Furthermore, my first monograph, *God and Knowledge*, included a section on theological anthropology, situated within a work that focused on Bavinck's account of human knowledge.[14] There, I gestured toward the social nature of the image of God and the ways in which human knowing is situated and dependent on pre-theoretical and bodily affects. I envision this present monograph as a kind of sequel to *God and Knowledge*.

Furthermore, providing a panoramic view of humanity's metaphysical condition here also provides a resource for further studies that explore and apply Bavinck's thought to other matters of theological anthropology. As Michael Allen has noted in his conclusion to the recent *Oxford Handbook of Reformed Theology*, we do well to give proper attention to the primary theological context of the topics at hand.[15] It is tempting for systematic theology to succumb to what John Webster

---

12. Eglinton, *Bavinck*, pp. 244–9, 258–9, 267–9; Irwyn Ince, *Beautiful Community: Unity, Diversity, and the Church at Its Best* (Downers Grove: InterVarsity Press, 2020); Jemar Tisby, *How to Fight Racism: Courageous Christianity and the Journey Toward Racial Justice* (Grand Rapids: Zondervan, 2021), pp. 29–30.

13. Sutanto, 'Herman Bavinck on the Image of God and Original Sin'; N. Gray Sutanto, 'Egocentricity, Metaphysics, and Organism: Sin and Renewal in Bavinck's *Ethics*', *Studies in Christian Ethics* 34 (2021): pp. 223–40; 'Consummation Anyway: A Reformed Proposal', *Journal of Analytic Theology* 9 (2021): pp. 223–37. The latter essays appear in a revised form as Chapter 5 and 8 of this present work, respectively.

14. Sutanto, *God and Knowledge*, chapter 2.

15. Michael Allen, 'Future Prospects for Reformed Theology', in *Oxford Handbook to Reformed Theology*, Michael Allen and Scott Swain (eds) (Oxford: Oxford University Press, 2021), pp. 623–30.

denotes as 'a process of assimilation', whereby Christian doctrine lends itself unduly to other disciplines first to set the terms and agenda for its construal.[16] Yet, by paying attention to the subject matter of Christian dogmatics and metaphysics, one can and must turn to their immanent manifestations and implications for human existence. While this book applies Bavinck's thought on core doctrines that relate to anthropology and contemporary issues – such as embodiment, cognitive science of religion, race, covenant and the beatific vision – I see my argument here as providing the proper theological backdrop for other future explorations.

Outline of Chapters

The chapters of this book are ordered according to a logical sequence that follows a common order of exposition, from human ontology, through the fall, sin, renewal, and consummation. The book also considers humanity as individuals and as a corporate whole. Chapters 2 to 4 explore the individual religious self as created and fallen, whereas Chapters 5 to 9 explore humanity as a whole in original sin, as a unity-in-diversity, and in redemption and consummation. Bavinck argues that the intrinsically religious self is embedded, psychologically situated and thus socially habituated, and this shapes his account of humanity as a singular organic whole.

After this introductory chapter, the second chapter focuses on the self and the body–soul relation, and traces Bavinck's thoughts on the matter chronologically from 1897 to 1915. What emerges is Bavinck's foregrounding of the unconscious and personality, which, in his mind, are fundamental aspects of the religious self that have been neglected in the earlier Reformed tradition's articulation of theological anthropology. While arguing that this older Reformed tradition still possesses the richest insights on the human person, he argues that one should enrich that tradition by observing the modern findings on the importance of the unconscious and personality.

Chapters 2 thus serves as an expository building block for the more constructive material in Chapters 3 and 4. The third chapter puts Bavinck in dialogue with some of the generative findings of religious affect theory, phenomenology, and the cognitive science of religion, while the fourth chapter proposes an account of human embodiment that situates the reception of divine revelation, which, in turn, provides a granular description of what I call the psychical effects of sin. I indicate that Bavinck refuses to isolate human cognition from its affective and embodied backdrop, while situating that backdrop within the context of exposure to divine revelation. Human beings are intrinsically religious creatures, and are constantly responsive to the affordances of that revelation in unconscious and conscious

---

16. John Webster, *Confessing God* (London: Bloomsbury T&T Clark, 2005), p. 22. Cf. Lewis Ayres, 'Seven Theses on Dogmatics and Patristics in Catholic Theology', *Modern Theology* 38 (2022): pp. 36–62.

ways. Such an experientially granular account of everyday human existence and revelation provides one way to bring together insights from both affect theory and the cognitive science of religion, while evading some of the pitfalls that conflate general revelation with propositional beliefs, as well as the reduction of the noetic effects of sin to human ignorance. Bavinck's holistic anthropology is thus attentive to the bodily dimensions of human existence, and the situatedness of our social habitation.

Chapters 5 to 9 of this book explore Bavinck's corporate understanding of the image of God, the unity and diversity of humanity, and of humanity's teleological ends. Chapter 5 describes Bavinck's understanding of the image of God as referring not merely to individuals, but to humanity as a corporate whole, as individuals are intrinsically related to one another and connected by ethical bonds. As an analogical ectype of the Trinity, humanity will bear an organic shape, consisting in a unity-and-diversity. The federal representations of Adam or Christ expressed in covenant, therefore, are no mere legal fictions but are an implications of the organic creation of humanity, and form the unity undergirding the diversity. This corporate account of humanity also shapes Bavinck's account of the principle of actual sin as egocentricity, and of renewal as restoring humanity as selves and as a corporate whole.

Chapters 6 and 7 then turn to Bavinck's critiques of Euro-centrism and racialization within his own context, which manifest themselves in the forms of German nationalism and the search for the 'primitive', original human community. Bavinck traces the racism he witnessed at the turn of the twentieth century to the failure to attend to divine revelation, which discloses the unity of humanity and a transcendent telos. Bavinck emphasized that it is through attending to divine special revelation and its global reception that we avoid the perils of racialization and nationalism, on the one hand, and embrace the good of cultural and ecclesial plurality, on the other. Humanity's intrinsically religious character also means that we do well to avoid tiered account of human existence, as if one group has privileged access to the divine. Bavinck's critiques of these racializing movements, as we shall see, indicate that his anthropological outlook is a significant improvement over his contemporary, Abraham Kuyper.

Chapters 8 and 9, finally, turn to the telos of humanity by exploring Bavinck's deployment of a Reformed covenant theology to produce a nuanced depiction of how humanity might obtain everlasting communion with God. By deploying the logic of covenant theology, Bavinck argued carefully that though human consummation is possible without the incarnation, Christ is the central focal point of God's decreed purposes for human salvation and the beatific vision. Furthermore, I shall show that Bavinck's covenant theology and Christology conditioned his description of the beatific vision, for, in his mind, these doctrines provide the principles according to which a doctrine of the beatific vision should be sketched. The conclusion of the book summarizes the argument of the whole and points to some potential generative ways forward for future study.

Bavinck on the Image of God: A Précis

It is helpful to offer here a brief sketch of the main contours of Bavinck's doctrine of the image of God as a framework presupposed in the following chapters. This précis will not be encumbered with copious documentation, for it summarizes the established findings of the contemporary scholarship, which draws not only from Bavinck's *Dogmatics*, but also his 1897 work *Foundations of Psychology*, his booklets, *Christian Worldview* (1904; 1913 2nd ed. 1929 3rd ed.) and *The Christian Family* (1908; 1912 2nd ed.), and his 1908 Stone Lectures, *The Philosophy of Revelation*.[17] Where relevant, however, I will provide references from his 1920 work, *Bijbelsche en religieuze psychologie*, partly because it is underexplored and less well-known, but mainly because it contains Bavinck's mature summary of his theological anthropology.[18] This précis has two steps that anticipate the two dimensions of humanity explored in this volume: first, humanity considered as organic individuals, and second, humanity as a corporate organic whole.

First, then, it is important to consider the human individual as made in God's image. To grasp his account of the image of God, a review of the organic motif in Bavinck is important. The organic motif is Bavinck's way of describing the way in which creation is shaped by its triune Creator. In God, there is an absolute unity-in-diversity, as this simple God exists in three persons. If God is the archetype, and creation the ectype, then creation, too, will be shaped by patterns of unities-in-diversities. Human beings, made in God's image, are those creatures who mirror God's being most: 'God is the supposition, the archetype, the example, the original from which humanity [stems], and humanity is his likeness, his correlating image, though in a very small way.'[19] It follows that if image-bearers of God are the pinnacles of creation, then we shall see this pattern of unity in diversity most clearly in human beings, though in an analogical fashion.[20] Furthermore, if human beings are image-bearers, three material ideas are entailed: (1) that original righteousness is intrinsic to the image of God and organically belongs to it; (2) that the body–soul relationship must be construed holistically rather than dualistically; and (3) that

---

17. Herman Bavinck, *Beginselen der psychologie* (Kampen: Bos, 1897); *Christelijke wereldbeschouwing*, 3rd ed. (Kampen: Kok, 1929); *Het christelijke huisgezin*, 2nd ed. (Kampen: Kok, 1912); *Wijsbegeerte der openbaring* (Kampen: Kok, 1908); ET: 'Foundations of Psychology', Jack Vanden Born, Nelson Kloosterman, and John Bolt (trans.), *The Bavinck Review* 9 (2018): pp. 1–270; *Christian Worldview*, Nathaniel Gray Sutanto, James Eglinton, and Cory Brock (eds and trans.) (Wheaton: Crossway, 2019); *The Christian Family*, Nelson Kloosterman (trans.) (Grand Rapids: Christian's Library Press, 2012); *Philosophy of Revelation: A New Annotated Edition*, Cory Brock and Nathaniel Gray Sutanto (eds) (Peabody: Hendricksen, 2018). Hereafter, *PoR*.

18. Herman Bavinck, *Bijbelsche en religieuze psychologie* (Kampen: Kok, 1920).

19. Bavinck, *Bijbelsche en religieuze psychologie*, p. 86. Unless otherwise noted, translations are my own.

20. Bavinck, *Bijbelsche en religieuze psychologie*, pp. 21–2.

the faculties of the self were created and redeemed to be organized in unity by an undivided heart and thus an undivided personality.

This organicism means that human individuals are intrinsically made in God's image – and that the image is non-partitive and not limited to one aspect of the human being. Bavinck's definition is ostensive, pointing to the humans as image-bearers. Furthermore, the image is not a *donum superadditum*, mechanically attached to human nature. Such a view, Bavinck argues, betrays the nature-grace dualism of Roman Catholic anthropology and was directly countered by the Reformation's distinction between the broad and narrow senses of the image of God.[21] The fall did not entail the loss of a superadded gift that was extrinsic to human nature, but rather led to an ethical distortion of human nature itself, as human beings are led away from God and toward sin. If original righteousness – knowledge, righteousness, and holiness – belongs intrinsically to the being of the human self, then the loss of original righteousness in the fall means that the whole self has become spiritually darkened. Bavinck writes: 'If he loses it, he does not cease to be a human being, with body and soul, understanding and reason; but he ceases to be a spiritually sound person; he is no longer what he ought to be according to the idea he should be (the idea that God has concerning him); he becomes a sick man, a sinner, dead in sins and trespasses, as Paul calls him.'[22] This loss is catastrophic, as the human being is called to represent God and to spread God's glory on earth, and so original righteousness properly belongs to this calling. Knowledge corresponds to humanity's prophetic office, righteousness to its kingship, and holiness to its priesthood. Original righteousness points to humanity as an intrinsically religious creature, properly oriented toward God in order to fulfil its calling.

The body, too, should be considered part and parcel of the image of God.[23] Three doctrinal strands testify to the holiness of the body: creation, incarnation, and resurrection. God is the creator of heaven and earth, and all of creation reflects his glory; God enters into human flesh, and the incarnation is not something incompatible with or beneath the dignity of the divine nature – rather the human body is made fitting for it; and God resurrects human bodies and renews creation in the last day, showing that the body was indeed created good.[24] Body and soul were not created separately and then brought together by force; rather, God formed body and soul together and as such the human individual 'forms an organic unity [*Als zoodanig vormt de mensche eene organische eenheid*]'.[25] This organic unity between body and soul means that neither is reducible to the other – the distinction between the two is fixed as the human self has an external and internal side. Yet, this is no dualism 'in the sense of Plato and Descartes', as if the

---

21. Bavinck, *Bijbelsche en religieuze psychologie*, pp. 88–9.
22. Bavinck, *Bijbelsche en religieuze psychologie*, p. 86.
23. Bavinck, *RD* 2: p. 559; *Reformed Ethics*, vol. 2, *The Duties of the Christian Life*, John Bolt (ed. and trans.) (Grand Rapids: Baker Academic, 2022), p. 296. Hereafter, *RE*.
24. Bavinck, *Bijbelsche en religieuze psychologie*, pp. 22–30, 90.
25. Bavinck, *Bijbelsche en religieuze psychologie*, p. 18.

body is less important than the soul, or as if each enjoys independence from the other in a kind of parallelism.[26] Organic unity maintains unity-in-diversity, and a holism where body and soul reciprocally influence one another and act together intimately: 'the spiritual component in [humanity] (unlike that of the angels) is adapted to and organized for a body and is bound, also for his intellectual and spiritual life, to the sensory and external faculties ... [The human] is a rational animal, a thinking reed, a being existing between angels and animals, related to but distinct from both.'[27] The resurrection of the body and the reunification of body with soul on the last day show that the temporary separation of the two is unnatural, and only arose due to the entrance of death and sin.

Hence, though at times Bavinck admitted that the 'image of God comes out more clearly in one part than another, more in the soul than in the body',[28] and that the body is an 'organ' of the soul, an 'instrument of the soul in its formal perfection',[29] he would also write that there is a reciprocal relation between the two that is irreducible to one-way causation: 'soul and body together make up the essence of a person and have as their subject that unique sensory-spiritual essence we call "a human being"'.[30] As such, Bavinck emphasizes that the soul's intellectual functions are never independent of the body, and are in fact dependent on the brain as its 'bearer and organ'.[31] Indeed, the body is 'just as constitutive for the essence of humanity as the soul'.[32] Although the soul may *epistemically* reflect the image of God more clearly than the body, the body remains *metaphysically* just as constitutive for that image. Just as the material world reveals the glory of God the Creator, then, so do the bodies of human beings image God.[33] In its unity and disclosure of personality it images *God*, and in its finitude and physicality it shows itself to be *image*, dependent on God and not itself divine. What the human personality does with its body further impacts its environment, and the world that humanity inhabits conditions the body and thus also impacts personality.[34]

There is a unity that animates the operations of soul and body. Indeed, organic unity is 'of fundamental significance' for psychology.[35] For Bavinck, the heart, which is the locus of the individual's unique personality, is the seat and core of the exercise of the faculties. The faculties are fundamentally two: willing (desiring) and knowing, with feeling or affection subordinated to them.[36] The faculties of

---

26. Bavinck, *Bijbelsche en religieuze psychologie*, pp. 20–1.
27. Bavinck, *RD* 2: p. 556.
28. Bavinck, *RD* 2: p. 555.
29. Bavinck, *RD* 2: p. 560. Cf. Petrus van Mastricht on the body's 'formal perfection', *Theoretical-Practical Theology*, vol. 3, p. 285.
30. Bavinck, 'Foundations of Psychology', p. 214.
31. Bavinck, *RD* 4: p. 616.
32. Bavinck, *RD* 2: p. 559.
33. Bavinck, *RD* 2: pp. 556, 561–2.
34. Bavinck, *RD* 2: p. 561.
35. Bavinck, *Bijbelsche en religieuze psychologie*, p. 18.
36. See especially 'Foundations of Psychology', and the briefer, less detailed summary in Bavinck, *Bijbelsche en religieuze psychologie*, pp. 59–71.

knowing and will presuppose the workings of the heart, which manifests itself in unconscious intuitions and desires. In line with *Foundations of Psychology* and his early essay 'The Kingdom of God, the Highest Good', Bavinck argues that sin tears asunder the organic unity of the human personality, as it takes root in the heart and causes the faculties of the soul to wage war against each other.[37] He finds unsatisfying mechanical theories of sin that identify it with merely one faculty, and prefers an organic conception that sees sin as corrupting every faculty precisely because it corrupts the human heart. Eschatologically, Bavinck envisions renewal as reunifying the human self, such that the law is no longer obeyed externally but internally, as glorified human persons follow the law in freedom, not compulsion. While the diversity of psychological phenomena seems disparate now (thoughts, impressions, memories, affections, desires, and so on), there remains a natural unity between them that will be consummately restored on the last day.[38]

Second, there is the social dimension in Bavinck's account of the image. Due to the infinite perfections of the triune God, only human beings taken as a corporate whole, together, can image God fully, leading to an eschatological understanding of the image that envisions corporate humanity obeying God in all its diverse parts. No single individual can display the fullness of the glory of God analogically, and each image-bearer has a role to play in reflecting that image. The corporation of the whole is greater than the sum of its individual parts. This presupposes a fundamentally singular human nature that is shared by all human beings together.[39] Ontologically, all human beings are made in God's image, and share the same structure of body and soul and the same capacities for desiring and thinking.

This natural unity is also the basis for a federal unity as humanity is represented ethically by Adam and by Christ. Humanity's organic character means that this federal representation is no legal fiction – it was fitting for God to unite the human race by a federal head because of humanity's organic shape.[40] An emphasis on the structure of the human being as that which bears the image of God does not preclude but rather includes the importance of ethical relations in identifying the image.[41] Once again, the pattern of the Trinity's absolute unity-in-diversity will find an analogical reflection in the ectype of humanity as a whole, as human beings are related to one another not simply and perichoretically but socially and ethically.

---

37. Herman Bavinck, 'The Kingdom of God the Highest Good', Nelson Kloosterman (trans.), *The Bavinck Review* 2 (2011): p. 142.
38. Bavinck, *Bijbelsche en religieuze psychologie*, pp. 21–2.
39. Bavinck, *Bijbelsche en religieuze psychologie*, p. 18.
40. See especially, Bavinck, *RD* 2: pp. 576–9.
41. '[Humanity] is a unity, a body with many members, a tree with many branches, a kingdom with many citizens … Physically, humanity is one on account of it being one in blood; legally and ethically, it is one on account of the foundation of natural unity; it is placed under the same divine law, the law of the covenant of works.' Herman Bavinck, *Guidebook for the Christian Religion*, Gregory Parker Jr. and Cameron Clausing (eds and trans.) (Peabody: Hendickson Academic, 2022), p. 91.

If human beings are united together socially, then sin, too, can be individual or social: 'there are individual sins, but also, family, class, social, and national sins.'[42] The corporate character of humanity leads Bavinck to recognize that human communities manifest a variety of cultures and patterns, for good or ill.

In Bavinck one finds a third way that cuts across certain impulses of so-called social trinitarianism and some contemporary presentations of classical theism.[43] While some social trinitarians have found it fitting to modify classical trinitarian metaphysics, emphasizing distinct centers of consciousness and affirming a correlation between God's triune self and social programs, contemporary classical theists have generally emphasized the ineffability of the triune and simple God. Indeed, for some classical theists, the unity-in-diversity of human beings and the church is not to be grounded in God's self at all, for the triune being of God highlights the absolute uniqueness and transcendence of the Godhead.[44] Critics of social trinitarianism, further, accuse it of wrongly prioritizing the reshaping of theology proper in light of human experience and social action, which ends up projecting those horizontal experiences onto God himself.[45] These are concerns with which Bavinck himself would agree, as he gladly affirms classical metaphysical descriptions of God's triune and simple being, and would place epistemic priority on God's self-revelation, rather than the horizontal axis of human experience.[46] Yet, by drawing from the Reformed scholastic paradigm of God's being as the archetype, and humanity in particular as created in the ectype of God, Bavinck maintains that *patterns* of unity-in-diversity can still be witnessed in human beings (in a way that harkens back to Augustine's *vestigia*).[47] This, however, does not motivate or baptize, as it were, a particular social agenda, but rather supplies the theological and macro-level shape of covenant theology: humanity's individuals (the diversity) are united together ethically by way of a federal head (unity). The analogy between God and the shape of humankind is theological first, grounded in God's self-revelation. As such, Bavinck was able to maintain classical doctrines like divine simplicity and a gloss of the divine persons as relations of origin, and yet argue that these very doctrines inform our understanding – however modestly – of human ontology and social relations.

---

42. Bavinck, *Guidebook*, p. 92.
43. See Thomas McCall, "What's Not to Love?" Rethinking Appeals to Tradition in Contemporary Debates in Trinitarian Theology', *International Journal of Systematic Theology* 25 (2023): pp. 610–32; the current binary does not reflect the tradition's commitments.
44. Cf. McCall, 'What's Not to Love?' Lewis Ayres, *Nicaea and Its Legacy: An Approach to Fourth Century Trinitarian Theology* (Oxford: Oxford University Press, 2004), pp. 408–9, 417 n. 64.
45. Cf. Karen Kilby, *God, Evil, and the Limits of Theology* (London: Bloomsbury, 2020), esp. chapters 1–6.
46. On the classical contours of Bavinck's doctrine of God, see my *God and Knowledge*, chapter. 2.
47. Cf. McCall, 'What's Not to Love?', p. 9.

Just as a central core such as the heart animates the parts of a living organism, so was it fitting that humans would rise or fall by way of an ethical center. Relations are ontologically constitutive for Bavinck's account of the human being. In Adam, the organism of humanity fell, inheriting both original guilt and corruption from his disobedience. Sin tears asunder not only the relationship of our bodies, souls, and faculties, but also our relationships with one another, as we choose to curve in on ourselves rather than love each other. In Christ, the organism of humanity is once again renewed, as ethical allegiance and union with this second Adam restore our ethical relations to one another in and through the Spirit, forming the Kingdom of God. Christ, as the head of the church, unifies God's people and consummates them in the resurrection as a single organism who would image God and enjoy God as prophets, priests, and kings.

The chapters ahead presuppose these basic parameters of Bavinck's anthropology that have been established in the recent scholarship.

Chapter 2

PERSONALITY AND THE UNCONSCIOUS: CHARTING BAVINCK ON THE UNITY OF BODY AND SOUL

The purpose of this chapter is to trace out Bavinck's thoughts on the features of the body–soul relation, and concomitantly, on personality. This is done through a close reading of papers and booklets that most directly discuss the matter from 1897 to 1916. I argue that a close reading of these texts reveals a consistent picture of the reciprocal character of the body–soul relation that depends not merely on older Christian-Aristotelian conceptions of psychology but also on more modern observations of the unconscious.[1] Embedded within this picture is an increasing concern to foreground the term 'personality' to describe the activity and identity of the soul as a whole. Personality is that persisting self-identity through physical changes over time, that pre-conscious unity of direction that animates the soul's faculties of knowing and desiring, and that incommunicable reality that distinguishes one person from another.[2]

The chapter moves in four steps: attending in turn to (1) Bavinck's 1897 *Foundations of Psychology* (*Beginselen der psychologie*), which documents Bavinck's observations on the importance of the studies on the unconscious within the history of psychology, (2) his lecture on religious experience in the 1908 *Philosophy of Revelation*, (3) his 1915 essay on the Unconscious, and (4) his 1916 booklet *De overwinning der ziel*. The importance of personality and of the unconscious emerged already in his earlier writings and was developed throughout the later

---

1. On the suggestion that Bavinck's *De overwinning der ziel* serves as a repudiation of his earlier views, see the 'Translator's Introduction: Bavinck's Motives', in 'Foundations of Psychology', p. xix; Cornelius Jaarsma, *The Educational Philosophy of Herman Bavinck: A Textbook in Education* (Grand Rapids: Eerdmans, 1935), p. 78; and repeated in Helm, *Human Nature from Calvin to Edwards*, p. 245. I offer an alternative reading and address their interpretation by the end of this chapter.

2. Bavinck's view is consistent with Turretin's on this point: 'Finally, personality is neither an integral nor essential part of a nature, but as it were the terminus'. *Institutes of Elenctic Theology*, 3 vols, 1: p. 316.

texts. Following the trajectory of Bavinck's thought will uncover a theologically complex and affective account of human existence.

Bavinck's association of the soul with the term 'personality' serves to distinguish the soul from the body and to locate the soul's operations within the body simultaneously. The unconscious operations of the soul that animates each individual's distinct personality are manifested in the body's habits and are paralleled in the body's own unconscious physiological and psychological activity.[3] This emphasis on the distinctness and mysteriousness of one's personality also serves as a polemic against materialism and the over-reaching claims of the secularized natural sciences: the more empirical investigation does its work, the more it discovers a mysterious reality that exceeds the merely natural and encroaches upon the heavenly – personality, the uniting 'I' that moves and animates the body. My close reading of key texts will also demonstrate that an analysis of Bavinck's faculty psychology and his treatment of the unconscious life of personality again displays a desire to relate older orthodox ideas to modern research and investigation.

This chapter's focus on exposition should not eclipse how it functions within the context of the over-arching constructive argument of this section of the book. Indeed, this chapter serves as an expository building block for the next two chapters that follow on Bavinck's account of the religious self. Following chapters will consider how a constructive theological synthesis of Bavinck's position with some current material from the cognitive science of religion and religious affect theory can produce an affectively rich account of religious awareness and the psychical effects of sin.

1897: Foundations of Psychology

This section turns to this early text from Bavinck to consider his comments on the body–soul relation in general, especially as he attends to the history of psychology, and then on how the unconscious self lies behind the two faculties of the soul that Bavinck identifies: knowing and desiring. What emerges is Bavinck's argument that recent advancements on the unconscious life and personality improve on and supplement the older Christian-Aristotelian paradigm of human nature, and that the personality is indicative of the unity of body and soul.

---

3. Helm's pre-occupation with Bavinck's connection to earlier faculty psychology leads him to eclipse these emphases in Bavinck's overall thought. Indeed, attending to the ideas of the unconscious and of personality answers Helm's query regarding the lack of clarity in Bavinck's theological anthropology: 'It is not made clear exactly what Bavinck means by such explanations in a situation in which he stresses the individuality and uniqueness of the human person and the mysteriousness of the interaction between soul and body.' Helm, *Human Nature*, p. 253.

Physiological Methodology, the History of Psychology, and the Emergence of Unconscious Personality

This work attends to the study of the soul (*zieleleven*): specifically, its metaphysical, psychological, physiological, and specialized character.[4] Introducing this material, Bavinck argues that consciousness recognizes the necessary distinction and relation between the subject and the object – that is, between the internal life of human consciousness and the objective world on which it depends. Studying the internal life of the self, the soul, then, requires studying how the soul interacts with the external world through the body, as the activities of the soul 'are all tied to the working of the body, and through it to the whole physical world'.[5] There is a 'close relationship' between body and soul, and '[n]othing happens in the soul in which the body does not participate and vice versa'.[6] There is, clearly, a reciprocal relation between body and soul.

This close relation between body and soul leads Bavinck to consider the various means by which one might study the nature and activity of the soul. One might, for instance, seek to understand the soul by consulting the subjective life of the self, that is, of first-person phenomenology. This means studying the internal phenomena of our own consciousness, making one's self the object of study, since 'the source of knowledge for psychology is, in the first place, the psychic life that we observe in ourselves'.[7] Yet, the awareness of some modern objections – that it is difficult to make one's self the object of perception, that we are often a mystery to ourselves, and that self-deception risks distorting the findings of our investigation – does prompt Bavinck to consider 'still other sources for psychology', namely *objective* psychology, which provides information about the psyche from a more objective, third-person perspective.[8] This involves taking into consideration historical scholarship, as humanity reveals itself in all of its diversity through literature, science, and art, as well as Scripture, which also discloses to us who we are.

In addition to objective psychological studies, Bavinck argues that *physiological* and biological experimental methods can aid the study of the soul, as he once again reminds readers that 'an intimate relationship exists between body and soul'.[9] Bavinck points to the work of Alfred Binet (1857–1911) on the formation of child perception as one example of the fruitfulness of this method. The 'valuable contributions to our knowledge of the phenomena of consciousness' from physiological investigations include 'much greater clarity on the following: the intimate relationship between soul and body, the conditions under which perceptions originate, the duration of elementary psychic phenomena, the limitations of consciousness, the strength or weakness of attention, and the

---

4. Bavinck, 'Foundations of Psychology', pp. 1–3. Hereafter *FP*.
5. Bavinck, *FP*, p. 2.
6. Bavinck, *FP*, p. 2.
7. Bavinck, *FP*, p. 7.
8. Bavinck, *FP*, p. 10.
9. Bavinck, *FP*, p. 12.

reproduction and association of ideas'.[10] To be sure, physiological studies at times risk reducing the discipline of psychology to a purely materialist and descriptive exercise. But when taken as one method that complements metaphysical and introspective (rational) analyses, it is a fruitful endeavour that deserves theologians' serious attention.

Bavinck moves on to a section briefly outlining the history of psychological studies, and in this section his emphasis on the importance of the body and the body–soul relation becomes more focused. He argues that Christian psychology up until the period of the early modern Reformed scholastics more closely followed Aristotle and his hylomorphism than Plato. While, for Aristotle, the soul is valued still as the principle of life, 'the human soul is built on a body and is designed for this. The body is not the soul's prison but its natural organ'.[11] Aristotle's tripartite distinction of the vegetative, sensitive, and rational soul was generally accepted, with the highest activity consisting in the intellectual activities of the two faculties of understanding and will.[12]

Although Bavinck considered this Christian-Aristotelian account of the soul to be superior to a Platonic one, he registers two critiques against it.[13] First, he writes, 'the unity of psychic life and the mutual relationship of these three psychic activities are not adequately emphasized'.[14] Anticipating his later discussions on the unity of the ego (*Ik-heid*) that animates the self's manifold activities manifesting as one's personality, Bavinck argues here that while the tripartite soul better distinguishes aspects of the soul's activity, it lacks a proper account of their unity. Second, he notes, 'the connection of soul and body and the bond between physiology and psychology are frequently absent'.[15] The Christian-Aristotelian account of the soul, in other words, failed to attend to the unconscious and physiological backdrop of the rational intellect, and thus needs to be re-evaluated in light of the modern findings on these issues. Bavinck's evaluation here is worth quoting in full, as he elaborates on his critique and suggests that the misguided Greek dualism

10. Bavinck, *FP*, p. 12.
11. Bavinck, *FP*, p. 23.
12. Cf. Mastricht, *Theoretical-Practical Theology*, vol. 3, pp. 253–61.
13. Matthew Lapine's reading that Bavinck's psychology here is 'Thomistic-like … in conversation with contemporary psychology' is apt, though Lapine underappreciates the turn toward the unconscious and personality, and their significance in Bavinck's thought. *The Logic of the Body: Retrieving Theological Psychology* (Lexham: Bellingham, 2020), p. 211; the same could be said of Paul Helm's appendix on Bavinck in *Human Nature*, pp. 243–53. For the broader reception of Aquinas and Aristotle in early Reformed orthodoxy on the subject of affection, see David Sytsma, 'The Logic of the Heart: Analyzing the Affections in Early Reformed Orthodoxy', in *Church and School in Early Modern Protestantism: Studies in Honor of Richard A. Muller on the Maturation of a Theological Tradition*, Jordan Ballor, David Systsma, and Jason Zuidema (eds) (Leiden: Brill, 2013), pp. 471–88.
14. Bavinck, *FP*, p. 25.
15. Bavinck, *FP*, p. 26.

between body and rationality is still at work in much of this Christian-Aristotelian psychology:

> The notions of a vegetative soul and a sensitive soul definitely take the body into account. But with the rational soul the body completely fades into the background. The subdivisions of a vegetative soul and sensitive soul lack sufficient insight into the physiological significance of various organs and their functions, such as circulation of the blood, respiration, digestion, the heart, the lungs, etc. In connection with these, the different conditions and activities of the soul are not sufficiently appreciated, *especially the unconscious, imagination, and emotions*. The ancient Greek antithesis between sensuality and reason still seems to be operative here. In general, all manner of distinctions, analyses and divisions occupy the place of explanation. The most difficult problems are occasionally solved with words and concepts.[16]

Bavinck maintains that this older Christian psychology still offers deeper insights than those of his contemporaries, yet he argues that particular issues were left underdeveloped – issues that he would focus on in the rest of this work and his later writings. Helm's observation that Bavinck's view offers merely 'occasional suggestions' of 'hylomorphism' is apt, as Bavinck 'comments on the disjointedness of this approach', and seems only to welcome it insofar as it contributes to his emphasis on resisting 'reductionism'.[17] Indeed, Bavinck later focuses precisely on these aspects that he reckoned to be lacking in this earlier psychology: the unconscious, the unity of the self and the connectedness between soul and body.[18] He saw these more recent advancements as offering improvements on the older Aristotelian paradigm.

Bavinck's section on theism's view of the soul summarizes a classical Christian understanding that relies on a biblical modification of Aristotelian hylomorphism, while gesturing briefly toward the role of consciousness as a means of identifying the soul. It argues that the soul is distinct from the body and yet is manifested by and organically connected to the body. In contrast to pantheism and materialism, theism recognizes the reality of the soul and does not reduce it to a more fundamental reality. The human soul animates the body as it exercises its two faculties of knowing and desiring. Human beings can form concepts, abstracting universals from particulars, willing resistance to their basic animal impulses, and desiring higher, spiritual realities.[19] While these activities highlight the distinct character of the human soul vis-à-vis the body, and indeed the human soul from

---

16. Bavinck, *FP*, p. 26. Emphasis mine. By way of contrast, then, Bavinck emphasizes that the soul's intellectual functions are never independent of the body, and are in fact dependent on the brain as its 'bearer and organ'. *RD* 4: p. 616.

17. Helm, *Human Nature*, p. 247.

18. See the section on the knowing faculty below for a further elaboration of this point. Helm, too, recognizes that lack in the older tradition: 'Reformed scholasticism does not of course have a theory of the unconscious in the modern sense.' Helm, *Human Nature*, p. 171.

19. These observations dovetail consistently with Bavinck's later work 'Triumph of the Soul'.

animals, Bavinck is keen to emphasize that 'perception, consciousness, thinking, self-consciousness, willing, and personal identity in all the changes of the material body by language, religion, morality, art, science, and history refer back to the human soul as a spiritual principle'.[20] Furthermore, though the precise relationship of body and soul is 'in fact completely unknown', Bavinck maintains that the 'soul is the form, the moving power, the foundation of the body; and the body is the matter, the material, and the possibility of soul'.[21] The two are so intertwined that the separation of soul and body at death is 'indeed unnatural and violent', and thus this 'temporary rupture must be restored at the resurrection'.[22]

It is instructive to observe the ways in which Bavinck's account of the individual image-bearer is consistent with and yet develops that of the *Leiden Synopsis* – a classic statement of Dutch Reformed orthodoxy, a new edition of which was edited by Bavinck in 1881.[23] While Bavinck follows the main lines of reasoning from the Synopsis (especially on the body's integral place in the image of God), certain features of innovation are clearly seen in Bavinck's account. Indeed, the more constructive areas of Bavinck's anthropology show up again in his emphasis on the importance of the unconscious life and personality as representative of the soul and its mysteries, yet with an intrinsic connection to the body. The unconscious and personality are terms that elucidate each other – the personality is the direction of the self that precedes and forms conscious thinking and willing.[24] Let us now observe Bavinck's inclusion and discussion of the unconscious and personality, for here, his distinctive voice clearly emerges.

The Unconscious and Personality

This creative exploration of the unconscious and personality impacts three areas: (1) in his discussion of feeling as a subset of either knowing or desiring, (2) in his view of the role of the unconscious in the activity of knowing, and (3) in his take on

20. Bavinck, *FP*, p. 44.
21. Bavinck, *FP*, p. 49.
22. Bavinck, *FP*, p. 50. In this passage, Bavinck does not specify precisely how the soul can exist outside of the body during the intermediate state. Elsewhere, Bavinck argues that because 'the body, too, is created in the image and likeness of God', we 'have duties toward our bodies' – duties which are implied in the second table of the Ten Commandments. Bavinck, *RE 2*: p. 296.
23. See *Synopsis purioris theologie*, Herman Bavinck (ed.) (Leiden: D. Donner, 1881). *Synopsis of a Purer Theology: Latin Text and English Translation*, vol. 1, *Disputations 1-23*, Dolf te Velde (ed.), Riemer A. Faber (trans.) (Leiden: Brill, 2014), p. 13 (pp. 315–31). On paragraph 13. 36, Bavinck repeats that 'the whole man in both soul and body is "created in the image of God and according to his likeness"', p. 329. See also Eglinton, *Bavinck*, pp. 112–13.
24. Bavinck commonly traces the idea of the unconscious to pre-Freudian sources, especially to Eduard von Hartmann (1842–1906). On Bavinck and Eduard von Hartmann, see my *God and Knowledge*, chapter 6.

the role of the unconscious in the activity of desiring. I shall explore each in turn below, and shall also highlight the way in which Bavinck relates the unconscious activities of the psyche to the unconscious activities of the body, and in turn, how identity and personality are formed unconsciously. The unconscious in Bavinck, therefore, is not reducible to animal instinct or the mere bodily activity that occurs without our conscious consent, but consists in the particular characteristics of each individual's personality. To use the biblical metaphor, the unconscious is the locus of the 'heart' of a person.

First, then, we turn to Bavinck's discussion of feeling. It is important to note that feeling is not to be conflated with emotion, but rather refers to the immediacy of consciousness, self-consciousness, and the perception of internal intuitions and external conditions. Feeling is, '[a]s Schopenhauer rightly said, "referring to all that immediate and direct knowledge that precedes thinking and reflection, which stands in contrast to the knowledge consisting in abstract ideas and argumentation".[25] Bavinck considers feeling not to identify a third faculty alongside willing and knowing, but rather as an activity of willing or knowing. Considered as the means by which one accumulates pre-theoretical knowledge, 'as perception or consciousness, feeling belongs, together with all awareness, impressions, perceptions, ideas, etc., to the faculty of knowing'.[26] Feeling considered in this way is akin to that phenomenological experience of entertaining particular intuitions – that a proposition just seems true or false, or of the inner conditions of 'I feel that I am thirsty', and so on.[27] Feeling, considered as a subset of knowing, is what accounts for that intuition that precedes and directs explicit, conceptual reasoning.

As Bavinck subsequently makes clear, there are two species of knowing: a conceptual knowledge and a non-conceptual (or pre-theoretical) knowledge:

> This [latter] manner of cognizance is highly important. It is distinguished from and precedes cognizance by means of argumentation and thinking. Intuitive knowledge is no less certain than this manner of knowing, but it far surpasses it. But it is indeed less clear and less conscious, precisely because it is not a knowledge in concepts [*zij geen kennis in begrippen*] and because it is not a fruit of intentional reflection and argumentation.[28]

Intuitive, felt, knowing is not a lower form of knowledge, but provides the backdrop for theoretical reasoning. 'Intentional reflection', therefore, does not hang in the air but is actualized within the context of prior intuitions. This association of feeling as non-conceptual knowing anticipates later sections of this text, where Bavinck

---

25. Bavinck, *FP*, p. 83.
26. Bavinck, *FP*, p. 82.
27. Bavinck, *FP*, p. 84.
28. Bavinck, *FP*, p. 85; *Beginselen der Psychologie*, pp. 57–8. I modified the English translation to include Bavinck's identification of this nonconceptual knowing as indeed *kennis* – a knowledge without concepts. The English translation merely says that this is not 'conceptual' and omits the word '*kennis*'.

argues that knowledge is gained unconsciously by the soul, which in turn forms a person's personality in a similarly pre-conscious fashion.[29]

Feeling can also be considered as a subset of the faculty of desiring. Bavinck circles around to this aspect of feeling in his discussion of desire, which he construes broadly as a kind of propulsion of human beings toward either attraction or repulsion. Following then-recent studies, Bavinck distinguishes between moods, feelings, passions, and emotions. Moods represent general, 'vague, unspecified, feelings, whose source people do not know precisely and therefore usually cannot explain'.[30] Feelings proper, by contrast, are '*conditions of the soul* that originate more in particular sensations or representations, whether sensory (feelings of hunger, thirst, cold, warmth) or spiritual (shame, aversion, disgust, gratitude, reverence, respect, fear, love, compassion)'.[31] Emotions are often shocking and acute, but pass by quickly, whereas passions reflect a particularly strong desire that can often blind one's reason and freedom. These distinctions are helpful but are not meant to be separations: these phenomena overlap one another as psychic activities.

The psychic functions of feeling, and of attraction and repulsion, manifest themselves in the body. At times, the body's sensations affect the psyche, whereas at other times a psychic mood or feeling might affect the body. There exists a 'reciprocal' relation between them.[32] In any case, what is significant here is that, as we shall soon elaborate, *what* attracts and repulses us far precedes our conscious willing and desiring. Furthermore, one's personality determines which object might elicit this or that affect. It is worth noting the parallel between knowing and desiring: pre-conscious intuitions and dispositions, which differ from individual to individual, form the backdrop for what it is that individuals consciously attend to in thoughts and desires.

In concluding his discussion of the faculties, Bavinck thus warns that we should never isolate or separate the faculties, or consider them independently from the subject that animates the faculties. Bavinck writes:

> It is not in the will, but the *I*, that consciousness finds its basis and unity. Indeed, the will itself would fall apart into a series of loose, disconnected volitions, if it did not have its unity in the *I*. Just like representations, the will is carried by the subject, the *I* itself, and thus always points back to it. Just as we speak of *my* representations, we speak also of *my* will. There is therefore a subject that stands above all representations, all phenomena of feeling and willing, a subject that possesses all of them and that to a certain extent, governs them.[33]

---

29. For a more thorough analysis of this and its epistemological implications, see Sutanto, *God and Knowledge*, especially chapter 7.
30. Bavinck, *FP*, p. 201.
31. Bavinck, *FP*, p. 201. Emphasis mine.
32. Bavinck, *FP*, pp. 209–18.
33. Bavinck, *FP*, pp. 97–8. Emphases original.

Bavinck thus resists an abstract consideration of the faculties, for the attentions and exercises of the faculties are manifesting the personalities of the human person. He then appeals to the words of Jesus when he argues that the heart 'frequently rules the head': 'According to the saying of Jesus, misunderstanding also comes from the heart.'[34] The self, in other words, animates the workings, attentions, and inclinations of the faculties.

Second, then, Bavinck continues to elaborate on the importance of attending to pre-conscious states in his discussion of how humans know. Bavinck's discussion of the knowing faculty is rich, but here we will focus on three salient aspects: the first involves the (lower) unconscious life, sensation, and the formation of representations, and second and third involve the conscious and 'higher' activities of self-consciousness and language. The predicates of lower and higher, as we shall see, denote not so much a devaluation of the former as less than the latter, but rather a phenomenological priority or progression. A subject reasons *from* an unconscious self, and the unconscious acts of knowing form the trajectories *for* conscious reflection.

As Bavinck recognizes, sensation is the beginning of consciousness and the proximate starting point of knowledge. Sensation arises when our physiological stimuli are engaged by the external world, and as the psyche begins to distinguish between conscious and unconscious sensations. From birth, we are thrown into a world of sight, smell, touch, taste, and sound, and we feel ourselves able to distinguish between objects, functioning purposively and appropriately within our situatedness. At the end of Bavinck's section on perception, and turning toward the discussion on unconscious representations, he reflects on the importance of sensations and impressions that form the self from their youth: 'They are acquired in the early years. What is learned later is constructed on this foundation. They are freshly introduced into the soul; they lie at the soul's deepest level, remain the longest, and have the most far-reaching effects.'[35] Bavinck refers to these formative and pre-conscious impressions as presuppositions – they form one's noetic intuitions prior to active knowing, and hence determine substantively how we use our cognitive faculties. Here, Bavinck is imbuing the Romantic tinge of Fichte's subjective idealist philosophy with the scholastic dictum that action follows being – our doing follows our heart; our personality determines our decisions and intuitions. The following passage is paradigmatic of Bavinck's account of the self, pertaining primarily to the faculty of knowing but also encompassing that of desiring:

34. Bavinck, *FP*, pp. 100–1. Despite this emphasis, Bavinck still maintained in this work 'the *primacy of the intellect*'. *FP*, p. 239. Emphasis original. In his more mature work, however, Bavinck will revise his position and hold that the intellect and will are equally basic, both being driven as they are by the heart. See the 1921 work: Herman Bavinck, 'The Primacy of the Intellect or the Will', in *Essays on Religion, Science, and Society*, John Bolt (ed.), Harry Boonstra and Gerrit Sheeres (trans.) (Grand Rapids: Baker Academic, 2008), pp. 199–204.

35. Bavinck, *FP*, p. 126.

For that reason, no one undertakes any endeavour while being free of presuppositions, least of all the endeavour of science. To be presuppositionless, one would have to get rid of oneself, since these notions and impressions, sensations, and representations are of all sorts and have connections to everything. They are physical and psychic, religious, ethical, and aesthetic. And they precede all conscious life, reflection, and thinking by quite some time. It is indeed an impoverished psychology that limits the faculty of knowing to understanding or to reason. The richest and deepest life, also of the faculty of knowing, lies behind understanding and reason in the human *heart*. This is affirmed by Scripture: 'Keep thy heart with all diligence; for out of it are the issues of life' (Prov. 4:23). Out of the heart proceeds thoughts and deliberations. Folly has its origin in the heart. The philosophy a person has, Fichte rightly said, depends on the kind of person one is. One's philosophy is nothing but the history of one's heart. The tree precedes the fruit, and doing follows being [*operari sequitur esse, het werken volgt op het zijn*].[36]

If being precedes action, then, personality precedes conscious reflection. After this passage, Bavinck begins his discussion of the unconscious representations proper, noting that Gottfried Leibniz and Eduard von Hartmann have brought attention to these important phenomena. Once more, Bavinck notes that 'scholasticism' overlooked them almost entirely, despite their implicit presence in works of ancient mysticism:

Indeed this unconscious activity of the soul in the faculty of knowing was previously almost completely overlooked in psychology. Scholasticism did speak of consciousness in a general sense and also considered the reflection of the knowing subject about itself (self-consciousness). But that there existed activities of the faculty of knowing apart from consciousness was not considered.[37]

Bavinck is thus explicit concerning the way in which modern psychology improves on the older scholastic accounts of faculty psychology: scholasticism neglected attending to the unconscious. Unconscious representations are those acts of the soul that occur outside of our conscious awareness, and this occurs in multiple levels. Physiologically, this occurs during moments of sleep-walking, intoxication, etc., which cause memory loss of the body's actions. These acts of the soul also happen when we are fully alert, and here Bavinck gives a few vivid examples: that of conversing with someone while our mind is consciously thinking of something else, 'thus we really do not hear what that person is saying, but we still know later on what we are told'; of passing by streets and houses while our minds are

---

36. Bavinck, *FP*, p. 126. The comment on Fichte is repeated in Bavinck, *Certainty of Faith*, Harry der Nederlanden (trans.) (Ontario: Paideia Press, 1980), p. 23: 'J.G. Fichte (1762–1814) said that the philosophy a man chooses determines what kind of man he will be. The shape of one's thought is often nothing more than the history of his heart.'
37. Bavinck, *FP*, p. 127.

occupied, but still somehow remembering what we encountered the next day; or of a 'soldier [who] may notice nothing of his wound in the heat of battle'.[38] Bavinck then concludes this section by arguing that the faculty of knowing is filled with activity prior to understanding and reasoning:

> All these facts and events demonstrate that there is an unexpectedly rich life in the faculty of knowing preceding understanding and reason, preceding even consciousness and self-consciousness. Understanding and reason represent so little of the essence of humanity and so little of the entire contents of the faculty of knowing, that they are but particular activities of that faculty and, as such, begin their work only after the fundamental sensations, perceptions, and representations are laid down broadly and deeply, into the unconscious.[39]

Observing the importance of the unconscious underpinnings of knowing does not mean that reasoning becomes devalued for Bavinck. Rather, to repeat, it means that all conscious acts of deliberate reasoning work with a prior unconscious foundation. Memory, imagination, reason, and understanding work with prior unconscious knowledge and conditions. There is no act of 'reasoning' in the abstract; all reasoning is situated within an embodied context, and is shaped by an unconscious self, and as will further be clarified below, a personality.

Hence, when Bavinck then turns to self-consciousness and language, he again notes that these two phenomena rely on unconscious foundations, and that self-consciousness and language often function apart from active reasoning. Self-consciousness takes the unconscious representations that we have in common with other animals and makes them our possession. These are the representations of *myself*. It is an activity of 'understanding and not of reason. After all, self-consciousness is not the conclusion of a syllogism. Human beings do not acquire self-consciousness by ratiocination, but rather, in self-consciousness they know themselves immediately, as it were by intuition, and that is an attribute of understanding.'[40] As such, Bavinck argues that self-consciousness is a direct indication of the presence of a soul as the subject. It is an immediate awareness of the self, and thus of the subject, the pre-condition of the possibility of active reasoning. When, in 1904, Bavinck discusses the process of how human beings engage in perception, he is explicit in arguing that even perception presupposes the activity of the personality: 'Indeed, it is not the eye or the ear that perceives but the person who sees through the eye and hears through the ear. Perception is a psychical activity – not a passive state but a positive action by which the subject makes its influence felt.'[41] No act of cognition stands above the self and its personality.

---

38. Bavinck, *FP*, p. 129.
39. Bavinck, *FP*, p. 130.
40. Bavinck, *FP*, p. 167.
41. Bavinck, *Christianity and Science*, pp. 94–5.

Furthermore, though language is an activity of humanity's higher intellectual and rational capacities, it, too, is rooted in pre-theoretical and pre-ratiocinative phenomena. Language, as the highest mark of human cognition, is also the capacity through which one sees the body–soul reciprocation in the highest degree. Phenomenologically, Bavinck argues that the body is intelligible to us – there is a language of the body: 'of facial features; a language of gestures, a language of the often involuntary movement of facial muscles, of nerves, and of body parts'.[42] In other words, the soul often communicates itself by unarticulated bodily movements and sounds, and human beings have an understanding of this mode of communication. Language is the 'totality of the signs by which human beings reveal their thoughts'.[43] Then, when human beings use words in speech, they are dependent on prior thoughts and feelings that they are seeking to convey in articulated sounds. At times we know a concept by learning a word, but then retain only the concept without remembering the word; at other times, unconscious representations are known while we are searching for the word that best communicates them: 'words can be completely forgotten, and yet the thought can be retained and expressed using different sounds … A sign and the thing signified are not one and the same. Often we have a representation, a concept, a thought, for which we still search for a word.'[44] The phenomenon of language, then, is not just indicative of the reciprocal relation between body and soul, but also of the nobility of human beings as image-bearers: 'In the final analysis, language rests on the one single Logos who created spirit and matter, soul and body, subject and object, along with creating thought and language, concept and word, in relationship with each other.'[45] Bavinck is suggesting, rather provocatively, that as image-bearers with linguistic capacities, humans are thus analogically imitating the God who created all things through the Word.

Third, the natural faculty of desire works in conjunction with the faculty of knowing. Unconscious and conscious representations are the objects of desire: 'each of them, the lower and higher faculty of knowing, offer their representations to the entire faculty of desiring, thus also to actual desiring.'[46] Once again, Bavinck argues that desiring has to take into account both conscious and unconscious acts, in parallel with the faculty of knowing:

> Just as the faculty of knowing includes far more than actual knowing but includes also sensation, impression, representation, etc., so too the faculty of desiring is far broader than the term suggests. Desire is only one of the activities of the faculty of desiring. This faculty includes every action in which the soul establishes its real relation to things and thus includes not only desire and will but also inclination and temperament, attraction and repulsion, emotion and

---

42. Bavinck, *FP*, p. 170.
43. Bavinck, *FP*, p. 170.
44. Bavinck, *FP*, p. 173.
45. Bavinck, *FP*, p. 176.
46. Bavinck, *FP*, p. 195.

passion. This faculty is just as rich as the faculty of knowing and testifies once again to the amazing organization of the soul.[47]

Just as the faculty of knowing is divided into lower and higher functions, so too is the faculty of desiring. The higher functions refer to conscious acts of free will, but the lower functions refer to the unconscious. The unconscious function of desiring involves that 'unconscious pursuit, in all creatures, even if only to be and to preserve their existence'.[48] This pursuit for self-preservation and advancement is manifested as love, that desire for the infinite, as defined by Plato and Augustine. Human beings, 'in whom the faculty of desiring rises to its highest level, assimilate and incorporate within themselves all those lower forms. With them, a rich life of pursuing precedes all consciousness and desiring.'[49] Bavinck locates this ultimate longing for the infinite in the locus of the unconscious. Unconscious pursuits (that take place without active, conscious desiring), in turn, become a basis on which our personality arises: 'Beneath the conscious, will-directed life, a world of unconscious representations and automatic actions is expanding. And the personality, with its self-consciousness and self-direction, rises on this broad foundation like a pyramid.'[50] While this natural longing for preservation is in itself good and is supposed to direct one to the Good, namely, God, sin has darkened us such that we direct even these unconscious longings toward things that fail to advance our existence: 'The sinner chases after sin under the illusion that it is good and despises virtue under the illusion that it is evil.'[51] Later, Bavinck argues that this striving and chasing can be referred to as a kind of unconscious 'penchant', which can take the shape of a conscious striving of the will toward a more particularized end.[52]

This explains why, in his discussion on the freedom of the will, Bavinck argues that 'indeterminism is usually presented in a form that makes it untenable, not only theologically, religiously, and ethically, but also *psychologically*.'[53] Though conscious acts of the will could still be considered a higher, mature act of the soul, they arise from the preceding unconscious realities that already determine the direction of the self. As he writes: 'Frequently, the will has no control over the lower faculty of desiring, over sympathy or antipathy, over liking or disliking,

---

47. Bavinck, *FP*, p. 182.
48. Bavinck, *FP*, p. 183. Interestingly, on the same page, Bavinck critiques Schelling, Schopenhauer, and Von Hartmann here since they 'identify this urge in every creature as will', when, in his judgment, this urge for self-preservation takes place without 'reason and self-consciousness'.
49. Bavinck, *FP*, p. 184.
50. Bavinck, *FP*, p. 187.
51. Bavinck, *FP*, p. 189.
52. Bavinck, *FP*, p. 193.
53. Bavinck, *FP*, p. 233. Emphasis mine.

over drives or passions, over urges and desires.'[54] The will follows through on these prior inclinations, many, if not most, of which one has no control.

Let us take stock. In Bavinck's *Beginselen der psychologie*, one sees a holistic theological anthropology that sees human beings as psychosomatic unities. Cognizant of both the methodological and historical nuances of psychology, Bavinck argued that Christian Aristotelianism is stronger than its modern counterparts in offering a holistic account of the body–soul relation, yet regards it as insufficient in its account of the unity of the self, personality, and the reciprocal relationship between body and soul. What begins to emerge in the latter half of this work is an analysis of the unconscious self as a way to account for that unity and reciprocation. Personality arises out of the unconscious, and the unconscious informs the faculties of both knowing and desiring. Just as the body has physiological functions that occur without consciousness, the *direction* of the body, determined by the soul, is itself formed on the basis of unconscious activity. Hence, Bavinck argues that attending to the unconscious life of persons discloses the mystery of personalities. One's personality animates and attends every conscious act of knowing and desiring, as it provides the intuitions and dispositions that direct the self's attentions and desires.

1908: Philosophy of Revelation

Bavinck further reflects on the body–soul relation and the unconscious in the *Philosophy of Revelation*, though here his comments on the matter are more indirect. The focus in these Stone Lectures is on demonstrating the way in which divine revelation underpins every domain of study: it is the 'secret of all that exists', and the 'deeper science pushes its investigation, the more clearly will it discover that revelation underlies all created being'.[55] One of Bavinck's key claims is that revelation penetrates the psyche in a way that precedes conscious reflection and desiring. In consciousness, we always feel 'dependent' on 'everything around us', and absolutely dependent on God, precisely because God has not left himself without a witness.[56] Thus, two implications follow from this observation on the impact of God's revelation: first, one can give a richer analysis of revelation's impact on the self by studying the psychological dimensions of religious experience, and second that consciousness cannot be studied from an empirical standpoint alone.

As Bavinck argues, 'we may acknowledge that dogmatics, especially in the doctrine of the *ordo salutis* ("order of salvation"), must become more psychological and must reckon more fully with religious experience'.[57] Because the psyche is the locus of revelation's reception, psychology enriches our understanding and perception of the empirical dimensions of God's work. Again, one topic of recent

---

54. Bavinck, *FP*, p. 226.
55. Bavinck, *PoR*, p. 24.
56. Bavinck, *PoR*, pp. 57, 63–5.
57. Bavinck, *PoR*, p. 168.

psychological study that Bavinck emphasizes is the study of the unconscious. Bavinck observes:

> [T]he psychical life of the human being is much richer than his conscious intelligence and action. One may disagree over the names; but whether we speak of waking and dreaming, day and night, supraliminal and subliminal, intuitive and reflexive consciousness, in any case there is a great difference between what happens beneath and above the threshold of consciousness.[58]

The unconscious, however, is not just the domain of physiological and dormant perception but also of one's character, talents, and habits: 'Beneath consciousness there is a world of instincts and habits, notions and inclinations, abilities and capacities, which continually sets on fire the course of nature. Beneath the head lies the heart, from which are the gates of life.'[59] When one investigates the depths of the human consciousness, one finds there not merely physiological processes but also instincts and dispositions that bear a moral, even religious character. While studying consciousness from an empirical, third-person perspective might produce observations about the material conditions that correspond to consciousness, the inner life of that consciousness is irreducible to those material conditions and contains features that are inexplicable without an appeal to immaterial realities.

When one encounters these dispositions and intuitions within consciousness about morality and the divine, one has to make a judgment about the sources of those intuitions, and when empirical psychology reduces them to be nothing more than illusory, or reduces them to the material, they have gone beyond empirical observation into the domain of metaphysical adjudication. The presence of these moral and theological impressions in the psyche can be explained in another way: the religious consciousness points to the intrinsic human attunement to divine revelation: 'religious experience arises out of preceding revelation'.[60] In other words, the empirical method can observe *that* there is something underlying explicit consciousness, and can observe its physical features, but fails to explain why it is that the unconscious includes intuitions about these immaterial realities that determine the life-direction of individuals. When it seeks to give an account of the substance and direction of the unconscious, empirical psychology begins to cross disciplinary boundaries to the domain of metaphysics. As Bavinck argues:

> For this reason, empirical psychology will never be able fully to know and explain the psychical life. It may with the utmost closeness examine the phenomena of consciousness, the sensations, the feelings, the passions, and it may try to conceive their working mechanically; it may even endeavor to explain the ego or the self-consciousness by association of ideas; but naturally it cannot penetrate to what lies behind and beneath consciousness and can kindle no light

---

58. Bavinck, *PoR*, p. 172.
59. Bavinck, *PoR*, p. 173.
60. Bavinck, *PoR*, p. 167.

in the secret places of the heart. Herein the declaration may find its application that God alone knows the heart and tests the inner-life. Empirical psychology can inquire into the conditions of consciousness, can even investigate the self-consciousness which slowly arises in the human and is subject to all kinds of changes. But the question whether a hidden ego [*ik*] or an independent soul lies behind it is beyond its reach. So soon as it occupies itself with this question it passes beyond itself into metaphysics.[61]

Studying the phenomena of consciousness from a third-person perspective exclusively lacks the means to identify and adjudicate upon the soul and its hidden powers, and hence lacks also the ability properly to understand the body. It 'always takes its start from an abstraction … it degenerates into psychologism, historicism, and relativism and the fullness and richness of life are curtailed'.[62] By way of contrast, Bavinck advocates for an organic approach that seeks to do justice to the richness of the phenomena in its unity and diversity, for it refuses to reduce the unconscious to nature or nurture, to materialism or to the conditions of one's upbringing, and refuses to conclude that the fact of an unconscious life means all moral evaluation is excluded. As Bavinck writes, the empirical psychologist is always ever rubbing up against an irreducibly metaphysical and *personal* reality:

> In reality all these phenomena of consciousness, so far from being isolated, exist only in intimate mutual relations, *and ever spring out of the depths of personality.* The whole cannot be explained in an atomistic manner by a combination of its parts; but on the contrary the parts must be conceived in an organic way by unfolding the totality. Behind the particular lies the general, and the whole precedes the parts.[63]

Here, Bavinck is giving a directly theological account of the unconscious. One discovers in the mysterious depths of human psychology a world of freedom and normativity that transcends mere physicality, and hence a locus of divine revelation's activity: the soul. In Bavinck's words: 'If psychology leads by serious reflection to a metaphysical reality, and this again to the idea of revelation, we are not far removed from the conviction that humanity, in the hidden places of the soul, yet belongs to another and a higher world than that of this earthly existence.'[64] As Bavinck concludes in this chapter, though psychology and experience are not the norms or sources of religion, by studying them scientifically one can give a more granular account of revelation's impact, and of the Spirit's work in conversion. Divine activity is 'psychologically mediated'.[65] Underneath the threshold of one's consciousness, one encounters an irreducibly supernatural work of God on the

61. Bavinck, *PoR*, p. 173.
62. Bavinck, *PoR*, p. 173.
63. Bavinck, *PoR*, p. 173. Emphasis mine.
64. Bavinck, *PoR*, p. 174.
65. Bavinck, *PoR*, p. 190.

soul. Bavinck writes: 'Though [revelation] occur[s] thus in a psychological way, which takes into account each one's character and environment, yet they are a revelation of that will which works in us both to will and to do anything according to his good pleasure.'[66] By failing to avail itself of the categories of metaphysics, and also of the fact of revelation, empirical psychology fails to do justice to this irreducibly personal character of the unconscious: 'It is the intuitive, organic life which in sensations, in thoughts and actions, gives an impulse to us and shows us the way. Instinct and capacity, norm and law, precede the life of reflection.'[67] In other words, while the empirical psychologist might be tempted to reduce human character into a deterministic by-product of his or her nature or upbringing, she is confronted in each individual with a direction that is at once moral, free, and personal.

This theological and revelational account of the unconscious in *Philosophy of Revelation* should be kept in mind as we now proceed to Bavinck's more direct and sustained engagement with the phenomena of the unconscious itself in Bavinck's 1915 booklet *Over het onbewuste*.

1915: Over het Onbewuste

This 1915 work places a further emphasis on the unconscious' relation to the soul and the importance of the unconscious to human personality.[68] Prompted by the observations of Haeckel that referred to consciousness as a profound mystery and the burgeoning interest on the unconscious in the psychological literature, Bavinck argued that 'there is no conceivable psychology today that does not try to pay some attention to it'.[69] This treatise seeks to answer a basic question: is the unconscious a function and reference of the soul itself, or is it an independent reality alongside the soul, carrying the faculties of the soul as a separate energy? In Bavinck's words: 'Of what do these unconscious-psychical phenomena consist? Are they references to the soul itself, with its powers and dispositions, its habits or activities? Or do the facts also allow us to speak of the unconscious impressions, feeling, and acts of the will?'[70] Bavinck's answer at the end of the booklet is clear: the unconscious is a property and function of the soul rather than a separate energy – the former view correctly presupposes that unconscious phenomena are predicated on a substantial unity (an identity and a soul), whereas the latter erroneously marks a

---

66. Bavinck, *PoR*, p. 191.
67. Bavinck, *PoR*, p. 173.
68. Herman Bavinck, *Over het onbewuste: Wetenschappelijke samenkomst op 7 juli 1915* (Amsterdam: Kirchner, 1915). ET: Herman Bavinck, 'The Unconscious', in *Essays on Religion, Science, and Society*, John Bolt (ed.), Harry Boonstra and Gerrit Sheeres (trans.) (Grand Rapids: Baker Academic, 2008), pp. 175–98.
69. Bavinck, 'The Unconscious', p. 184. See also Bavinck, *Bijbelsche en religieuze psychologie*, p. 61.
70. Bavinck, 'The Unconscious', p. 179.

return to occultism that specifies some unknowable force or energy that animates human existence. Furthermore, Bavinck argues that the 'theory of the unconscious that has gained such prominence in psychology of late is proof that "psychology without a soul" is untenable, and in this respect is a recovery of the old theory of the soul'.[71] The recent psychologies of the unconscious, in other words, are a kind of contemporary updating and re-establishment of the older idea that the soul has its own substance and activity, and establish that it is not to be viewed 'purely as an *ens* [being] but that it also has to be understood as an *agent*'.[72] The unconscious, in turn, is useful in the study of a variety of theological loci and is also found in Scripture:

> The theory of the unconscious finds support in Holy Scripture insofar as [Scripture] definitely takes the view that the soul is much richer and deeper than the consciousness (Ps. 44:21; Prov. 4:23; Jer. 17:9-10; 1 Cor. 14:25; 1 Pet. 3:4; etc.), and it posits this thought as basic to its doctrine of sin (Gen. 8:21; Pss. 19:12; 51:10; Jer. 17:9; Mark 7:21), of regeneration (Jer. 31:33; John 3:8), of the mystical union (Rom. 8:16, Gal. 2:20), of inspiration (2 Pet. 1:21) and of obsession (John 13:2; Acts 5:3).[73]

In effect, Bavinck is arguing that Christianity can account for and accommodate the recent psychological findings on the importance of the unconscious to understand human agency and have them inform its theology, and all this without having radically to revise its classical understanding of the soul as distinct from and yet intimately connected to the body. The following analysis focuses on Bavinck's comments on the unconscious' relation to the soul and personality in correspondence to the three sections of this work: definition (*begripsbepaling*), history (*geschiedenis*), and phenomena (*verschijnselen*).[74]

The first two sections can be treated together. In his section on defining the concept, Bavinck couches the unconscious in relation to consciousness, which refers to 'an immediate awareness of a state of things, with a direct psychic experience … Only by being conscious can we understand something of consciousness; it makes itself known by itself'.[75] More precisely, consciousness includes two elements, and here Bavinck invokes Augustine and Kant to illumine the matter:

> First, it is an awareness on the part of the subject regarding phenomena that occur within by which we come to know all sorts of things that are part of our consciousness. These include observing, remembering, judging, knowing; but

---

71. Bavinck, 'The Unconscious', p. 196.
72. Bavinck, 'The Unconscious', p. 196. This interplay and co-dependency of older orthodoxy and modern ideas is a common theme in Bavinck's writings.
73. Bavinck, 'The Unconscious', p. 197.
74. Bavinck, *Over het onbewuste*, pp. 5, 12, 19.
75. Bavinck, 'The Unconscious', p. 175. On Bavinck's understanding of consciousness in general, see Brock, *Orthodox yet Modern*.

also feelings, both sensory and spiritual; wishing, desiring, striving, wanting, and acting experiences .... Consciousness is knowledge, awareness, 'knowing' what goes on inside of me. And second, it is an immediate awareness. It is a knowledge obtained not through external sense organs or through deliberate research and serious study but directly through immediate experience, through 'an inner sense' [*inneren Sinn*], as Kant called it, in imitation of the *sensus interior* of Augustine and the Scholastics. This 'inner sense' is nothing but consciousness itself. Some phenomena in the life of our soul (some inner phenomena) have the peculiarity that they are conscious and that they exist in no other way; if I know anything, I also know that I know I; without the latter, the former could not happen.[76]

The two elements of consciousness, therefore, are the awareness of the sensations, impressions, and representations of our inner life, which include the memory, one's feelings concerning those impressions and ideas, and the consciousness of the *self*.

For Bavinck, consciousness is best regarded as a means of identifying a soul, but he is well aware that pantheism and materialism deny the soul, which leads to the reduction of the same to mere phenomena: a series of disparate moments and experienced content without a unity. His immediate response is that in consciousness one identifies a self – these are *my* experiences, *my* thoughts – and one also perceives the enduring character of identity: 'the relationship to a subject, to a "self," is always implied in consciousness.'[77] Once one identifies this self that is mine, however, an encounter occurs with something beyond or behind the self that is not so easily identified: 'something enduring hides.'[78] One can sense things falling into the center or periphery of one's conscious reflections, and things arise that were previously forgotten, or there is the awareness (feeling) that there remains a self that persists through waking or sleeping. It is these phenomena that lead one to accept the reality of an unconscious and to hypothesize the existence of a soul or life-force. Bavinck argues that the unconscious, though a term of 'more recent origin', has been recognized from older times.[79] He repeats his analysis that Christianity improved on the older Platonic and Aristotelian concepts of the soul while emphasizing the need to accommodate the studies on the unconscious phenomena, which he traces to Eduard von Hartmann and Schopenhauer.[80]

Finally, then, Bavinck turns to the possible types of unconscious phenomena, and divides these into five categories. The first, and most uncontroversial, is that of physiological phenomena: that the bodily functions of the lungs, heart, stomach, etc. all work apart from conscious willing. The second refers to the 'psychical' unconscious. While keeping in mind that it is hard 'to draw boundaries between

---

76. Bavinck, 'The Unconscious', pp. 175–6.
77. Bavinck, 'The Unconscious', p. 176.
78. Bavinck, 'The Unconscious', p. 178.
79. Bavinck, 'The Unconscious', p. 179.
80. Bavinck, 'The Unconscious', pp. 180–4.

physiology and psychology', for 'phenomena that at one time were considered to be psychic were later explained quite easily physiologically', the psychical unconscious accounts for the phenomena of instinct and of the variability of personality and genius.[81] The third set of phenomena relates to the forgotten objects of our attention, having to do with memory, both mental and physical, and habits. The fourth refers to the subconscious or subliminal consciousness, having to do with the ability of the mind to fixate on another topic while the body is busy doing something else, and the distinction between the 'two groups of impressions present in our consciousness, one at the center and one at the periphery, one in the upper floor and one on the ground floor'.[82] As such, this fourth category is not about unconscious phenomena per se, but of those relating to a dim or unlit consciousness, having to do with dreams and hypnosis. Fifthly, and finally, there are phenomena of the unconscious that are often linked with what he calls a new occultism, whereby one might seek to unlock the secrets of nature, or seek to bring oneself into a higher unity with nature or more absolute unconscious mind. This occultism, Bavinck argues, is 'a renewal of the old mysticism and the even older animism … but it connects these old ideas with the modern theory of evolution'.[83]

What emerges here in Bavinck's survey is his observation that the denial of the soul is correlative to the denial of personality. Instead of seeing mental illness, for example, as a corruption of the soul and hence of personality, others see it merely as an alteration of the content of consciousness: 'they first dissolved the soul, the substantial unity of a person, into a series of conscious contents and self-impressions'.[84] Likewise, in occultism the self is at best seen as an obstruction and is to be reduced into Nature, or is a mere illusion that veils the metaphysical oneness with the Absolute (as in Von Hartmann).

It is the second phenomenon that dovetails most clearly with the present purposes of this chapter. The second phenomenon looks at the mystery that attends the variability of personalities, and the porous boundary between 'heredity and variability'.[85] The human being is always embodied and situated, and thus has 'much in common with his parents, family, nation, humanity, and yet at the same time differs from them in certain respects. Every human being, as Emerson said, is a citation of his ancestors; and yet he is also an independent thought and word.'[86] There are individualizing features of each person that are not reducible to one's parents, upbringing, and social location.

This leads Bavinck to observe the inexplicable psychological *ongelijkheid* in human beings.[87] The English translation renders this word simply into 'inequality' or 'unequal', which can have a negative connotation, but *ongelijkheid* is rather

---

81. Bavinck, 'The Unconscious', p. 184.
82. Bavinck, 'The Unconscious', p. 190.
83. Bavinck, 'The Unconscious', p. 194.
84. Bavinck, 'The Unconscious', p. 192.
85. Bavinck, 'The Unconscious', p. 186.
86. Bavinck, 'The Unconscious', p. 186.
87. Bavinck, *Over het onbewuste*, p. 23.

2. Personality and the Unconscious

generic; the word could well be rendered the 'difference', 'dissimilarity', or 'diversity' instead of inequality.[88] Hence, though Bavinck will invoke examples of geniuses – a fascination of the nineteenth-century Romantic intellectual milieu – as being inexplicable from the point of view of nature or nurture, he has in view first and foremost the basic reality that human beings have irreducibly different personalities, traits, talents, and tendencies. As he observes:

> The difference [*verschil*] in human beings shows up in everything: in the physical and no less in the spiritual; in sensation, observation, memory, imagination, feeling, emotion, desire, will, character, temperament, and so forth; and not only in these aptitudes by themselves but equally so in their mutual relationships. We have innate capabilities, qualities, habits, dispositions, inclinations, conditions, actions, and whatever else one wants to call them; *prior to our consciousness and our will, they shape us to be what we are and lay the foundation for our own thinking and acting.*[89]

Human beings come into existence with personalities that individuate their characters, distinguishing one's self from another. Bavinck goes on to advance an arresting and important line of reasoning:

> Without our will or knowledge, all of that unconscious [dimension] affects our conscious life and gives direction and guidance. And this does not happen only now and then, by way of exception, but it is the rule: our conscious life is continuously born and animated by the unconscious. Our becoming aware and our observations, our feeling and our wanting, our thinking and speaking; all our convictions in religion, morality, science, the arts; our insights and our prejudices, our sympathies and aversions – *these all are rooted far and deep behind the consciousness in our soul*. Often they make us impervious to all reasoning and proof, and often so strongly that we ourselves with all our willpower are powerless to resist them. Who is able to sufficiently account for why he fosters sympathies for and sides with one or another of the warring nations these days? Later, after having fostered such sympathies and having taken sides, we try to justify them with reasons, but such proof is usually not the basis but the outcome of our convictions. *The root of a human being's personality lies in the subconscious, in the soul itself, with all that is innate to it. Soul and consciousness definitely do not coincide. The self is much richer than the 'I'.*[90]

Two comments are worth making with regard to this passage. Bavinck is recognizing that the space of reasons and linguistic communication is not usually sufficient to transform the dispositions of the self. Humans are more than thinking things, and the heart is formed and fixed in ways that go deeper and further

---

88. Bavinck, 'The Unconscious', p. 186.
89. Bavinck, 'The Unconscious', p. 186; *Over het onbewuste*, p. 23. Emphasis mine.
90. Bavinck, 'The Unconscious', pp. 186–7. Emphases mine.

than reasoning. Our basic personalities and tendencies are deeply wired in one's embodied souls that cannot be fully explained. Transformation, then, is possible but must be understood in light of this bodily intransigence. In other words, Bavinck's comments about the fixedness and differences that emerge in human personalities are not meant to be deterministic, as if our inclinations and prejudices cannot be changed with much effort and time. In this regard, his comments on the unconscious self and personality here have to be situated within his broader theology and writings – conversions are possible, and sanctification is precisely that work of transforming the self and its inclinations or habits. But as regeneration and sanctification renews and redirects the self, it renews one's *self*, and does so *as* a self, rather than creating a new uni-personal sanctified humanity that eradicates individuality and freedom. In other words, one is renewed into the kingdom of God precisely with one's distinct personality intact: Paul, Peter, and John, Bavinck argues, retain their distinct personalities even as all are transformed by the Spirit.[91] Elsewhere, Bavinck connects this to a creationist view of the soul, whereby God creates each specific soul as each individual is conceived under the conditions of concrete humanity: 'Creationism preserves the organic – both physical and moral – unity of humanity and *at the same time it respects the mystery of the individual personality*.'[92] The individuation and mystery of personality is unsurprising, given that God creates each human soul at the moment of conception.

Again, a consistent picture emerges: Bavinck understands the soul to be distinct from the body and deeply intertwined with it. Furthermore, the soul is deeper than consciousness – much underlies the threshold of one's consciousness, such that we are often a mystery to ourselves, and without our conscious consent, we come to exist with pre-established personalities and tendencies, which in turn explains the habits of the faculties and our bodies. To repeat Bavinck's conclusion, Holy Scripture recognizes that 'the soul is much richer and deeper than consciousness'.[93]

1916: De overwinning der ziel

Finally, Bavinck's 'Triumph of the Soul' is an address to a conference of philologists that celebrates the persistence of the soul's presence in contemporary discourse and functions as a subtle apologetic. Specifically, it seeks to establish two claims. First, Bavinck develops a narrative according to which materialist accounts of humanity have given way to a renewed focus on the irreducibly immaterial

---

91. Herman Bavinck, *Reformed Ethics*, vol. 1: *Created, Fallen, and Converted Humanity*, John Bolt (ed.) (Grand Rapids: Baker Academic, 2019), p. 420.
92. Bavinck, *RD* 2: p. 587.
93. Bavinck, 'The Unconscious', p. 197.

and vitalist character of reality, including the human person.[94] Second, Bavinck highlights that the soul is manifested in embodied cultural activities, especially in science and art, and that the persistence of the soul points to a life beyond this earth.[95] Bavinck's aim of establishing the importance and distinctness of the soul in this text does not contradict his earlier claims regarding the body–soul relation. All of the earlier themes of the reciprocation between body and soul, personality, and the unconscious are present within this text; they are simply now deployed in service of an expanded theological vision.

The soul, identified as personality, manifests itself distinctly not just through the body but also in the body's very physical endeavors. In science, culture, and art, one discerns the activities of the soul and its triumph over matter precisely because human personalities are disclosed in those cultural spheres.[96] The study of the soul takes place by a close investigation of the maturation of personality as a child matures into adulthood. Here, the psychological studies are 'endlessly differentiated [*eindeloos gedifferenciëerd*]': there are studies on the psychologies 'of the child at home and in school … of male and female … [There is] a genetic, individual, social, pathological, and criminal psychology, a psychology of each psychical function, of representation, understanding and will, of reflection and language, feelings [*aandoeningen*] and passions, of the religious, ethical, and aesthetic feeling [*gevoel*] etc.'[97] Yet, through all these there is a clear development detected in the development of a human being's psyche: one from 'receptivity to spontaneity, from the concrete to the abstract, or, following Augustine, from memory to intellect and will'.[98] The development of the body and its activities manifests the soul.

This spontaneous freedom and action lead to the mastery of material realities, and are irreducible to those same realities. There is 'no direct bridge [*geen directe brug*]' from 'mechanical causality to choice [*mechanische causaliteit tot den*

---

94. This movement from a kind of materialist and mechanical worldview to a dynamic and vitalist one receives a parallel treatment in Bavinck's Stone Lectures, especially in relation to the topics of natural science and history (*PoR*, chapters 4–5). See also Nathaniel Gray Sutanto, 'Divine Providence's *Wetenschappelijke* Benefits: A Bavinckian Model', in *Divine Action and Providence: Explorations in Constructive Dogmatics*, Fred Sanders and Oliver Crisp (eds) (Grand Rapids: Zondervan, 2019), pp. 96–114.

95. Herman Bavinck, *De overwinning der ziel: rede uitgesproken in de algemeene vergardering van het achste Nederlandsche philogencongres te Utrecht, 26 April 1916* (Kampen: Kok, 1916), pp. 10–16. He points to the works of Gustav Theodor Fechner and Dubois-Reymond, among others, as representatives of this 'reaction' against materialism, and further refers to a concession of Ernst Haeckel, a renowned materialist of the day: 'Haeckel himself was overcome, and began to present his materialism as a monism, and he himself, in any case, began to speak of inspired, living atoms … there is a spirit in all things, that atoms are not dead material, but living elements', p. 13.

96. Bavinck, *De overwinning der ziel*, p. 16.
97. Bavinck, *De overwinning der ziel*, pp. 17–18.
98. Bavinck, *De overwinning der ziel*, p. 18.

kiezenden]'.[99] The soul manifests itself in this emergence of personality, where the human being freely chooses, desires, knows, and recognizes him- or herself as a subject. Yet, in all of this, the independent personality remains tethered to the material:

> Hence, humanity ascends through understanding and heart [*gemoed*], through reason and will, to the height of free independent personality. He remains bound to earth, and does not lose his natural base ... man rests both of his feet on the earth, but his head is directed toward the stars. He remains a sensuous being, but with his higher psychical organs [*zielsorganen*] he presses into the realm of invisible things. Enrolled in the natural order, he is also a citizen of a higher world, the world of ideas and norms, of the true, good, and beautiful.[100]

The personality has a general, formal character, to be sure, and can be filled with all sorts of content. However, in its freedom and flexibility there is to be found the individuality of each human being, and its enduring identity that persists through the changing circumstances of the body. As our spiritual property, the soul rises above time: 'It is the soul, which, as personality, overcomes sensuousness and receives a spiritual and eternal portion.'[101] This enduring identity, and the way in which each personality is manifested in one's earthly work, is precisely that which indicates humanity's heavenly origins.

The last two sections of the booklet then reflect on how the soul's triumph over sensuousness and materiality is precisely reflected in humanity's cultural endeavors. Bavinck elaborates on the two spheres of science and art.[102] Science, taken broadly as both the empirical sciences and the industrial sciences, showcases the mastery of the soul over the material, as it organizes, studies, and codifies the raw nature around us. In art, we see the victory of the realm of ideas as humans deploy visual imagery to depict those ideals. Art projects a future reality, and though it does not have any intrinsic resources to bring that future to realization, it witnesses to the human longing for the triumph of good over evil.[103] The apologetic tinge of Bavinck's descriptions is further displayed in his warning to philologists to take seriously the presence of strife within human beings, a deeper strife than that which exists between 'sensuality and spirit' ('*zinnelijkheid en geest*'), one which bears an 'ethical character' ('*etisch karakter*'): a strife within one's self, against one's self.[104] Bavinck, it seems, is referring here to the presence of sin within the soul, and claims in this regard that the most 'beautiful and richest victory is that which

---

99. Bavinck, *De overwinning der ziel*, p. 24.
100. Bavinck, *De overwinning der ziel*, p. 24.
101. Bavinck, *De overwinning der ziel*, p. 26.
102. Bavinck, *De overwinning der ziel*, pp. 28–33.
103. Bavinck, *De overwinning der ziel*, pp. 32–3.
104. Bavinck, *De overwinning der ziel*, p. 29.

the soul obtains over itself'.[105] To find that victory is to reach beyond the bounds of reason, and to a faith beyond one's earthly existence.[106]

Having an overview of the text in hand, it is indicative that *De overwinning der ziel* paints a picture consistent with his writings as a whole – it is a development within an intelligible trajectory of thought, not a contradiction of it. The booklet emphasizes the necessity of recognizing the soul, and the connection of the soul to the body as witnessed in its cultural activities.

Looking Ahead

Let us take stock. In the 1916 booklet on the triumph of the soul, one sees several emphases are anticipated by and organically emerge from his earliest works. As the preceding analysis has shown, his *Beginselen der psychologie* already included extended reflections on the importance of subconscious life, even if the language of the organic personality emerges only later. To be sure, in *De overwinning der ziel*, Bavinck re-emphasizes the importance of Augustinian insights that endure in light of recent psychological findings, depend less on Aristotelian faculty psychology, and put the concept of personality front and center. Furthermore, though the purpose of this booklet is to highlight the triumph of the soul over material realities, it achieves this precisely by showcasing the unique earthly work of human beings – earthly work made possible by the spiritual character of the soul and its manifestation in human personality. Here, however, one sees not a contradiction but rather a logical maturation in Bavinck's thought on the body-soul relation. Far from departing from the older insights, Bavinck presupposed them, and, contrary to Jaarsma's conjecture that Bavinck rejects the use of faculty psychology in his mature writings, as late as 1921, Bavinck continued to speak of the faculties of knowing and desiring.[107] Furthermore, as we have shown, Bavinck's positive comments on Aristotelian hylomorphism in the earlier writings were not without some reservations and went alongside his argument that the newer studies on the unconscious and personality needed to be taken seriously. The textual evidence thus does not support the interpretation that Bavinck 'refutes' his earlier writings in his more mature texts, despite the shifts of emphases that he places on modern sources on personality and the unconscious.[108]

More importantly, the preceding analysis has shown that, for Bavinck, the unity behind body and soul is the personality. The personality showcases the unconscious depths of the soul and the mystery of the human heart as well as the incommunicable property that distinguishes self from others. It informs the heart's desires and thoughts in ways that seem to elude our grasp, and in turn further illumines the way in which each human being is unique in expressing

---

105. Bavinck, *De overwinning der ziel*, p. 32.
106. Bavinck, *De overwinning der ziel*, p. 34.
107. Bavinck, 'Primacy of the Intellect or the Will', pp. 199–204.
108. Jaarsma, *Educational Philosophy of Herman Bavinck*, p. 83.

personality. This hiddenness and mystery of personality also manifest themselves in the unconscious workings of the body, showing that the body knows, feels, and functions in rich ways that precede conscious willing and knowing, and this also eludes our comprehension.[109] To connect this more explicitly to Bavinck's organicism: the soul, its faculties, and the body constitute a diversity that is united by the mystery of personality. There is a discernible pattern of unity-in-diversity in Bavinck's account of the human individual. Here, there is a decisively structural and psychological view of the human subject, but in later chapters, we shall see that it also provides the seeds for the social account of corporate humanity that Bavinck will emphasize, for in the depths of the human heart one sees a direction toward relationships – or a *being-toward-relation*. For Bavinck, the human being's relationality has metaphysical significance – it is exemplified in every human individual's connection to one another and ultimately to Adam and to Christ.

In Bavinck's view, taking seriously the subconscious life is an implication of an Augustinian theological anthropology and the doctrine of general revelation. Observing the affective dimensions of Bavinck's anthropology will further demonstrate how it might intersect with some current trajectories in affect theory, phenomenology, and the cognitive science of religion.[110] It is to these topics that we now turn.

---

109. Bavinck's perspective thus confirms what Lucy Peppiatt has called the 'apophatic' aspect of the imago Dei, in *The Imago Dei: Humanity Made in the Image of God* (Eugene: Cascade, 2022), pp. 19, 60.

110. Jaarsma has already recognized the potential fruitfulness of putting Bavinck's thought in dialogue with phenomenology, in his *Educational Philosophy of Herman Bavinck*, p. 82.

Chapter 3

RELIGIOUS CREATURES: REVELATION, AFFECT THEORY, AND THE COGNITIVE SCIENCE OF RELIGION

The Leiden Synopsis argues that God reveals himself in creation, and that human beings are so exposed to that revelation that 'the notion of God has been inscribed on the human soul as a first truth and a first principle'.[1] Indeed, the Leiden Synopsis is codifying in a succinct way the Christian teaching that human beings exist in a fundamental relation to God. The heavens declare his glory, the Psalmist says (Ps. 19), and thus his divinity has been clearly 'perceived' (Rom. 1:20). If human beings are image-bearers of God, then they are simultaneously accountable to and dependent on him at every point of their existence (Ps. 8). Image-bearers live *coram deo*.

Two contemporary trajectories emphasize two differing loci for the reception of this creational awareness of God: affect and cognition. On one level, affect theory argues that the body is already formed in particular ways that precede and inform cognition.[2] Religiosity here is not predicated upon the unique cognitive (and linguistic) features of the human self, but rather upon something it has in common with other animals. Human bodies produce and are affected by particular social, physiological, and cultural affects that inform and nurture religiosity. Religious affect theory thus posits an animalistic and naturalistic explanation for religious practices and phenomena. Rather than signifying the uniqueness of the human being, it actually points to the way in which its existence shares common traits with other animals, and offers a more granular account of how it is that bodies are moved. As we shall see, the focus on religious affects is consonant with the findings in Heideggerian phenomenology with regard to the pre-discursive existence of

---

1. *Synopsis of a Purer Theology: Latin Text and English Translation*, vol. 1: 6. 4. (p. 153).
2. For a summary of how affect theory has emerged and has been utilized in religious studies, see Simeon Zahl, *Holy Spirit and Christian Experience* (Oxford: Oxford University Press, 2020), pp. 146–9. Especially relevant for our purposes here is the work of Donovan O. Schaefer, *Religious Affects: Animality, Evolution, and Power* (Durham: Duke University Press, 2015).

human everydayness.³ On another level, the cognitive science of religion shows through empirical studies that human agents spontaneously believe in a higher mind or agency that bestows meaning on particular events. During particular instances, a propositional belief in some higher mind is produced in a properly basic way as an immediate result. Thus, a particular focus of this science is the recognition that something unique in the human being – its cognition – points to some higher divine reality as brains produce cognitive beliefs about the existence of some higher agent.

The purpose of this chapter is to exposit Bavinck's own position on the primordially religious character of the human self, and to put it in dialogue with the trends in affect theory and the cognitive science of religion. This dialogue will ready us to develop further Bavinck's understanding of the human being as a fundamentally religious creature who is in contact with God, to apply Bavinck's insights in dialogue with affect theory and cognitive science, and to show ways in which his affective theological anthropology can enfold the insights of both trajectories in a rather harmonious fashion.

This chapter thus moves in four steps. In the first section, I draw from the primary texts, and the current scholarship on Bavinck's retrieval of Schleiermacher's account of affection and Romantic phenomenology to provide an exposition of Bavinck on the primordially religious character of human beings. In the second and third sections of this chapter, I outline some current insights from religious affect theory and Heideggerian phenomenology, while applying our findings in Bavinck's thought to the question of human religiosity in dialogue with these trajectories. The picture of the human developed here is one that is primordially responding to God in ways that precede the development of cognitive belief in God. God is the first 'thing' *felt* by the human heart, though cognitive belief in God itself does arise spontaneously and naturally after the fact. The fourth section examines the findings of the cognitive science of religion, and shows how the insights from this generative field might be rendered consistent with the findings of affect theory outlined in Sections 2 and 3. The final section shows how the insights of both affect theory and the cognitive science of religion can be fruitfully deployed from a Bavinckian perspective. These arguments thus contribute to the overarching thesis of this book concerning Bavinck's holistic anthropology as an account of the human self that is neither primarily cognitive nor animalistic, while meshing particular instincts from both classical and more recent accounts of theological anthropology.

---

3. As we shall see, deploying Heideggerian phenomenology also has some benefits in that it offers a philosophical language that meshes well with the concerns of Eve Sedgwick and others more usefully than a Deleuzian account, as outlined in Schaefer, *Religious Affects*, pp. 28–35, and Donovan O. Schaefer, *The Evolution of Affect Theory: The Humanities, the Sciences, and the Study of Power* (Cambridge: Cambridge University Press, 2019), pp. 1–53.

Religious Creatures: Human Awareness and Dependence on God

If the depths of the human personality are a mystery that yet informs the way in which the human lives as a psychosomatic unity, in the core of that personality is a deep-seated awareness of dependence on God. To grapple with Bavinck's understanding of human beings as religious creatures, it is therefore necessary to understand how he utilizes particular nineteenth-century terminology and patterns of reasoning. Drawing from the Romantic, mediating, and ethical theologians, Bavinck argues that Calvin's *sensus divinitatis* is best construed not primarily as a rational capacity or habit created within us, but rather as Schleiermacher's 'feeling of absolute dependence'. One has to do with cognition, the other with affection; the former's effect is the acquisition of knowledge as a result of its proper use, while the latter is a *given* from the moment of self-consciousness.

A helpful starting point for grasping Bavinck's account of the self in dependence on God is in the chapter on general revelation in *Wonderful Works of God* (1908):

> In the first place, a sense of absolute dependency is characteristic of it. Underneath the mind and will, underneath our thought and action, there is in us a self-consciousness which is interdependent with our self-existence and seems to coincide with it. Before we think, before we will, we *are*, we *exist*. We exist in a *definite* way, and in indissoluble unity with this existence we have a *sense* of existence and a sense of existing *as* we are. And the core of this near identity of self-existence and self-consciousness is the feeling of dependency. In our inmost selves, we are immediately, without benefit of reasoning, that is, and prior to all reasoning – conscious of ourselves as created, limited, dependent beings ... Man is a 'dependent' of the universe. And, further, he is dependent, *together with* other created things, and dependent this time in an absolute sense, on God, who is the one, eternal, and real being.[4]

Human existence is concomitant with the reception of the feeling of absolute dependence. This affect of absolute dependence is the result of God's self-revelation in the human psyche and creation itself. Both within and without themselves, human beings encounter their own dependence on God. Cory Brock's recent monograph, *Orthodox yet Modern*, usefully brings out the Romantic philosophical backdrop that undergirds Bavinck's construction. Brock comments that Bavinck's statements here distinguish 'an awareness of divinity ... from discursive, propositional knowing'.[5] As a case of non-propositional knowing (underneath the mind and will), dependence is 'felt' rather than consciously thought about.[6] In his Stone lectures, Bavinck further tethered this feeling of dependence on one's

---

4. Herman Bavinck, *Wonderful Works of God*, Henry Zylstra (trans.) (Glenside: Westminster Seminary Press, 2019), pp. 26–7.
5. Brock, *Orthodox yet Modern*, p. 252.
6. On feeling as a kind of knowing, see Brock, *Orthodox yet Modern*, 144–6, and Sutanto, *God and Knowledge*, chapter 7.

self-consciousness: 'The core of our self-consciousness is, as Schleiermacher perceived much more clearly than Kant, not autonomy, but a feeling of dependence. In the act of becoming conscious of ourselves we become conscious of ourselves as creatures …. We feel ourselves dependent on everything around us; we are not alone.'[7] Self-consciousness is the consciousness of our beings as creatures, and thus of our dependence on the Creator.

Brock notes that the reference to self-consciousness is important for two reasons. First, consciousness and self-consciousness are more basic than our acts of thinking and desiring. They sit underneath both, while also giving thinking and desiring their legitimacy and direction: 'For Bavinck, Schleiermacher's immediacy of self-consciousness is a pre-discursive awareness of self that renders the possibility of all forms of thinking and doing.'[8] Second, however, although the feeling of absolute dependence is unmediated by thinking and willing and is in fact beneath both, the feeling produced by self-consciousness is still the result of God's created order outside of the self: 'For Bavinck, because revelatory creation is the secret of the universe, God's witness is everywhere presenting God both objectively and subjectively, directly and indirectly.'[9] Feeling here is not reducible to conscious emotions, but is that which is prior to them – it is that direct awareness that is the result of everyday exposure to God's revelation in creation.

Bavinck consistently deploys the language of feeling in conjunction with the use of Schleiermacher's terms. Language of consciousness, subjects and objects, conscience, representations, and intuition ubiquitously attends Bavinck's talk of feeling.[10] The sense of the divine is thus an affect – a feeling not reducible to explicit notions or propositions. Though Bavinck would not deny either that there are common notions 'acknowledged intuitively or by direct apprehension by all human beings' or that there is a 'potency' implanted within us in order to know God via reasoning, feeling is always prior to these ways of knowing. In other words, *feeling* and *affect* are irreducible and lie under conceptual forms of knowing, being indicative of humanity's utter dependence upon God existentially.[11] It is not merely

---

7. Bavinck, *PoR*, p. 57. The older edition's English translation of the word '*afhankelijkheidsgevoel*' into 'sense of dependence' veils the allusion to Schleiermacher, and hence the word 'feeling' is to be preferred.

8. Brock, *Orthodox yet Modern*, p. 87.

9. Brock, *Orthodox yet Modern*, p. 252. Cf. Bavinck, *RD* 2: p. 73. This important observation responds to Duby's worries about an 'intuitive' revelation that 'bypasses the creaturely media of revelation altogether', which would more properly characterize the knowledge of the blessed in heaven. Steven J. Duby, *God in Himself: Scripture, Metaphysics, and the Task of Christian Theology* (Downers Grove: IVP Academic, 2019), p. 99 n. 132.

10. See the analyses throughout chapters 3–5 in Brock's *Orthodox yet Modern* that expound the intricate grammar through which Bavinck elaborates on the nature of *gevoel*.

11. Duby, *God in Himself*, pp. 98–9.

pre-ratiocinative but also affective.[12] If one were to gloss it as a *sensus divinitatis*, one would have to specify that it is not a faculty that produces conceptual beliefs about God, but rather an ever-present pre-categorical intuition produced by God himself.

As Brock shows, this language draws from the post-Kantian understanding of affect as a pre-categorical intuition. It is simultaneously not reducible to and precedes the Reformed-scholastic understanding of implanted knowledge as common notions. Not to be confused with emotions, intuition here refers to that awareness of the world yet to be cognized by the categories of the understanding, which forms the groundwork for everyday phenomenology. As I will further demonstrate in the next chapter, this provides a theological re-interpretation of what Heidegger means when he describes this daily experience:

> we may then say that that which already shows itself in the appearance as prior to the 'phenomenon' as ordinarily understood and as accompanying it in every case, can, even though it thus shows itself unthematically, be brought thematically to show itself; and what thus shows itself in itself (the 'forms of the intuition') will be the 'phenomena' of phenomenology.[13]

As Hubert Dreyfus comments, these forms of intuition are nonconceptual and yet *meaningful*: 'We must accept the possibility that our ground-level coping opens up the world by opening us up to a *meaningful* Given – a Given that is *nonconceptual* but not *bare*.'[14] Andrew Inkpin shows that this means the consideration of 'propositional truth' is incorporated 'within a broader phenomenon' of 'unbreached contact with [*Dasein's*] surroundings'.[15]

Reading the doctrine of general revelation along with these Romantic emphases from Bavinck prompts us toward not merely reflection on the cognitive, but that which is phenomenological and itself underneath explicit cognition, irreducible to an immediate knowledge of common notions or propositions. Inkpin notes that Heidegger shared similar concerns. Though Heidegger might not find his motivation to ground the human being's basic embeddedness within the world by drawing from the Reformed doctrine of general revelation, he desires to deny 'a

---

12. Anticipating our discussion of Augustine, James K. A. Smith's description of Augustine's view of human beings as 'fundamentally noncognitive, affective creatures' is apt. *Desiring the Kingdom: Worship, Worldviews, and Cultural Formation* (Grand Rapids: Baker Academic, 2009), p. 53.

13. Martin Heidegger, *Being and Time*, John Macquarrie and Edward Robinson (trans.) (Oxford: Blackwell, 1962), pp. 54–5. Hereafter, *BT*.

14. Hubert Dreyfus, 'Overcoming the Myth of the Mental: How Philosophers Can Benefit from the Phenomenology of Everyday Expertise', in *Skillful Coping: Essays on the Phenomenology of Everyday Perception and Action*, Mark Wrathall (ed.) (Oxford: Oxford University Press, 2014), p. 116.

15. Andrew Inkpin, *Disclosing the World: On the Phenomenology of Language* (Cambridge: MIT Press, 2016), p. 62.

basic subject-object dichotomy in favour of the notion of being-in-the-world', such that 'the idea of being radically out of touch with the world, or with truth, makes no sense'.[16] Human beings are already always in touch with truth, and indeed, are always *in* the truth, in the sense that they are involved within 'the broader phenomenon of openness to and contact with the world, and as encompassing subpropositional, propositional, and suprapropositional levels'.[17] We shall return to these phenomenological themes below in the discussion on affect theory.

Bavinck, like the Reformed scholastics before him (and the Romantic tradition), was seeking to describe universal and everyday *human* experience on this point. One feels God at every moment as one feels one's own self. In addition to general revelation, Bavinck and others suppose that this feeling is a result of common grace: 'Common grace is first found in the fact of consciousness, where the self is the substratum of the possibility of all knowing and willing, of science, art, and ethics.'[18] The *ego* is upheld by grace – and as such, before the *ego* apprehends or thinks of the world, it feels its dependence.[19] This further explains Bavinck's own preference for the terms 'general and special revelation' over natural and supernatural theology[20]: 'Scripture … makes no distinction between "natural" and "supernatural" revelation … Actually, according to Scripture, all revelation, also that in nature, is supernatural.'[21] All awareness of God is due to revelation, and because revelation is from the *divine*, no revelation, technically speaking, is natural.

Bavinck emphasizes that natural theology should be viewed under the purview of common grace rather than creation as such:

---

16. Inkpin, *Disclosing the World*, p. 62. However, on the theological (and Augustinian) roots of Heidegger's thought, see Judith Wolfe, *Heidegger's Eschatology: Theological Horizons in Martin Heidegger's Early Work* (Oxford: Oxford University Press, 2013).

17. Inkpin, *Disclosing the World*, p. 62.

18. Brock, *Orthodox yet Modern*, p. 125.

19. This can be considered as a deepening and extension of what Steven Duby has observed about natural theology's prior dependence on '*natural* grace' that is given to the subjective inner life of the psyche: God is the gracious source of all that is natural and supernatural. Duby, *God in Himself*, p. 97. Emphasis original. In my judgment, this emphasis on natural grace as the foundation for natural theology is not brought out enough in other dogmatic statements on this subject matter and is worth further teasing out. Arguably it is key to alleviating many contemporary Kuyperian and Bavinckian anxieties about properly articulating natural theology's place.

20. 'Hence the distinction between natural and supernatural revelation is not identical with the distinction between general and special revelation. To describe the twofold revelation that underlies pagan religions and the religion of Scripture, the latter distinction is preferable to the former.' Bavinck, *RD* 1: pp. 311–12.

21. Bavinck, *RD* 1: p. 307. This is consistent with Duby's emphasis: '*God* gives this knowledge.' *God in Himself*, p. 126. Emphasis original.

> From the fall onward, human life and humanity itself is not simply grounded in the order of creation ... the fruit of common grace – being allowed to retain something of what we by nature possessed by Adam ... is a gift of grace .... It is in this sense that we also speak of natural theology, natural morality, and natural law .... This is better than seeing it under the purview of creation.[22]

This is an addition to Bavinck's judgment that the term 'natural theology' is ambiguous, especially after the eighteenth-century rationalist programs, for it could refer to an autonomous way by which humans reason unto God, instead of to that sense of the divine produced by being exposed to God's common grace and creational revelation.[23] Though fallen, human beings continue to live in dependence on God due to this common grace.

Lest we receive the wrong impression that Bavinck was wholly motivated by a nineteenth-century Romantic program in his account of the affective dimensions of general revelation, Brock rightly notes that Bavinck identified this trajectory in Augustine's turn to the subject and in an Augustinian account of illumination.[24] In Bavinck's words:

> Augustine was the first to understand self-consciousness .... But when the Christian religion revealed to us the greatness of God's heart, and in the dayspring from on high visited us with his tender mercy, it at the same time cast its light on man and on the riches and value of his soul. It imparted to him a new certainty, the certainty of faith (*de verzekerheid des geloof*); it restored to him his confidence in God, and therewith his confidence in himself. And by this light of revelation Augustine descended deep into his own inner life; forgetting nature, he desired to know naught else but God and himself. There he found thought, to be sure, but not thought alone; beneath thought he penetrated to the essence of the soul, for in himself always life preceded thought; faith, knowledge;

---

22. Herman Bavinck, *RE* 1: p. 149.

23. Bavinck, *RD* 2: p. 78. Paul Gould and James Dew articulate the distinction between natural theology and natural revelation helpfully: 'To see this, it will be helpful to draw the word "natural" from them, at least for the moment, and see the difference between "revelation" and "theology" more generally. Revelation, as understood by the Christian tradition, refers to what God has done or said or given. Revelation is God's self-disclosure of himself that allows human beings to know and understand who he is. As such, revelation is something that God does and/or something that God gives. Theology, by contrast, is a derivative of revelation. It refers to what human beings to with revelation, as a human response to God's self-disclosure'. *Philosophy: A Christian Introduction* (Grand Rapids: Baker Academic, 2019), pp. 73–4.

24. What Bavinck appreciates in Schleiermacher, therefore, is traceable back to Augustine: 'In other words, Bavinck makes a subtle declaration in his adoption of an argument built upon the immediate self-consciousness and the feeling of dependence that this project is inaugurated first in Augustine before taken up by Schleiermacher'. Brock, *Orthodox yet Modern*, p. 218.

self-consciousness (*zelfbesef*), reflection; experience, science (*het kennen de ervaring*); he first lived through the things which later he thought and wrote. Thus Augustine went back behind thought to the essence of the soul, and found in it not a simple unity, but a marvellously rich totality; he found there the ideas, the norms, the laws of the true and the good, the solution of the problem of the certainty of knowledge, of the cause of all things, of the supreme good; he found there the seeds and germs of all knowledge and science and art; he found there even, in the triad of *memoria, intellectus*, and *voluntas*, a reflection (*afdruk*) of the triune being of God. Augustine was the philosopher of self-examination, and in self-consciousness he discovered the starting-point of a new metaphysics.[25]

Bavinck is recognizing here that Augustine was the first to recognize that the reception of divine revelation resides deep within the self's consciousness. Though ultimately 'Bavinck does not turn to the adoption of Augustine's details', for, in Bavinck's judgment, Augustine did include fully formed rational propositions within the mind, Bavinck identified Augustine's turn toward 'humble interiority' with 'Schleiermacher's dependent self'.[26] In other words, Bavinck recognized that in Augustine, there is found a theologian who calls the self to attend to itself, to look inward precisely so that the self might be led to look upward toward God. As Rowan Williams has argued, the Augustinian turn to the self is precisely to recognize that 'neither God nor the self is a kind of *thing*, an object with material boundaries: it is an agency essentially unconfined by matter and space, and this becomes plain only when we "look within", as Augustine repeatedly encourages us

---

25. Bavinck, *Philosophy of Revelation*, p. 55. Here is one place where Bavinck potentially contradicts Duby's account, for Duby argues that 'the human mind is a *tabula rasa* with respect to such knowledge'. *God in Himself*, p. 98. However, Bavinck seemingly argues to the contrary that 'The mind of man is indeed no *tabula rasa*, no empty form, but a totality of life from the very first moment of its existence. And when it becomes conscious of itself, this self-consciousness is not a mere formal apprehension of existence but always includes within it an apprehension of a peculiar nature, a particular quality of mind.' *Philosophy of Revelation*, p. 55. Then again, in context Duby is arguing against 'fully formed propositions,' while Bavinck later argues that this consciousness is more properly articulated as simply a feeling of absolute dependence (which is a more modest account than Augustine's proposal of what the subject knows by illumination).

26. Brock, *Orthodox yet Modern*, p. 220. Scott MacDonald's recent summary of Augustine's epistemology is consistent with Bavinck's reading: 'The central epistemological idea in this model is that intellectual seeing – direct acquaintance or direct cognitive contact of the knower with what is known – is the paradigm and foundation of knowledge. The model's focal analogy articulates this idea: just as the bodily eye sees visible corporeal objects when they are present and illumined by sunlight, the mind's eye "sees" intelligible objects when the conditions are right, where the right conditions include the presence or activity of a kind of intelligible light.' 'Augustine', in *The Oxford Handbook of the Epistemology of Theology*, William Abraham and Frederick Aquino (eds) (Oxford: Oxford University Press, 2017), p. 356.

to do, to find something that does not alter in step with our material conditions'.[27] Turning inward leads toward an acknowledgment of 'dependence on the strictly unconditioned and unlimited act of God's gift'.[28] There, one encounters the very realities that one desires but cannot grasp, in other words, a desire for the eternal. Crucially, Williams then argues that the Augustinian sense of self is a 'sign', for the self is 'profoundly mysterious to us … and the locus of our deepest awareness of frustration'.[29] The mystery of the self's depths and its longings for stability point to our need for humility, that recognition that we are at every moment dependent on God. Human beings are made in the *image* of God, after all, 'a sign of [their] maker'.[30] Bavinck was observing precisely this Augustinian turn to the interiority of the self as a sign to God in Schleiermacher's account of the feeling of absolute dependence.

With this sketch of the unconscious personality and the religious core of human beings from Bavinck in view, one can now turn to the contemporary conversations and bring Bavinck and them into constructive dialogue.

Affect Theory and Phenomenology

In this section, I observe some findings within affect theory and particular strands of Heideggerian phenomenology. In so doing, the observations here display the backdrop to show that Bavinck provides theological resources to situate those insights from within a dogmatic framework in the next section. Furthermore, I argue that reading the fruits of these works from religious studies and phenomenology through Bavinck helps us avoid interpreting religious practice through an exclusively naturalist paradigm, and that Christian theology can accommodate and perhaps offer a richer theological account of why religious beliefs emerge out of the embodied human condition. What follows here is a constructive reading of four categories drawn from Donovan O. Schaefer's *Religious Affects*: (1) the linguistic fallacy, (2) onto-phenomenology, (3) para-cognition, and (4) intransigence. My interest here is not to regurgitate Schaefer's discussion of these features of affects, but, again, to offer a constructive reading of them while utilizing tools from Heideggerian phenomenology, and where useful, analytic philosophy, with a view to applying their insights into Bavinck's own theological anthropology. The use of Heideggerian phenomenology in this section is also fruitful because Heidegger's thought dovetails well with Schaefer's concern for the interplay between the pre-categorical and categorical, and sees a continuity between affects (the unconscious) and emotions (consciousness), for such a rubric of boundaries

---

27. Rowan Williams, *On Augustine* (London: Bloomsbury, 2016), p. 22. It is important to note, as Williams does, that this takes place without eliding the place of the body as constitutive for the self.
28. Williams, *On Augustine*, p. 23.
29. Williams, *On Augustine*, p. 35.
30. Williams, *On Augustine*, p. 196.

'presupposes in advance that structure and awareness can be comfortably set aside from the pre-structured or pre-conscious forces that make them up'.[31] Heidegger rejects the view that human beings relate with the world representationally first and phenomenologically second, but rather considers that the phenomenological always informs and is the backdrop against which cognition arises, and offers philosophical language that helps articulate this basic feature of reality.[32]

Affect theory observes that there is a kind of bodily knowing prior to and alongside linguistic and propositional expression, and that these affects from and on the body form behavior and belief. It is, in Schaefer's words, the study of those 'propulsive elements of experience, thought, sensation, feeling, and action that are not necessarily captured or capturable by language of self-sovereign "consciousness"'.[33] Affect theory, by these lights, subverts the notion that religion forms our behavior unidirectionally – from linguistic themes to habits. It indicates that the roots of religion are natural and physical (in a non-reductionist way), and that religion arises out of the basic power relations and affections that have already shaped our bodies and hence who we are.

Bavinck himself was aware of this newer consciousness of the animalistic dimensions of religion.[34] But if Bavinck is right regarding the pervasiveness of general revelation and our embodied attunement to that revelation, then the possibility arises that the basic 'animality' and pre-cognitive realities of our bodies are already primordially religious not because of a reducibly naturalist cause, but because animality itself is created as directed toward God. On this account, religious expression may arise out of basic affects precisely because our bodies have been formed by an unconsciously religious psyche and an environment of revelation. And so too, revelation may not just be disclosed in one's 'pneumatic side, but equally in terms of [one's] somatic side'.[35] It may then be that religiosity goes all the way down, precisely because revelation goes all the way down: religious animality, read theologically in this way, is not a defeater but a confirmation of the affective dimensions of general revelation. We now turn to the four concepts mentioned above.

---

31. Schaefer, *Religious Affects*, p. 32. As Mark Wrathall describes Dreyfus's deployment of Heidegger: 'Dreyfus rejects any account that builds a mind/world distinction into the logic of action, even in the minimal form of the distinction between the experience of acting (mind) and the bodily movement that accompanies that experience (world)'. 'Introduction', in *Skillful Coping: Essays on the Phenomenology of Everyday Perception and Action*, Hubert Dreyfus and Mark Wrathall (eds) (Oxford: Oxford University Press, 2014), p. 15.

32. Practice thus precedes and forms cognition: 'Dreyfus starts with the premise that skillful activity itself is the consummate form and foundation of human intelligence, and derives an account of cognition from coping.' Wrathall, 'Introduction', p. 3.

33. Schaefer, *Religious Affects*, p. 23.

34. Bavinck, *RD* 1: p. 316.

35. Bavinck, *RD* 2: p. 561. See also the stimulating comments in Paul Dafydd Jones, *Patience – A Theological Exploration: Part One, from Creation to Christ* (London: Bloomsbury T&T Clark, 2022), pp. 349–50.

Linguistic Fallacy

The linguistic fallacy, in brief, mistakenly supposes that the direction of power and influence comes primarily (or solely) through the formation of concepts and the space of reasons. It is, in Schaefer's reading, the 'myth that the medium of power is language'.[36] The identification of the linguistic fallacy thus follows the lead of the so-called 'materialist shift' in religious studies that sees religious concepts, beliefs, narratives, and cosmologies as emerging *out of* discernable bodily behaviors prior to linguistic articulation.[37] This explains the empirical observation that differing religious themes and beliefs can give rise to similar behavior patterns, and the obverse: that differing religious beliefs emerge from and satiate similar bodily patterns.

The linguistic fallacy is part and parcel of what Hubert Dreyfus has called the 'epistemological tradition' synonymous with the Cartesian turn toward self-consciousness.[38] This tradition trades in the idea that the human subject is most functional when it is detached, rational, and self-aware. However, most of human living is not in the theoretical and detached, but in the lived existence of involvement with one's physical environment. Human beings are always *being-there – Dasein*. Thus it is that for Heidegger, human existence – that is, human *being* – is an existence prior to the *study* of its existence. Human *onticity* is prior to *ontology*, and to get at the existence of human beings, we need to give an account of their existence that is prior to their own self-awareness. Indeed, when any human being studies a field, that study is rooted in that primordial embeddedness and in the pre-theoretical awareness of the human self. As Heidegger wrote, 'whenever an ontology takes for its theme entities whose character of Being is other than that of Dasein, it has its own foundation and motivation in Dasein's own ontical structure, in which a pre-ontological understanding of Being is comprised as a definite character'.[39] More tersely, '"Being-ontological" is not yet tantamount to "developing an ontology"'.[40] Being precedes theoretical knowing.

Onto-phenomenology

This study of being prior to the *study* of being is consonant with what Schaefer has described (drawing from political theorist William Connolly) as a 'methodological approach to religion that emphasizes precognitive, affective dimensions … rather than the primacy of texts'.[41] In other words, there are '*phenomenological affects*, affects woven into the textures of experience, hovering around, rather than beneath, the line of "conscious" awareness … [providing] religious studies resources for

---

36. Schaefer, *Religious Affects*, p. 22.
37. Schaefer, *Religious Affects*, p. 22.
38. Hubert Dreyfus, *Being-in-the-World: A Commentary on Heidegger's Being and Time, Division I* (Massachusetts: MIT Press, 1999), pp. 45–6.
39. Heidegger, *BT*, p. 33.
40. Heidegger, *BT*, p. 32.
41. Schaefer, *Religious Affects*, p. 27.

studying the named (shame, happiness, fear, anger, etc.) and the as-yet-unnamed emotions of embodied affective palettes'.[42] The reason why Schaefer prefers to speak of affects as hovering around, rather than beneath, conscious awareness is because of the phenomenological blurriness of when self-consciousness ends and begins. Taken together with the linguistic fallacy, onto-phenomenology shows that 'discourses attach to bodies' which are motivated by pre-linguistic phenomenology, such as involvement, belonging, fear, shame, and the like, which in turn inform and shape religious discourse.[43]

The 'onto' in 'onto-phenomenology' then refers to the *essence* of the human being – its lived existence. This use of the term 'essence' is itself self-consciously non-Platonic and non-Aristotelian, in so far as it does not refer to a kind of stable and rational soul.[44] Rather, the evolutionary and animalistic origin of the human self – which determine it precisely as a biologically involved body with affects that elude linguistic expression – is that which determines its *being*. As Schaefer writes, 'Onto-phenomenology diagrams these moving, overlapping, bodily technologies' – it is a study of epistemology that has as its object not the space of reasons but the realities of human behavior – an 'onto-epistemology'.[45]

Despite the intimidating language of onto-phenomenology here, Heidegger observes that this sort of study is actually the closest to us, for it is an observation of the human being in its *everydayness*:

> We must rather choose such a way of access and such a kind of interpretation that this entity can show itself in itself and from itself. And this means that it is to be shown as it is *proximally and for the most part* – in its average *everydayness*. In this everydayness there are certain structures which we shall exhibit – not just any accidental structures, but essential ones which, in every kind of Being that factical Dasein may have, persist as determinative for the character of its being.[46]

The human being, in its *essence*, is something that we *are* in our everyday living. As such, to study ourselves is actually a most difficult discipline, for by studying ourselves, we make ourselves our conscious object for conceptualization, when what we want to study is ourselves in our everydayness, that is, apart from our self-awareness and that life that precedes explicit rational cognition. To emphasize the point, if the 'onto' in onto-phenomenology refers to that everyday manifestation of the human essence, the phenomenology itself refers to the human beings

---

42. Schaefer, *Religious Affects*, p. 28. Emphasis original. Schaefer here is drawing from Silvan Tomkin's work.

43. Schaefer, *Religious Affects*, 32.

44. Drawing from Stephen Jay Gould, Schaefer writes: 'essences need not be Platonic in cast: we can rehabilitate "essence" as a concept by viewing it as a long-term pattern expressing a slow-motion trajectory of change within an expansive evolutionary dynamic.' *Religious Affects*, p. 47.

45. Schaefer, *Religious Affects*, p. 51.

46. Heidegger, *BT*, p. 38. Emphasis original.

receptivity and responsiveness to its environment prior to thematization. This phenomenological reading isolates Kant's *intuitions* and treats them as are prior to the processes of the *categories*: 'what thus shows itself in itself (the "forms of the intuition") will be the "phenomena" of phenomenology'.[47] The upshot of studying the human being in its everydayness is that, prior to conscious reasoning, humanity is always already attuned and connected to its environment.

This focus on the everyday attunement of human bodies to its environment anticipates the focus on Dreyfus's *skilful coping* in the next chapter, and dovetails well with the observations often made in particular strands of affect theory and cognitive science of religion that the human mind is not reducible to data-processing computers or machines. The human capacity to recognize and form linguistic and pre-linguistic transmitters of meaning demonstrates a kind of mastery quite distinct from computational machinery.

Para-cognition

This third point is a much-needed clarification, for while the preceding sections emphasize the importance of the pre-conscious life for understanding human existence, they are not meant to undermine the role that conscious cognition plays in human behavior. The issue at stake is not that cognition plays no role, but the rejection of the claim that explicit cognition plays the dominant or exclusive role in shaping behavior, given that cognition often arises from pre-cognitive affects. It recognizes that affect and rationality are in a complex and interwoven relationship, such that affects are at times 'not exactly noncognitive but extra- or paracognitive, *coassembling* with the cognitive (Silvan Tomkin's word) to shape the contours of thought, action, and experience'.[48] Affects are 'the flexible architecture of our animal lifeways, the experiential shapes that herd together and carry religion on their backs'.[49] Conscious reasoning is predicated upon the embodied affections.

In this respect, two further terms help describe the importance of recognizing that cognition never functions alone: *entrainment* and *compulsion*. Entrainment is the 'transmission of an affective state felt by one body to another body through proximity'.[50] This is done through close physical contact – whether through the sights, sounds, smells, and 'feel' of that social environment. Entrainment explains the way in which how we respond in self-consciousness after we 'feel' the room, and indeed, we might comment that so and so a person has failed to 'feel' the room when they make an insensitive comment. In those situations, the cognitive rides on and alongside the affective – a reading of body language, tone of voice, facial expressions, and one's place that constantly informs and is informed by discursive reasoning. In this regard, entrainment nurtures impressions that form and teach us: 'impressions transform us, instruct our bodies in an ongoing

---

47. Heidegger, *BT*, p. 55.
48. Schaefer, *Religious Affects*, p. 24. Emphasis original.
49. Schaefer, *Religious Affects*, p. 24.
50. Schaefer, *Religious Affects*, p. 65.

pedagogic encounter with the world.'[51] Through entrainment, one learns how to feel and react in particular situations, and also learns what kinds of affections are inappropriate to the encounter at hand. Schaefer points to the way in which Christian sub-groups (or denominations) attend to the affective dimensions of the worship 'experience' to carve out boundary markers of who is in and who is out, showing that what we think of a community cognitively arises out of how our body reacts within shared space.

Graham Ward recently reiterated the importance of recognizing that beliefs are always arising out of a kind of embodied attunement, noting that

> there is a mode of liminal processing, related to embodiment and affectivity, which 'thinks' more quickly and reacts more instinctively than our conscious rational deliberation. Beneath and prior to interpretation, and the conflicts of meaning, lie sets of remembered associations and assumptions woven tightly into the processes of *how we make sense*.[52]

These associations and assumptions undergird what Pierre Bourdieu has called *habitus*, 'encultured dispositions, socialized mindsets, and biases'.[53] In this regard, Ward warns against some potential typical deformations within analytic philosophy:[54]

> It is to these dispositions and biases, emerging we know not how (yet) from the body's processing of its environment through the neutral, molecular, and ionic operations in and across the brain and the nervous system that I am pointing when I speak of 'beliefs'. Analytic philosophers (left-hemisphere doyens) often wish to speak of belief as 'propositional attitudes' and, as such, speak about 'judgments'. But there is too much evidence that the operations of belief come before judgment. Beliefs are 'dispositions toward judgments' or even 'dispositional attitudes' – where 'attitudes' picks up something of the affective as it pertains to believing. Just as Kihlstrom (among others) shows that our 'cognitive unconscious' arrives at judgments and impressions prior to conscious attentiveness, so we can infer that beliefs inform perception, interpretation, experience, and action prior to rationalization. Furthermore, there is no linear

---

51. Schaefer, *Religious Affects*, p. 66.
52. Graham Ward, *How the Light Gets In: Ethical Life I* (Oxford: Oxford University Press, 2016), p. 259. Emphasis original.
53. Ward, *How the Light Gets In*, p. 259.
54. I am following William Wood's use of the word 'deformation', from 'The Characteristic Deformations of Analytic Theology', in his *Analytic Theology and The Academic Study of Religion* (Oxford: Oxford University Press, 2021), pp. 45–7. Wood is thus not unaware of these charges against the analytic tradition, and argues in response that analytic philosophy is merely the systematization of ordinary, everyday forms of human intuition (see p. 100). For similar observations, see Dru Johnson, *Biblical Philosophy: A Hebraic Approach to the Old and New Testaments* (Cambridge: Cambridge University Press, 2021), p. 60.

route from perception, belief, and thought to experience, interpretation, and action. If actions can precede consciousness and interpretation (and they can), then we are examining not a linear process but a complex set of feedback and feed-forward loops in which believing is deeply implicated.[55]

Ward's observations here about beliefs as prior dispositions, and about the nexus of non-linear and nonconscious causes that inform our behavior, dovetail well with Schaefer's use of the term 'para-cognitive', and display once again the fact that human beings are organic wholes. It is difficult, if not impossible, to pinpoint where the unconscious ends and where rationality begins, and our bodies indicate that we relate to one another not as self-enclosed systems of reasons that negotiate the rationality of premises, but also as porous nervous systems that are environmentally formed.[56]

In popular media, para-cognitive dimensions of human reaction are increasingly recognized as pivotal for understanding the contemporary polarization in matters of politics and science. The 2021 documentary *15 Minutes of Shame*, produced by Monica Lewinsky and Max Joseph, explored a new modality of public shaming in view of the rise of social media in so-called 'cancel culture'.[57] The documentary emphasized two relevant features. First, social media interaction detaches statements and propositions from the bodily and facial 'language' that human brains need to recognize the personhood from which those statements come. It is much easier to hold negative beliefs about someone and to communicate shameful and offensive language through social media because the personhood of the ones attacked is not generally registered by the human brain. We can recognize personhood in others because we recognize facial and bodily language that is analogous to our own. Second, the human brain produces higher amounts of dopamine relief from consuming external misfortune or pain, in the phenomenon commonly called *Schadenfreude*. We are hardwired to be attracted to negative stories rather than positive ones (which also explain why it is that we tend to remember memories that are tethered to painful emotions rather than happy ones). Public shaming is addictive. Human reasoning is tethered to bodily functions.

Here is where *compulsion*, the abovementioned companion of 'entrainment' in the context of para-cognition, becomes important.[58] Drawing from Mark Johnson's

---

55. Ward, *How the Light Gets In*, p. 259.

56. Adam Green's observation that this illumines the doctrine of original sin's transmission is apt in this regard: 'original sin is maturationally natural, which is more associated with automatic, instinctive processing' that stems from one's social embeddedness. 'The Maturational Naturalness of Original Sin', *TheoLogica* 6 (2022): p. 40.

57. Monica Lewinsky and Max Joseph, *15 Minutes of Shame* (A+E Networks: Six West Media, 2021).

58. See also the discussion on compulsion in Schaefer, *Religious Affects*, pp. 92–119; Schaefer defines compulsion as 'th[e] set of affective properties that pull bodies independently of the linguistic index.' *Religious Affects*, p. 26.

The Body in the Mind, Dru Johnson argues that the body and its senses are involved even in the most abstract of propositional analysis, such as contemplating the veracity of necessary propositions that $1 + 1 = 2$.[59] Observing the sense of compulsion in everyday experience of cause and effect, like feeling the inevitability of the shopping cart drawing your body as you push it away, we now '*extend*' that sense of compulsion 'into our abstract reasoning'.[60] In other words: 'We use our conceptualized analog of COMPULSION – learned only through our body – and analogically *map* that sense of compulsion into the idea (the conviction, actually) of logical necessity. Mathematical solutions are compellingly true, like pushing a wheelbarrow is compelling it forward.'[61] What Mark Johnson and Dru Johnson are observing here is that even in areas of logical necessity, we rely on the body's sense of compulsion – that gut 'feeling' that compels us to believe that X is entailed by Y or that $1 + 1 = 2$. Logical analysis itself arises alongside the affective; it is para-cognitive.

Recognizing the importance of the body for knowing means that attentiveness to the way in which we are formed by socially embodied processes, for good and for ill, becomes key for the pursuit of intellectual virtue. Just as we can reason in deformed ways when we are unconsciously submerged by negative bodily influences (like our brains on social media), so can we pursue a more holistic account of moral formation by thinking through the kinds of social processes that are necessary for intellectual maturation.[62]

Intransigence

The fourth and final concept that follows from this foray into phenomenology and affect theory as applied to religious studies is *intransigence*. If religious forms arise out of affects that are deeply embedded in our bodily and physical histories, those affects are much more difficult to shift than propositional beliefs. In other words, onto-phenomenological features are far more stubborn and enduring than the traffic in the space of reason: 'They are recognized at the level of intransigent, onto-phenomenological features of our animal bodies at the same time as they are spun and maneuvered by systems of signification.'[63] The result of this recognition is fruitful for the study of religion, for it signals that mere information transmission and worldview dissemination is insufficient for behavioral modification and habituation. Crucially for Schaefer, intransigence goes some way to explaining why believers in the same religious system might sit at opposite ends of the ideological spectrum in other respects, especially with regard to political affiliation and intuitions. Adherence to particular religious ideas (or doctrines) does not

---

59. Mark Johnson, *The Body in the Mind: The Bodily Basis of Meaning, Imagination, and Reason* (Chicago: University of Chicago Press, 1987).
60. Johnson, *Biblical Philosophy*, p. 60. Emphasis original.
61. Johnson, *Biblical Philosophy*, p. 60.
62. Johnson, *Biblical Philosophy*, pp. 234–5.
63. Schaefer, *Religious Affects*, p. 56.

necessarily change the other intuitions that have been submerged over time in bodies.[64] Christians have long wrestled with the so-called 'gap' in our sanctification – that gulf between what we claim to believe and who we are, or why it is that more knowledge of Christian doctrine does not guarantee further growth in sanctified maturity. Intransigence is that feature of human bodily life that explains the need for further exercise in ritual practice and habit-formation in order to facilitate a change in behavior and intuition.

Furthermore, for Schaefer, intransigence also explains why it is that differing religious forms can produce and satiate similar affects. 'Affect theory proposes that we need to consider the possibility that although distribution, significations, and permutations of bodily practices (including discourses) are varied, they nonetheless can yield more or less consistent effects and affects across bodies.'[65] In everyday language, the same shame and guilt that may lead the Muslim to undertake the *Hajj* for a clear conscience may lead the Christian to pray some version of the sinner's prayer. Similar bodily patterns and affects can be observed across religious boundaries. Indeed, in Simeon Zahl's reading, intransigence is attested in daily human experience:

> We see this resistance to intentionality in our experience all the time: the bereaved person does not 'choose' the pattern, duration, or intensity of their grief; in the experience of falling powerfully in love; in the way that fears of the severely anxious are rarely allayed through 'rational' reflection; in the resistance of political convictions to transformation through political argument; in the phenomenon of addiction.[66]

Indeed, the space of reasons is often rendered mute by the intransigent heart, or retooled as a way of bias-confirmation. What the heart wants, the mind justifies.

Herman Bavinck and Affect Theory

Now that these four observations from affect theory and phenomenology stand in view, we are in a position to make explicit the way in which they are conceptually paralleled in Bavinck's theological anthropology. That Bavinck affirmed a (version of the) critique of the linguistic fallacy and the importance of onto-phenomenology can be treated together, and I will then turn to those passages in which Bavinck approximates the para-cognitive and the intransigence of the body. Consider again

---

64. Sally Haslanger's comment on the persistence of racial injustice despite shifts in cognitive beliefs is apt: 'Racial injustice (and other forms of injustice) persists despite substantial changes in "common sense" or shared belief… This suggests that the role of belief in coordination may not be as central as sometimes assumed.' 'Racism, Ideology, and Social Movements', *Res Philosophica* 94 (2017): p. 10.
65. Schaefer, *Religious Affects*, p. 57.
66. Zahl, *Holy Spirit and Christian Experience*, p. 149.

Bavinck's account of language, taken from his *Foundations of Psychology* and the *Reformed Dogmatics*:

(a) Understanding precedes reasoning and language: 'Human beings do not acquire self-consciousness by ratiocination, but rather, in self-consciousness they know themselves immediately, as it were by intuition, and that is an attribute of understanding.'[67]
(b) Bodily language is irreducible to conceptual vocabulary: there is a language 'of facial features, a language of gestures; a language of the often involuntary movement of facial muscles, of nerves, and of body parts'.[68]
(c) Meaning is prior to the use of words: 'words can be completely forgotten, and yet the thought can be retained and expressed using different sounds ... A sign and the thing signified are not one and the same. Often we have a representation, a concept, a thought, for which we still search a word.'[69] Hence, there is meaning found with or without the use of language: 'Intimately related, first of all, are thought and word, thinking and speaking. Indeed they are not, as Max Müller thinks, identical, for there is also a kind of thinking, a consciousness, a sense, however unclear, which is non-verbal.'[70]
(d) Furthermore, the personality, i.e., the human heart drives the intellect and will in a primordial fashion: 'Beneath the conscious, will-directed life, a world of unconscious representations and automatic actions is expanding. And the personality, with its self-consciousness and self-direction, rises on this broad foundation like a pyramid.'[71] The unconscious personality animates the explicit exercise of the faculties of the self.

To elaborate on these four points, Bavinck's *Philosophy of Revelation* is worth revisiting. There, (1) he reiterates that the heart informs consciousness from underneath its threshold and that (2) the locus of (general) revelation is prior to all conscious experience – or, to use the Heideggerian language, onto-phenomenological: 'Beneath consciousness there is a world of instincts and habits, notions and inclinations, abilities and capacities, which continually sets on fire the course of nature. Beneath the head lies the heart, from which are the gates of life.'[72] One's explicit patterns of reasoning, therefore, do not determine the course of one's worldview, but emerge from personality:

---

67. Bavinck, *FP*, p. 167.
68. Bavinck, *FP*, p. 170.
69. Bavinck, *FP*, p. 173.
70. Bavinck, *RD* 1: p. 377.
71. Bavinck, *FP*, p. 187.
72. Bavinck, *PoR*, p. 173. Bavinck emphasizes the same material in 'Hoofd en Hart', in *Christophilus: Jaarboekje Nederlandsch Jongelings-Verbond* (1892): pp. 71–5. ET: Herman Bavinck, 'Head and Heart', Gregory Parker Jr. (trans.), *Modern Reformation* (2021): https://modernreformation.org/resource-library/articles/head-and-heart/ (accessed November 10, 2021).

In reality all these phenomena of consciousness, so far from being isolated, exist only in intimate mutual relations, *and ever spring out of the depths of personality.* The whole cannot be explained in an atomistic manner by a combination of its parts; but on the contrary the parts must be conceived in an organic way by unfolding the totality. Behind the particular lies the general, and the whole precedes the parts.[73]

This personality, then, harkens one back to the biblical idea of the heart, the soul that is the form of the body, but signifies more than that. As we saw in Chapter 2, personality accounts for the individuation of one individual to another, is thus that which determines the direction or bodily intuition of an individual. Personality is always wrestling with the affordances of divine revelation – the heart wrestles with a pre-theoretical divine revelation, and the observations of empirical psychology merely describe the activities of that heart. 'If psychology leads by serious reflection to a metaphysical reality, and this again to the idea of revelation, we are not far removed from the conviction that humanity, in the hidden places of the soul, yet belongs to another and a higher world than that of this earthly existence.'[74] Beneath the conscious acts of willing and thinking, human beings are already always attuned to and coping with the unconscious realities that inform the psyche and the affordances of the world around us.

None of this, however, is meant to deny the importance of pre-conscious affects or their relationship to human rationality and explicit linguistic formulation; in that sense affects are *paracognitive*. Once one is aware that conscious rationality arises from and with the pre-conscious personality, one can then be self-critical, and is aware that no one comes to an argument in a neutral state. One can thus hone one's reasoning with the goal of clarity, humility, and logical rigor: 'certainly a word is primarily the fully matured, independent, and therefore lucid thought – an indispensable tool for conscious thinking.'[75] The observation here thus does not deny the importance of human reasoning, but rather recognizes that it is never untethered from the person who wields it: 'It is indeed an impoverished psychology that limits the faculty of knowing to understanding or to reason. The richest and deepest life, also of the faculty of knowing, lies behind understanding and reason in the human *heart*.'[76] Reason is personal, because it is always tethered to the heart.

Finally, Bavinck recognizes, therefore, that the heart is *intransigent*, and is deeply connected with the body's physicality. Notice the way in which Bavinck speaks of the soul:

> Our becoming aware and our observations, our feeling and our wanting, our thinking and speaking; all our convictions in religion, morality, science, the arts;

---

73. Bavinck, *PoR*, p. 173. Emphasis mine.
74. Bavinck, *PoR*, p. 174.
75. Bavinck, *RD* 1: p. 377.
76. Bavinck, *FP*, p. 126. Emphasis original.

our insights and our prejudices, our sympathies and aversions – *these all are rooted far and deep behind the consciousness in our soul.* Often they make us impervious to all reasoning and proof, and often so strongly that we ourselves with all our willpower are nevertheless powerless to resist them. Who is able to sufficiently account for the reason why he fosters sympathies for and sides with one or another of the warring nations these days? Later, after having fostered such sympathies and having taken sides, we try to justify them with reasons, but such proof is usually not the basis but the outcome of our convictions. *The root of a human being's personality lies in the subconscious, in the soul itself, with all that is innate to it. Soul and consciousness definitely do not coincide. The self is much richer than the 'I'.*[77]

Hence, in Bavinck, the soul is invoked not to fund a linguistic or mentalist picture of human beings, but rather to show that the human being's behavior and personality precede mental activity, and hence far elude it. Far from depending on an account of the soul as that which grounds the human being's stable and changeless rationality, the soul is that which precedes and often eludes reason's conscious grasp.

Three benefits follow from these observations. First, it shows that Bavinck's theological anthropology can be fruitfully brought into conversation with current strands in phenomenology and affect theory, especially in religious studies, and he accommodated those insights while locating them in a dogmatic context, nested within the doctrines of the image of God and general revelation. He was quite prescient in anticipating the ways in which contemporary psychological studies of the depths of the human self and its concrete existence in everyday life would shape the way we understood religion and the reception of revelation.

Second, then, Bavinck's anthropology helps re-interpret the empirical phenomena. The observations on affect theory by Schaefer and others noted above are offered alongside evolutionary and naturalist explanations of religious phenomena. Implied therein is a critique of the kind of study of religion that treats it as a disembodied idealized reality unaffected by evolutionary realities of power and history. Notice, however, that Bavinck was seeking to demonstrate that a belief in the revelatory origins of religion need not denigrate an account of revelation's psychological and historical mediation, or of the soul's embodied character. One can accommodate the insights of affect theory without naturalizing religion altogether. Bavinck's own critiques of what he called 'empirical psychology' in his chapter on religious experience in the *Philosophy of Revelation* were precisely against that sort of materialist reductionism:

For this reason, empirical psychology will never be able fully to know and explain the psychical life. It may with the utmost closeness examine the phenomena of consciousness, the sensations, the feelings, the passions, and it

---

77. Bavinck, 'The Unconscious', pp. 186–7. Emphases mine.

may try to conceive their working mechanically; it may even endeavor to explain the ego or the self-consciousness by association of ideas; but naturally it cannot penetrate to what lies behind and beneath consciousness and can kindle no light in the secret places of the heart. Herein the declaration may find its application that God alone knows the heart and tests the inner life. Empirical psychology can inquire into the conditions of consciousness, can even investigate the self-consciousness which slowly arises in the human and is subject to all kinds of changes. But the question whether a hidden ego (*ik*) or an independent soul lies behind it is beyond its reach. So soon as it occupies itself with this question it passes beyond itself into metaphysics.[78]

In other words, the empirical study of the phenomena of the embodied emergence of religious experience and expression should be wary of a kind of overreach – it might observe *how* religion emerges but not *why* or from *whence* it emerges.[79] To move from the former to the latter is to move beyond the purely empirical and into the realm of metaphysics. To observe that the embodied self explains the emergence of religious expression is not to reduce it to a merely materialist phenomenon. Rather, to observe the animality of religious expression is very much consonant with the convictions of the Christian tradition that human beings are a psychosomatic unity, and that all creatures under heaven, too, might declare the glory of God.

The previous sections of this chapter, then, show that a theological account of the human being as a primordially religious creature can include the findings of religious affect theory in a way that allows it to give a granular description of the ways in which human beings exhibit that primordial religiosity as image-bearers of God. If these sections indicate that bodily affects and behaviors can be considered not as signs of solely animalistic origins of religious affects, but rather of our theological origins and make-up, I turn now to the cognitive science of religion to emphasize that cognition, too, remains an important feature of who we are as religious beings. The emphasis above on para-cognition has already signaled the way in which the emphases on affect theory and phenomenology above are not meant to downplay the importance of belief formation and rational thought (though it does reject the view that cognition is the *locus* of our religiosity). Giving a theological reading of the findings of the cognitive science of religion will further enrich the sort of holistic theological anthropology we are pursuing here – a holism that seeks to do justice to both our affective and cognitive dimensions. The next section thus provides a constructive reading of some salient insights from

78. Bavinck, *PoR*, p. 173.
79. This parallels the observations on the limits and overreach that mark some trajectories within the cognitive science of religion. For a summary of these trajectories, see Lluis Oviedo, 'Explanatory Limits in the Cognitive Science of Religion: Theoretical Matrix and Evidence Levels', in *New Developments in the Cognitive Science of Religion: The Rationality of Religious Belief*, Hans Van Eyghen, Rik Peels, and Gijsbert van den Brink (eds) (Cham: Springer, 2018), pp. 15–35.

the cognitive science of religion (hereafter, CSR), while also deploying what we've learned from affect theory in conversation with CSR.

Theological Anthropology and the Cognitive Science of Religion

To grapple with how the affective theological anthropology canvassed above remains consonant with a robust affirmation of the importance of cognition and the findings of CSR, we do well to begin with a description of CSR. As a field CSR is relatively young at about thirty-forty years old. Though its findings have been mined for multiple trajectories in philosophy, religious studies, and theology, it is an empirical and psychological study about whether and how religious beliefs originate from common cognitive and neurophysiological processes.[80] Justin Barrett usefully summarizes its emergence:

> Neuroscience, as well as cognitive, developmental, evolutionary, and social psychology, have matured enough in their theories and methods to begin making real headway concerning how beliefs are formed, and this progress has been turned to studying the causes of religious belief. Most prominent in these efforts is the interdisciplinary space known as the cognitive science of religion .... As in times past, these scientific treatments of religious beliefs have been quickly followed by philosophical treatments concerning what the science means for whether religious beliefs are good or bad, justified or not, rational or irrational.[81]

The findings of CSR on the causes of religious belief have been used to argue for and against the rationality of the same. On one side, some suggest that the origin of religious belief in 'normal' cognitive processes undermines such rationality because, assuming a generally evolutionary account of the human brain, religious belief is a 'by-product' of our physiological make-up, or somehow the result of error-filled and accidental naturalistic origins.[82] On the other side, some have sought to show that these naturalist arguments are *non sequiturs*, for showing the physiological and cognitive origins of religious belief is an independent

---

80. CSR thus focuses on cognition in all of its dimensions: 'It is called "cognitive" since its focus is on *cognitions*: mental activities – both conscious and unconscious, both rational and experiential – involved in the processing of information and the acquisition of knowledge and understanding… The cognitive science of *religion* studies mental processes that concern religious phenomena, such as religious experiences, beliefs, practices, and dispositions.' Gijsbert van den Brink, *Reformed Theology and Evolutionary Theory* (Grand Rapids: Eerdmans, 2020), p. 243.

81. Justin Barrett, 'Foreword', in *God and the Brain: The Rationality of Belief*, Kelly James Clark (ed.) (Grand Rapids: Eerdmans, 2019), p. x. See also Justin Barrett, *Why Would Anyone Believe in God?* (Walnut Creek: Altamitra Press, 2004).

82. E.g. Daniel Dennett, *Breaking the Spell: Religion as a Natural Phenomenon* (New York: Penguin Books, 2006).

issue from the *rationality* of religious belief, and that the very existence of truth-aimed cognitive faculties fits much better in a theistic, rather than nontheistic, worldview.[83]

Notice the parallel between the study of religious affects and CSR: both have been used to point to the materialistic and animalistic origins of religiosity (the former in religious behavior and affection and the latter in the domain of mental states and cognition), yet neither an account of religious affects nor an interest in CSR *requires* a reductive mode of analysis. Given that my interest here are theological, rather, I presuppose that these findings in CSR are compatible with a theistic worldview.[84] I seek, more specifically, to show that the account of affective theological anthropology and general revelation above can accommodate and utilize the findings of CSR for a richer and fuller affective theological anthropology. As such, for the interests of space, I emphasize some of CSR's findings that seem most relevant for the current purposes.

Two sub-sections structure the discussion below. First, I describe the ways in which CSR shows that many of our beliefs originate from natural and unconscious processes. Second, I observe that belief in a divine mind, too, is a belief we find ourselves inclined toward pre-reflectively and naturally. Theological observations and our findings from affect theory will be peppered throughout.

Brains and Belief

An investigation of recent findings meshes well with the yields of affect theory. That is, if affect theory shows that religious behavioral traits are intransigent features ingrained in our bodies in ways that precede consciousness, CSR further confirms that our religious beliefs, too, spring from pre-conscious nonreflective processes. Despite the focus on cognition and propositional beliefs, CSR relies on the empirical evidence that humans are inclined to believe certain propositions without argument or reflection. Kelly James Clark's *God and the Brain* helpfully

---

83. For a recent concise survey of the research trajectories and debates, see Tyler Dalton McNabb, *Religious Epistemology* (Cambridge: Cambridge University Press, 2019), pp. 25–33, and Hans Van Eyghen, Rik Peels, and Gijsbert van den Brink, 'The Cognitive Science of Religion, Philosophy, and Theology: A Survey of the Issues', in *New Developments in the Cognitive Science of Religion: The Rationality of Religious Belief*, Hans Van Eyghen, Rik Peels, and Gijsbert van den Brink (eds) (Cham: Springer, 2018), pp. 1–15, and Van den Brink, *Reformed Theology and Evolutionary Theory*, pp. 241–65.

84. This is the conclusion offered by Kelly Clark, and others: 'Our cognitive faculties find their intellectual home in the worldview of supernaturalism, while the worldview of naturalism is intellectually inhospitable to reliable cognitive faculties.' Kelly James Clark, *God and the Brain: The Rationality of Belief* (Grand Rapids: Eerdmans, 2019), p. 118. See also Kelly Clark James and Justin Barrett, 'Reidian Religious Epistemology and the Cognitive Science of Religion', *Journal of the American Academy of Religion* 79 (2011): pp. 639–75; Adam Green, 'Cognitive Science and the Natural Knowledge of God', *The Monist* 96 (2013): pp. 399–416.

catalogues these findings.[85] We have developed the cognitive and unconscious faculties that attune us toward self-preservation – to find shelter, food, mates, and to fend off enemies.[86] As Clark observes, we are more likely to believe ourselves to be better than others, to insist on our own opinions when challenged by some disagreement, to listen to arguments that re-affirm our in-group, and to be suspicious of those who are perceived to be strangers and part of an out-group. Rather than being motivated exclusively by arguments, calm reflection, and detached reasoning, we are often unconsciously motivated to adopt beliefs for self-preservation, self-inflation, and self-assertion.

We are hard-wired to pay attention to those social cues that help us get ahead in the perceived hierarchies around us, and academics are no exception to this tendency. Conformity bias inclines us to accede to social norms about what we should wear, how we ought to smell, and whether to adopt a particular lifestyle. We find ourselves attracted to the newest items advertised, to the schedules and eating habits of the locals when we travel, and we can recall moments during which we succumbed to peer pressure. Prestige bias instills in us 'an unconscious preference for high-status individuals …. In highly competitive academic communities, people knowingly do all sorts of things to ingratiate themselves with and gain access to a "famous" scholar.'[87] If those who hold socially prestigious positions are inclined to believe in some political theory or religious view, that influences those (most of us) who are inclined toward those in high-status social positions. We find ourselves believing some political or religious theory not because of some argument or deep consideration, but because those who we admire say that they believe it. The combination of prestige and conformity bias together propels us toward belief in powerful and, to use a term discussed above in affect theory, *compulsive* ways: 'A well-timed horse laugh, a whispered comment over beers after a lecture, and a derisive snort are much more effective than an extended argument in a scholarly journal.'[88]

The affective theological anthropology that Bavinck offers can also accommodate some findings that might initially appear counter-intuitive. For instance, Clark observes that neurophysiological study has shown that our perception of how our wills interact with our intentional beliefs is more complex than we first think it to be. Consider the act of lifting your wrist. Conscious reflection on this process pictures the process this way: (1) an intentional thought that was freely willed: 'I

---

85. Clark rightly shows that CSR is often discussed in conjunction with Plantinga's philosophy and Reidian epistemology. For the similarities and differences between Bavinck, neo-Calvinism, and Plantinga's epistemology, see my *God and Knowledge*, especially chapters 5–7.

86. As Clark mentions rather humorously: 'These and other cognitive abilities developed in response to environment pressures in our hunter-gatherer past in accord with our most fundamental human needs (the famous four Fs – feeding, fleeing, fighting, and reproducing).' *God and the Brain*, p. 32.

87. Clark, *God and the Brain*, p. 129.

88. Clark, *God and the Brain*, p. 130.

shall now flick my wrist', and then, (2) the action itself – I flick my wrist. What the findings show, however, is that the 'subconscious brain' fired *prior to the 'subject's self-awareness* of their wish to act'.[89] The sequence is thus as follows: (1) the brain produces an electrical signal (2) I am self-aware that I shall now flick my wrist (3) the action, I flick my wrist. As Clark summarizes: 'The feeling of being consciously motivated to act comes *after* the unconsciously moved action; we then think, retrospectively but wrongly, that our beliefs motivated the action – we project our motivation onto the first cause.'[90] Though Clark concedes that this picture might be possible across the board as a general way of describing all human action, he makes a passing comment (without explanation), that he is disinclined to agree with such a generalization. One could speculate on those reasons – perhaps CSR gives some reason to think that because cognition is a unique-making feature of human beings, it should incline us to think that in at least some instances, cognitive reflection really does cause our behavior from the top-down. Whatever the reasons, however, the previous theological reading of affect theory shows that *even if* these neurophysiological studies are true across the board, it would still not lend us to the conclusion that we are exclusively materialistic beings reducible to naturalist origins, nor that our beliefs are reducible to our brain activity. An explication of the physiological processes by which belief formation arises does not compromise a theological construal of the human self.

Theory of Mind and Agency-Detecting Device

Among those beliefs that human cognition spontaneously generates are beliefs regarding the existence of supernatural entities that imbue meaning and purposiveness to the events around us. Referred to as the Theory of Mind (ToM), Oviedo provides a helpful definition: 'A central tenet of CSR claims that Theory of Mind (ToM) involves a capacity to conceive supernatural agents as being able to cause phenomena beyond the common traits attributed to ordinary subjects.'[91] It is important to recognize that ToM is a natural extension to other cognitive biases about beliefs and other minds, intentionality, and purposiveness, and is associated with an 'Agency-Detecting Device (ADD).'[92] Claire White summarizes these biases as follows:

> Some key cognitive biases that have been identified or proposed as underpinning religious ideas and behaviors include: anthropomorphism, the tendency to project human-like properties, including mental states and characteristics, to non-human things … folk-dualism, the intuition that minds are separate and independent from bodies … fairness or proportionality bias, the tendency to represent our actions and consequences as having proportionate consequences

---

89. Clark, *God and the Brain*, p. 116. Emphasis original.
90. Clark, *God and the Brain*, p. 116.
91. Oviedo, 'Explanatory Limits in the Cognitive Science of Religion', p. 26.
92. Clark, *God and the Brain*, p. 24.

... kinship detection and identity fusion, the ability to recognize and calibrate kinship – and by extension, fuse identity with the imagined kin ... teleology, a bias toward seeing things in the world as having a purpose, and being made for that purpose.[93]

The ToM, therefore, is what accounts for the human ability to infer information about the internal states of other agents. Aku Visala further catalogues the capacities of a higher-order Theory of Mind (HO-ToM) more unique to human beings:

Some nonhuman animals might have a basic first-order ToM, which is the ability to predict and explain the behavior of others by positing basic internal states, such as intentions, beliefs, and desires. These mental states have specific content that in turn explains the behavior involved. In this sense, I can understand that Justin is moving toward the other side of the road because he wants to get to the other side. Second-order ToM is the ability to attribute mental states, whose content refers to the content of other mental states, to first-order mental states. In this sense, I can say that Justin crossed the road because he believed there to be seeds on the other side, but Justin was mistaken. It seems that adult humans also have third-order (perhaps even fourth-order) ToM: I can understand that Justin believes that I falsely (in his mind) believe that there are no seeds on the other side of the road. The cognitive mechanisms that make the formation and processing of second- and third-order mental states are what we can call higher-order ToM.[94]

Cognitive biases that form the backdrop of our ordinary beliefs and the HO-ToM not only help with our survival – it makes a profound difference if you can perceive whether the person running toward you is rushing to attack or embrace you – but also explain the human tendency toward anthropomorphism ('attributing human characteristics to nonhuman things and events').[95] Just as we are inclined to believe, immediately and without argument, that the delicious meal prepared before us was cooked for our delight, we are inclined to believe that the good weather before us, for example, was a gift from some higher mind, designed purposively to make us glad, or the rain before us as somehow a consequence of some bad decision we made earlier in our lives, and so on. Despite the diversity of religious language and structures globally, these 'representations of supernatural agents –

---

93. Clair White, 'What Does Cognitive Science of Religion Explain?' in *New Developments in the Cognitive Science of Religion: The Rationality of Religious Belief*, Hans Van Eyghen, Rik Peels, and Gijsbert van den Brink (eds) (Cham: Springer, 2018), p. 41.

94. Aku Visala, 'Human Cognition and the Image of God', in *The Christian Doctrine of Humanity: Explorations in Constructive Dogmatics*, Fred Sanders and Oliver D. Crisp (eds) (Grand Rapids: Zondervan Academic, 2018), p. 105.

95. White, 'What Does Cognitive Science of Religion Explain?', p. 41.

are remarkably stable'.⁹⁶ As McNabb summarizes: 'Religious belief, then, is natural to human faculties … When one states that religion is natural, one just means that basic human psychology plays a meaningful role in explaining religious belief'.⁹⁷ Humans naturally form beliefs about the existence and states of other minds, and religious beliefs are an extension of this cognitive disposition.

Positing the existence of what has been called a God-faculty is the result of the conjunction of an agency-detecting device and theory of mind; human cognition is inclined to produce theistic beliefs. Human cognition inclines us naturally and spontaneously to believe in supernatural agents that somehow control our environment. It is important, however, not to overestimate the findings of CSR. CSR does not claim that particularly *Christian* theistic belief is natural. Rather, it observes that the belief that there is a purposive mind (teleology) behind particular events is natural. These beliefs are compossible with a specific religion, but need not be so. Furthermore, specifying the physical, psychological, and social causes of religious belief is, again, a distinct endeavor than adjudicating whether those beliefs are rational. These origins generate a double-edged sword, and both non-theist and theist alike might be guilty of a kind of overreach. Clark is right to argue that epistemic humility should be the mode by which we discuss these matters, for 'just as there are psychic, cultural, and non-alethic impulses involved in religious belief, so, too, there are psychic, cultural, and non-alethic impulses involved in unbelief'.⁹⁸ The non-theist might infer (hastily) that because theistic beliefs are naturally produced, they are merely by-products of the brain and hence lack rationality. The theist, however, might infer (hastily) that because theistic beliefs are natural, that non-theism is the result of some cognitive defect.

Looking Ahead: Bavinck, Affection, and Cognition

There are further theological questions that emerge from these findings. The focus on cognitive belief raises questions concerning the results and efficacy of general revelation. As I will show in the next chapter, some have also argued that the kind of religious belief that is natural cuts against the grain of the God of classical theism, and hence the God pictured by much of the orthodox Christian faith. The God of so-called classical theism, after all, is a highly mysterious and metaphysically rich Being, and descriptions of the same often go not only beyond but against the intuitions of the everyday person. Thus, the findings of CSR do not form a theological whole, but rather an attenuated collection of empirical data about the origins of religious beliefs that require interpretation. In the next chapter, I further explore a constructive and dogmatic reading of the findings of affect theory and CSR. The account provided will be rather complex, because, as much of Christian doctrine attests, what we often believe cognitively might not be consonant with

96. White, 'What Does Cognitive Science of Religion Explain?', p. 42.
97. McNabb, *Religious Epistemology*, pp. 26–7.
98. Clark, *God and the Brain*, p. 170.

what we know affectively. Paradoxically, as religious creatures exposed to God's general revelation, what we might know in our psyche might not be consistent with what we express intellectually. Because knowing is motivated by the heart (and its biases, as we saw), the motivations of the heart might yield cognitive beliefs that are self-inflating and self-preserving rather than truth-conducive.

I will return to these theological issues in the next chapter. For now, let us briefly consider how Bavinck's account of anthropology and general revelation might accommodate the findings of CSR.

In Bavinck's appraisal of the proofs of God's existence, he argued that belief in God is produced from 'the spontaneity with which our consciousness bears witness to the existence of God that urges itself upon us from all directions'.[99] Bavinck often links the immediate belief in the personality of God with the awareness of our own self-consciousness and one's immediate responsiveness to the world around us, in a way that parallels how CSR links the God-faculty with ToM and ADD:

> [T]he personality of God has remained firmly established, always and everywhere, among every nation and in every religion. Just as confidently as man is convinced of his self-consciousness of his own existence and of the reality of the external world, does he believe also in the reality and personality of God ... This belief [in God] is interwoven with his self-consciousness, more particularly with its double testimony to dependence and freedom .... The sense of dependence is the core of self-consciousness and the essence of religion, but it is not a mere *de facto* dependence, as the unconscious and the irrational creation is dependent on God; in man it is *feeling* of dependence.[100]

Theologically, for Bavinck, these convictions come naturally because of the pervasiveness of general revelation, and its efficacy in producing in us 'religious impressions and feelings that we humans receive and carry with us in our soul'.[101] Consistently, Bavinck argues that religious affection precedes syllogistic argumentation and propositional belief. God's revelation penetrates the soul (the psyche), in such a way that human beings know him prior to them expressing this knowledge in terms of propositional beliefs.[102] Revelation produces the *feeling* of absolute dependence (religious affects), which in turn produces beliefs spontaneously about God's existence and personality (cognition). Thus propositional beliefs about God also naturally arise. Bavinck shows conceptually how affect theory and the cognitive science of religion might be linked; in his perspective, affects form the backdrop for cognition. Contrary to the linguistic

---

99. Bavinck, *RD* 2: p. 90. See also Sutanto, *God and Knowledge*, chapters 5–6, and Nathaniel Sutanto, 'Herman Bavinck and Thomas Reid on Perception and Knowing God', *Harvard Theological Review* 111 (2018): pp. 115–34.

100. Bavinck, *PoR*, pp. 64–5.

101. Bavinck, *RD* 2: p. 90.

102. See my 'Neocalvinism and General Revelation: A Dogmatic Sketch', *International Journal of Systematic Theology* 20 (2018): pp. 494–516.

fallacy or much of the modern epistemological tradition, religious affects thus generate religious beliefs, rather than the other way around. Cognition might be a mark of human uniqueness but – as was seen above with reference to paracognition – cognition is not independent of affects.

This chapter has shown some ways in which Bavinck's affective theological anthropology intersects well with the yields of some concepts from affect theory and CSR. I began with a sketch of Bavinck's account of general revelation and the affects that it produces within the depths of personality. I then canvassed the findings of affect theory, before showing how such findings enrich Bavinck's anthropology. The latter half of this chapter then turned to the insights of CSR, which further furnishes Bavinck's observation that humans are inclined to believe in a divine mind. Again, however, there are further theological queries to follow, and we do well to chart the ways in which other theologians have sought to enfold these findings within the theological task before charting our own, which will be the task of the next chapter.

Chapter 4

KNOWING GOD AND INTRANSIGENT SIN

This chapter further explores how reading the yields of these non-theological disciplines through Bavinck's theological anthropology might provide constructive insights that support an experientially granular account of how human beings respond to the pervasiveness of God's general revelation as his image-bearers. This interest now brings us to a discussion of the noetic effects of sin, and I shall argue that a properly affective theological anthropology should primarily focus on the *psychical* effects of sin as a whole rather than on its merely cognitive or noetic dimensions. Indeed, if Bavinck's affective theological anthropology is taken on board, then a focus simply on cognition and its belief-output would be to miss the centrality of the heart as sin's corrupting locus and as that which drives cognition. Furthermore, the argument of this chapter bears significant implications as one considers Bavinck's corporate account of humanity and its ramifications for a theological rendering of humankind in the next chapters: exposure to God and his holy will, along with the intransigent resistance to that will, is shared in common by all of humanity, no matter one's ethnic, national, or geographically situated identity.

Focusing on Bavinck's affective anthropology and doctrine of general revelation in particular also makes good sense given the two current trajectories I explore in the first two sections of this chapter, both of which deploy affect theory and the cognitive science of religion (CSR) for theological ends. The first trajectory is Simeon Zahl's recent productive attempt to use the insights of affect theory to describe the importance of producing an experientially tangible account of doctrine in general, and sin's intransigence and the transformative powers of grace in particular. The second arises from a recent debate on the results of general revelation within the human mind and the cognitive consequences of sin in analytic theology. In a third section, I show that an affective and phenomenological account of the natural knowledge of God provides fruitful dogmatic resources to respond to worries about the usefulness of 'general revelation' as a theological category, and to avoid confusion over whether 'cognitively natural theism' is identifiable with the deliverances of general revelation. This leads us to the fourth section. Surveying these research trajectories situates my constructive proposal below on the usefulness of Hubert Dreyfus's phenomenological account of skillful coping – humanity's primordially affective and practical existence – for the description of an affectively salient and empirically granular doctrine of the human reception of general revelation and the effects of sin on the psyche. In a final section, I locate my description of Bavinck's affective theological anthropology in current discussions on the structural account of the image of God.

Zahl on the Affective Salience of Doctrine and Sin's Intransigence

Simeon Zahl's recent work has shown several of the benefits that arise when attending to religious affects for theological construction. Affect theory produces an account of human change that goes beneath and far beyond propositional transmission, and thus redirects Christian discipleship toward the reformation of dispositions and habit. Cognitive learning is still important, but it is no longer seen as the unilateral way by which lives are redirected.[1] Doctrinal and linguistic modification are insufficient to describe how bodies and affects are moved. As such, Zahl has called for theologians to pay attention to the *affective salience* of doctrine, and to articulate in empirically tangible ways how doctrines should have particular bodily affects.[2]

Zahl further highlights two benefits of deploying affective theory. First, and as I have sought to demonstrate in various ways in the previous chapter, affect theory 'provides a sophisticated theoretical vocabulary for describing a set of dynamics that lie close to the heart of Christian experiences of sin, salvation, and sanctification'.[3] Affect theory provides Christian doctrine with empirical granularity. Second, affective intransigence highlights the biblical witness on the necessity of the Holy Spirit to transform our desires and re-articulates the Lutheran doctrine of the bondage of the will by way of an empirical idiom.[4] This focus on intransigence also highlights the stable affective continuity (e.g., feelings of shame and the fear of death) that persists from one culture and generation to another despite 'substantial differences at the discursive level' that emerge from or address those intransigent affects (e.g., in ascetic monastic rules or cognitive therapy).[5]

Zahl describes how Luther and Melanchthon offer a theology of justification that provides a law/gospel distinction that tracks with the affects submerged beneath consciousness. Both reformers sought to show that the scriptural witness on justification, and in particular Pauline texts like Romans 3 and 5–7, should move the sinner through a tangible affective experience: from the felt intransigence of sin, the fear of death, and crippling guilt, to the joyous consolation of having been justified in Christ. Deploying affect theory to provide an account of the physiological and social phenomenology that attends these everyday bodily experiences and

---

1. Zahl, *Holy Spirit and Christian Experience*, p. 146.
2. Simeon Zahl, 'On the Affective Salience of Doctrine', *Modern Theology* 31 (2015): pp. 428–44.
3. Zahl, *Holy Spirit and Christian Experience*, p. 150.
4. Zahl, *Holy Spirit and Christian Experience*, p. 151.
5. Zahl, *Holy Spirit and Christian Experience*, p. 155.

the ways in which the Christian doctrines of sin and justification address them ameliorates the misperception that 'pneumatological activity' is detached from the material body.[6] Similar to Bavinck's insistence on the 'psychological mediation' of revelation, Zahl thus points to the Lutheran tradition to showcase how the law/gospel pattern exhibits a 'pedagogy of the affections' – a doctrinal account of justification that is at once biblically illuminating and experientially tangible.[7]

Zahl's deployment of affect theory thus provides a wonderful insight on the intersection between theology and affective phenomenology. Particularly illuminating is the way in which affect theory gives a granular description of sin's intransigence and the necessity of divine grace to address and transform the intransigent heart. However, though Zahl does recognize the intransigence of sin and an affective account of sin and grace at the point of receiving the justifying work of Christ, an affective and phenomenological description of sin's intransigence in light of God's pervasive *creational* revelation is not yet addressed. That is, though Zahl shows us the affective pedagogy of the law and gospel from Romans 3 and 5–7, this gospel comes within the context of a human phenomenology that is already responding to God in affectively salient ways. This is especially seen in the way in which Romans 1:18-32 describes human beings as both 'perceiving' and 'suppressing' simultaneously the creational knowledge of God. In other words, a theological deployment of affect theory illumines not only the affective salience of the doctrines of justification and sanctification, but also the understanding of human beings as fallen religious creatures that exhibit embodied responses to the affordances of God's general revelation. Providing such a phenomenology and affectively salient account of the fallen human reception of general revelation and of what I call the 'psychical effects' of sin would also further fortify Zahl's observation that theological description encompasses the everyday experience of human existence. It is precisely in this context that I shall draw from Dreyfus's Heideggerian phenomenology of skillful coping. Before I get to those constructive ends, however, one more trajectory of research should be surveyed to show the generative implications of my argument below: current discussions of the noetic effects of sin that are attentive to the findings of the CSR.

On the Cognitive Consequences of Sin

The diverse findings of the CSR have been deployed in dialogue with the Christian doctrine of the noetic effects of sin in a variety of ways, as will be shown below, and alerting oneself to some of these points of dialogue will further highlight the benefits of tending to the psychical dimensions of sin that I will develop. Because of the focus on particularly the *cognitive* dimensions of human knowing, deploying affect theory relating to the phenomenology of knowledge has some crucial

---

6. Zahl, *Holy Spirit and Christian Experience*, 179.
7. Zahl, *Holy Spirit and Christian Experience*, 168.

benefits for how we describe the doctrine of the natural knowledge of God and our suppression of it. As we shall see, paying exclusive attention to the malfunctioning of the human tendency to believe in some higher mind, or identifying the *sensus divinitatis* exclusively with humanity's cognitive apparatus, misses the phenomenological backdrop of the human knowledge of God, and recovering that phenomenological backdrop helps us avoid certain problems. To see how this is the case, I move first to the recent response from Peels, Eyghen, and Van den Brink to Helen De Cruz and Johan De Smedt concerning the compatibility of CSR with a Christian account of the cognitive consequences of sin. Second, I note that Peels' exegesis of the same passage produces some tensions – involving the experience of encountering non-theists who deny having propositional knowledge of God, and whether one should identify the propositional beliefs with the deliverances of general revelation – and that these tensions might benefit from again heeding the insights of the affective dimensions outlined in the previous sections.

Locating the Source of the Cognitive Consequences of Sin

Peels, Eyghen, and Van den Brink contest the claim made by Helen De Cruz and Johan De Smedt that CSR and a Christian account of the efficacy of general revelation along with the cognitive consequences of sin are incompatible. Briefly, the cognitive consequences of sin refer to the doctrine in which, due to original sin (and hence to original corruption), human beings have malfunctioning cognitive faculties that lead them to form unwarranted beliefs and non-alethic cognitive biases. In relation to the knowledge of God, this leads to the development of false beliefs about God, or to the loss of our initial beliefs about God, and to the loss of belief in God at all.[8]

It is the issue of theistic beliefs, or, rather, the propositional output of the sense of the divine, that is most relevant to our purposes. For De Cruz and De Smedt, CSR shows on an empirical basis that human beings have held to unwarranted and false beliefs from the very beginning due to their evolutionary history, and beliefs about the supernatural are no exception.[9] Human beings have evolved in such a way that theistic beliefs have helped to coordinate group co-operation for survival, and though the propensity to develop a theory of mind is useful, they may develop a hypersensitive agency-detecting device, producing all sorts of false-god beliefs. Furthermore, due to the lack of empirical evidence for a historic fall, it appears that monotheistic beliefs only emerged rather late in human history, and that false beliefs about God (from a Christian theological perspective) were the predominant output of early human cognitive faculties without exception. The resulting picture is the opposite one of the traditional Christian story, according

---

8. Cf. Rik Peels, 'Sin and Human Cognition of God', *Scottish Journal of Theology* 64 (2011): pp. 395–6.

9. Helen De Cruz and Johan De Smedt, 'Reformed and Evolutionary Epistemology and the Noetic Effects of Sin', *International Journal for the Philosophy of Religion* 74 (2012): pp. 54, 63.

to which an original period of communion with God and peace was disrupted by a fall into nontheistic disarray. Rather than viewing false god-beliefs as the result of the fall, a 'more natural reading of the evolutionary and cognitive empirical evidence is that off-track beliefs are results of our evolutionary history'.[10] Such a story would not only compromise the claim that the disposition to produce false beliefs about God is a fallen condition, but also the doctrine according to which God has revealed his existence universally, clearly, and efficaciously in creation. It seems difficult to affirm that God has disclosed himself universally in creation when false theistic beliefs have been the norm without exception.

In response, Peels, Eyghen, and Van den Brink offer the following story.[11] Assuming that the evolutionary account of human origins is true, suppose God isolated a representative community of humans so that they might be protected from evil and suffering, and that God might be present to them in a personal and intimate way. Suppose, however, that God withdrew from this people because they refused to obey him, and preferred to go their own way, determining for themselves what is good and evil. Because God is no longer present to them '*in that specific (close, intimate, etc.) way*' human beings are no longer prone to produce true beliefs about God.[12] As they write:

> An alternative way of thinking of this same scenario is that the mechanism that humans have when it comes to belief formation about gods is reliable – it is not broken, so to say, but that it is *not in the environment for which it was meant if it is not functioning in the intimate presence of God*. In that case, it produces all sorts of false beliefs. Thus, it would resemble a normal thermometer that is used on the moon; it is reliable, but just not in the sort of environment for which it was meant. It is not so much that the mechanism is broken, but that it is not functioning in the proper circumstances, which is now a sinful environment where God is not present in that particular way.[13]

---

10. De Cruz and De Smedt, 'Reformed and Evolutionary Epistemology and the Noetic Effects of Sin', 63. They further argue that natural-theological arguments stem from these same evolutionary features that form a stable part of human cognition in their *A Natural History of Natural Theology: The Cognitive Science of Theology and Philosophy of Religion* (Massachusetts: MIT Press, 2015). In the background to these discussions is Alvin Plantinga's influential account of the malfunctioning of the *sensus divinitatis*, defined as a cognitive faculty that produces beliefs in God in, e.g., *Warranted Christian Belief* (Oxford: Oxford University Press, 2000), pp. 203–15.

11. Rik Peels, Hans Van Eyghen, and Gijsbert van den Brink, 'Cognitive Science of Religion and the Cognitive Consequences of Sin', in *New Developments in the Cognitive Science of Religion: The Rationality of Religious Belief*, Hans Van Eyghen, Rik Peels, and Gijsbert van den Brink (eds) (Cham: Springer, 2018), pp. 210–11.

12. Peels, Eyghen, and Van den Brink, 'Cognitive Consequences of Sin', p. 210. Emphasis original.

13. Peels, Eyghen, and Van den Brink, 'Cognitive Consequences of Sin', p. 211. Emphasis original.

This response provides a twofold benefit. First, it is congruent with the positing of (a kind of) historical fall, according to which there was a point in history where human beings did enjoy a period of peace and communion with God, and then another point at which they were deprived of that state due to their own disobedience against God. Second, it is in keeping with the empirical data indicating that the false theistic beliefs have been the norm without exception, for here the shift is not from a properly functioning cognition to a malfunctioning one, but in the *environment* it is in – namely – the deprivation of God's intimate presence for this isolated representational community.

It is important to note for the purposes of this section that the authors are careful to qualify that the change in God's presence is one of *intimacy*. It is not that God was only present in one part of creation, and then due to human disobedience God is now absent everywhere. Rather, though the authors do not state this, it seems to me that they do not deny that God is present and revealing himself in all of creation (on pain of denying general revelation). Rather, God was present to that original human community in a personal and intimate way, and after their disobedience God is merely present to them in that general, creational sense. The shift is not from the presence of God to a lack of presence simpliciter, but from an intimate, personal (relational) presence, to a non-intimate one.

If one assumes the veracity of the evolutionary account of human cognition, Peels, Eyghen, and Van den Brink offer an elegant solution indeed. However, I suggest a tension exists between their solution and the scriptural testimony of the human awareness of God in Romans 1. Recall the Scriptural witness:

> For the wrath of God is revealed from heaven against all ungodliness and unrighteousness of men, who by their unrighteousness suppress the truth. For what can be known about God is plain to them, because God has shown it to them. For his invisible attributes, namely, his eternal power and divine nature, have been clearly perceived, ever since the creation of the world, in the things that have been made. So they are without excuse. For although they knew God, they did not honor him as God or give thanks to him, but they became futile in their thinking, and their foolish hearts were darkened.

Two relevant issues emerge from the text: one on the source of the cognitive consequences of sin and the second on the dynamic of revelation and suppression. I discuss the first one here and the second in the next section. First, then, the problem is that the noetic (and psychical) effects of sin, according to this passage, are not so much attributed to the change in the mode of God's presence, or to humanity's environment, but to human beings themselves who 'by their unrighteousness suppress the truth'. It is not a shift in environment, but a shift from human obedience to disobedience, that resulted in the darkening of their minds and the suppression of the truth disclosed. Furthermore, several texts alongside Romans 1 indicate that it was the hardening of the human heart behind the mind, and not a change in environment, that led to further idolatry – false beliefs about

God and the projecting of new gods.[14] The emphasis of Romans 1 is that God is 'plain' to them, and that humans have perceived him 'ever since the creation of the world'. The noetic effects of sin are not due to the result of God's withdrawal of intimacy, but to human disobedience that does, indeed, malform the direction of our cognitive faculties.[15] This is an important modification to the fall-like story offered by Van den Brink et al. The fall and its cognitive consequences are due not merely to loss of communion with God but also due to a corruption of human nature, such that the human heart becomes darkened. God's general revelation thus remains clear, and it is human beings who suppress their awareness of that revelation due to the darkness that has corrupted their minds and hearts. This will provide the backdrop for the later exploration of whether one is born a natural believer or a natural idolater.

The Limits of Cognition and Distinguishing 'Cognitively Natural Theism' from General Revelation

The second issue still persists, however, and it is this: the very *presence* of the knowledge of God is the context *within* which suppression takes place. What sort of knowledge is generated by general revelation, and what sort of suppression is this? While Rik Peels self-consciously avoids this issue, he does offer some hints in an earlier essay.[16] Peels argues that the mind is directed by the heart, and that this knowledge lies not merely within the intellect but also in the inner self-consciousness of the self. He thus recognizes that knowledge of God is obtained 'by instinctive recognition upon observing the world' rather than 'a complex process of reasoning'.[17] Peels further acknowledges that there are 'certain affective consequences of sin', such that 'our noetic faculties are *directed* towards things which they should not be directed towards, or not directed towards things which they should be directed towards'.[18] Peels recognizes that cognition is tethered to affect.

Peels, however, does not take these comments that hint at an affective reception toward an account of the knowledge of God as affective and phenomenological; he goes on to focus on this knowledge as cognitive and propositional, involving the formation of particular beliefs. Concerning this creational knowledge of God, Peels writes that it is a 'knowing that God exists, or, if you want, merely having *propositional* knowledge that there is such a being as God and that he exemplifies

---

14. E.g. Rom. 8:7; Col. 1:21; Eph. 4:17-19, 5:8.
15. In an earlier essay by Peels, one finds an account of the cognitive consequences of sin grounded in a philosophical-exegetical reflection on Romans 1 itself that elucidates the point I am making here, which is that our faulty beliefs about God do not come from a change in the divine presence or a withdrawal of general revelation but rather due to the corruption of human nature. See Peels, 'Sin and Human Cognition of God', pp. 400–6.
16. Peels, 'Sin and Human Cognition of God', p. 404.
17. Peels, 'Sin and Human Cognition of God', p. 405.
18. Peels, 'Sin and Human Cognition of God', p. 396.

certain properties, such as his being divine and powerful'.[19] As such, this propositional knowledge is either something all creatures have – or at least 'have had' – the noetic effects of sin thus might include a total loss of the knowledge of God.[20]

I suggest, however, that understanding the creational knowledge of God as primarily or exclusively propositional in character risks diluting the sense of Paul's text, which denotes that human beings always suppress the knowledge of God *within the context* of *possessing* that knowledge, of having 'clearly perceived' him because God himself has 'shown it to them'. A purely cognitive account of the natural knowledge of God seems to render the efficacy of God's general revelation dependent on whether human beings profess to believe particular propositions about God. Here, I suggest that unless one has a grasp of the possibility of a non-propositional *affective* and *phenomenological* account of knowing, one would be hard-pressed to do justice to the sense of Paul's meaning. In other words, in line with Paul's witness, human beings continue to know God, even while they hold false beliefs about him, and, indeed, human beings continue to know God, even while they profess *no propositional* beliefs about God, and even when they deny God.[21] A potential weakness of a propositional rendering of the knowledge of God disclosed in Romans 1 is that, upon encountering non-theists, one would have to say that God's revelation is somehow not plain to them, or that they do, in fact, lack a knowledge of God. Without such a phenomenological account, then, following Peels, Eyghen, and Van den Brink, when human beings lack God's intimate presence and hence begin to form false beliefs about God, they shift from knowing God to simply not knowing God, or, to follow Peels's earlier account, if they lack propositional beliefs about God, then they simply lack the knowledge of God.

However, affect theory and phenomenology have shown that cognition arises out of and alongside pre-conscious embodied affects. If one has a phenomenological account of knowing in view, then one can hold on to the *prima facie* paradox that one can know God without believing any explicit propositions about him and even while denying him. What is felt in the depths of personality, as Bavinck argues, precedes and is not necessarily articulated or professed by the intellect.[22] This phenomenological rendering of the efficacy of general revelation would also provide another way of responding to De Cruz and De Smedt: it would be a mistake to identify the professed theistic beliefs of humans across history with the deliverances of general revelation.

19. Peels, 'Sin and Human Cognition of God', p. 403.
20. Peels, 'Sin and Human Cognition of God', p. 405.
21. As indicated in the previous chapter, I am thus presupposing a broadly Heideggerian instead of a Husserlian account of phenomenology. This is the argument I shall draw out in the next few sections.
22. While I do not explore it further in this project, I suggest that this affective anthropology also avoids excluding persons with autism from imaging and knowing God. Cf. Joanna Leidenhag, 'The Challenge of Autism for Relational Approaches to Theological Anthropology', *International Journal of Systematic Theology* 23 (2021): pp. 109–34.

It is in this context that I return to the issue about whether the sort of theistic beliefs that are most naturally produced by our cognitive apparatus are a reliable way of arriving at a true theology. If a phenomenological knowledge of God is the result of general revelation, rather than a propositional awareness, then one has the benefit of being able to distinguish firmly between the theistic propositions that we come to believe (or disbelieve), on the one hand, and general revelation, on the other. In other words, one can resist identifying the beliefs of the surveys and polls conducted by CSR with the output of general revelation – no amount of propositional surveying, *in principle*, can prove or disprove the efficacy of general revelation. General revelation hits the locus of the inner self, the heart, and propositional beliefs are always the result of the heart having already processed that affective knowledge.

On 'Natural Knowledge' and 'Cognitively Natural' Theism

To see the payoff of this affective account of the knowledge of God, it is worth considering Ian McFarland's objections to general revelation and the natural knowledge of God, before turning to an argument by Lari Launonen and R. T. Mullins on open theism as more amenable to a cognitively natural version of theism.[23] Along the way, I shall also further elucidate the distinction between implicit beliefs and phenomenological knowing.

First, then, I suggest that these phenomenological emphases prove fruitful when put in dialogue with the recent dogmatic work of Ian McFarland against the natural knowledge of God.[24] His 2015 essay builds on the reasoning of his 2014 book, focusing on the epistemological implications of his understanding of divine transcendence and of God's exhaustive involvement within the world. In that essay, McFarland articulates a potent and theologically motivated rejection of the natural knowledge of God. He does not do so because, as some might predict, of a postulation of God's hiddenness or inactivity within the world, but rather because of God's immanence. Put positively, 'a maximally comprehensive vision of divine involvement in the world', he writes, makes 'untenable any direct line of inference from creature to Creator, in the form of claims that the beauty or order of the world reveal God'.[25] McFarland's line of argumentation climaxes in this arresting passage:

> Since all creatures are equally and absolutely dependent on God for every aspect of their existence and at every point of their existence, no aspect of created

---

23. Lari Launonen and R. T. Mullins, 'Why Open Theism Is Natural and Classical Theism Is Not', *Religions* 12, no. 956 (2021): pp. 1–16.

24. Ian McFarland, '"God, the Father Almighty": A Theological Excursus', *International Journal of Systematic Theology* 18 (2016): pp. 259-73; Ian McFarland, *From Nothing: A Theology of Creation* (Louisville: Westminster John Knox, 2014).

25. McFarland, 'God, the Father', p. 260.

reality can in itself provide any privileged line of access to the divine. Nor can the structure of the created order as a whole serve this purpose. Because God transcends all creatures, whether considered individually or as a collective, to the same infinite degree, one can no more ascend to God via the experience of any particular set of natural phenomena than Esther Summerson might infer the existence of Charles Dickens based on her experience of the novelistic world of Bleak House. The connection between God and the world, like that between the author and his novel, is visible only to one who has a view of both – and that is something we do not have – except insofar as God provides that perspective by revealing God's self within creation. Otherwise, creation remains opaque to God, not because God is distant from it, but precisely because God's all-encompassing relation to the world as 'the Father almighty' precludes the creature acquiring any point of epistemic leverage over against the Creator.[26]

McFarland's claims here concerning the implications of the opaqueness of creation and the inability of human reasoning to infer theological claims in a bottom-up fashion are complemented in the following passage from his From Nothing:

> [C]reation from nothing implies that God is *already* maximally "inside" the world: since God's sustaining presence is the one necessary and sufficient condition of every creature's existence at every moment of its existence, any degree of divine absence would result in the total and instantaneous dissolution of created being (see Ps. 104:29) .... Creation from nothing rules out talk of any creature existing apart from or at any distance from God. It follows that God is and cannot be *more* present in Jesus than in you or me or the lowliest sea slug.[27]

The creator-creature distinction means that from one creaturely phenomenon only another creaturely phenomenon can be inferred, and the doctrine of God's omnipresence and of his exhaustive involvement with the world means that no particular aspect of creation provides a privileged entryway toward knowledge of him. Theological reasoning with respect to creation and the being of God, therefore, belongs within the standpoint of a confessing faith rather than a set of deduced claims from empirical observation or by virtue of sheer logical acumen. McFarland's suspicion concerning the epistemic success of natural theological reasoning is thus similar to the broad disposition of Bavinck (and neo-Calvinism): both emphasize the necessity of starting with the Christian faith for proper dogmatic reflection, and hence both would render suspect the pre-dogmatic model of natural theology. Neo-Calvinist dogmaticians would also emphasize the transcendence of God and God's exhaustive preservation and governance of the world by way of concursus.[28] And McFarland's exegetical emphasis on Romans

---

26. McFarland, 'God, the Father', pp. 270–1.
27. McFarland, *From Nothing*, p. 102.
28. See Brock and Sutanto, *Neo-Calvinism*, chapter 4.

1 would also be shared by the neo-Calvinist: whatever knowledge or talk of God arises in the creature's experience of the world renders that creature's thinking 'futile' because 'they invariably confuse God with some lesser reality … with more abstract forms of first cause, unmoved mover, or most perfect being in what remains a worldly matrix of cause and effect'.[29] The emphasis in Romans 1:20 on the perception of God's 'eternal power and divine nature' is thus not the possibility of a 'perception of the invisible with a movement from phenomenal effect to transcendent cause', which would be to commit a 'category error', but about the 'One who comes to be known in questioning *us*'.[30] The direction must come from the top-down, from the God of Jesus Christ, who is recognized by those who are 'in faith'.[31]

However, as we have seen, Bavinck remained positive in his affirmation of the ubiquity of general revelation whereas McFarland deemed it fitting to deny it as a useful category altogether.[32] At least one reason this is the case, given the phenomenological account of general revelation, is that the natural knowledge of God is not primarily a rational category but an affective one. Creation reveals and bestows a knowledge of God that is not the product of reasoning from created effects toward a transcendent cause, but a pressure exerted by a ubiquitous divine revelation that incurs an ever-present and relational awareness first of the existence of the Creator and second of the creature's failure to honor the Creator. Just as the awareness that a spouse is angry arises when one enters into a room merely by recognizing the spouse's body language – without the attendance of words – God's pervasive presence means, in dogmatic terms, that for Bavinck, no creature exists without their awareness of their Creator and of their failures before their Creator. Furthermore, the talk of God that arises in those who do not stand in faith by virtue of that constant pressure, the neo-Calvinists would assert, remains futile, as they invariably confuse God with a lesser reality. Such talk of God is therefore to be distinguished from theological reasoning as a verbalized second moment, thereby preserving on the one hand the pervasiveness of general revelation and the futility of natural theologizing apart from faith. Those in Christ can, and do, behold the presence of God in creation in theologically richer terms that preserve the analogical mode (top-down) of theological predication. In these ways, it seems to me that the neo-Calvinist articulation of general revelation preserves McFarland's worries without paying the price of denying the doctrine of general revelation. As we saw in the previous chapter, general revelation elicits the feeling of absolute dependence, and propositional categorization is a second moment.

29. McFarland, 'God, the Father', p. 272.
30. McFarland, 'God, the Father', p. 273.
31. McFarland, 'God, the Father', p. 273.
32. 'I use the term "revelation" to designate what in some theological systems is called "special revelation", that is, the second person self-disclosure of the God of Jesus Christ. Given that I am arguing that there is no other means of coming to know God (that is, that there is no "general revelation"), the modifier is superfluous within the theological framework I employ.' McFarland, 'God, the Father', p. 261 n. 3.

Second, consider the application of this phenomenological line of reasoning to Launonen and Mullins's essay 'Why Open Theism Is Natural and Classical Theism Is Not'. This essay picks up on recent scholarship on the theological relevance of CSR and how it compares with particular models of theism, and in particular, classical theism. If the beliefs denoted by the CSR are identifiable with Christian beliefs about the natural knowledge of God, then what conclusions should one draw when those beliefs do not exactly match with particular models of God? If God has instilled in human beings a tendency to believe in God, should it not be rather easy for the common rational agent to arrive at a 'correct god' concept? In particular, Launonen and Mullins connect these issues with the doctrine of general revelation, and pose the question: 'Does CSR tend to support or undermine the doctrine of general revelation?'[33] The connection they are making is this: general revelation just is that doctrine which states that God has instilled in every person the appropriate cognitive faculties such that they would naturally or intuitively produce correct beliefs about God. Hence, 'the generation of theistic belief has been viewed as God's primary purpose for general revelation'.[34] While there are other theologically interesting claims in the article of Launonen and Mullins, I focus on this particular connection between CSR and general revelation.[35]

Specifically, Launonen and Mullins focus on whether our 'natural intuitions' are 'theism-tracking': 'natural cognitive biases and systems are theism-tracking if the god concept they give rise to approximates the theologically correct model of God.'[36] If the God-concept cognitive faculties produce is quite different than the Christian concept of God, then this might compromise the doctrine of general revelation and its efficacy, for general revelation, in their definition, among other things, at least involves the claim that our cognitive faculties are reliable enough to produce minimally correct beliefs of God. There is thus – from a Christian perspective – a correlation to be sought between the sort of theistic beliefs our cognitive apparatus naturally yields and the veracity and reliability of the doctrine of general revelation.

In this context, Launonen and Mullins draw on the distinction between implicit and explicit beliefs:

> First, a god concept is one's cognitively implicit blueprint of the basic attributes of a supernatural agent, be they ontological (e.g., incorporeality), mental (e.g., omniscience), or moral (e.g., benevolence) attributes. Second, models of God are theological theories of the divine attributes of what God is like. Such models are

---

33. Launonen and Mullins, 'Why Open Theism Is Natural and Classical Theism Is Not', p. 4.

34. Launonen and Mullins, 'Why Open Theism Is Natural and Classical Theism Is Not', p. 5.

35. There are, for instance, claims to the effect that the Bible itself does not warrant the conclusions of classical theism peppered throughout the article.

36. Launonen and Mullins, 'Why Open Theism Is Natural and Classical Theism Is Not', p. 4.

cognitively explicit. Since there are many versions of theism, we need to be clear which one we are talking about when considering whether Natural Religion is theism-tracking. Third, when does a god concept 'approximate' a theological model of God? Moreover, why do we employ such a criterion anyway? Would it not be simpler to just ask whether theism is natural? The reason is that the correct model of God does not need to have a perfect fit with Natural Religion for the doctrine of general revelation to be true. However, a model of God should not be too counter-intuitive either. Some counter-intuitiveness is allowed. After all, scholars, such as Boyer, argue that religious ideas are natural exactly because they are minimally counter-intuitive.[37]

The correct, explicit model of God should thus be minimally different from the implicit god-concept of our cognitive biases, and, again, whether our cognitive biases are 'theism-tracking' has direct implications for the veracity of the doctrine of general revelation.

The implicit theology of CSR, however, is far from the God of classical theism – the common report of the doctrine of God for most of Christian history through Augustine to the Protestant scholastics and advocated still by Herman Bavinck. Christian classical theism, after all, depicts God as simple, impassible, immutable, and Triune – not a being among other beings in the metaphysical furniture of the universe but Being himself. The divine that is described by CSR, however, is much more metaphysically limited. As Jong, Kavanagh, and Visala summarize:

> If they existed, the gods of the cognitive science of religion seem to be things in the world, effectively parts of the spatio-temporal universe; agents among other agents that interact with other things in the world in much the same way we do. They are more or less like normal agents, except more powerful. Indeed, *ex hypothesi*, gods are anthropomorphic entities generated by precisely those cognitive mechanisms that evolved to deal with other persons and non-human agents.[38]

The sort of Being described by classical theism is thus not cognitively 'natural', and thus our cognitive faculties would not be theism-tracking if classical theism is the model of God that one takes to be true. In fact, Launonen and Mullins claim, if classical theism is true, 'then true knowledge of God seems dependent on a particular cultural setting.'[39] However, as they observe, classical theism is not the only model of God on offer. Open theism, with its view (among other

---

37. Launonen and Mullins, 'Why Open Theism Is Natural and Classical Theism Is Not', p. 4.

38. Jonathan Jong, Christopher Kavanagh, and Aku Visala, 'Born Idolators: The Limits of the Philosophical Implications of the Cognitive Science of Religion', *Neue Zeitschrift für Systematische Theologie und Religionsphilosophie* 57 (2015): p. 251.

39. Launonen and Mullins, 'Why Open Theism Is Natural and Classical Theism Is Not', p. 8.

propositions) that God engages in reciprocal relationship with the world, is more amenable to the theological deliverances of CSR. Even if not all of the explicit claims of open theism are identifiable with the deliverances of CSR, 'the open theist could, thus, argue that God has created people with sufficient-theism tracking cognitive systems, such that it only takes a minimal amount of reflection and general scaffolding to arrive at a theistic-like god concept'.[40] Mullins and Launonen's argument, therefore, is similar to the argument offered by Peels in that both identify the propositional beliefs of humans with the deliverances of general revelation; while the former does so to deny the cognitive naturalness of classical theism, the latter concedes that the noetic effects of sin might just lead us to lose our natural knowledge of God altogether.

What might an advocate of classical theism and general revelation say about this analysis, given the deployment of Bavinck's theological account of humanity and revelation, affects and phenomenology, outlined above? I propose a three-pronged answer: first, a distinction between phenomenological knowing and implicit beliefs; second, an identification of phenomenological knowing as the locus of general revelation's effects (with a brief nod to John Calvin); and third, an elucidation of the relationship between implicit beliefs and our cognitive limitations.

The first two prongs go together. Recall that Launonen and Mullins associate the cognitive content of implicit beliefs with the doctrine of general revelation. If general revelation is true, then our implicit beliefs should be theism-tracking, and whether they are theism-tracking hangs on what explicit model of God we presuppose. If the explicit model of God we presuppose is classical theism, then our implicit beliefs are not theism-tracking, and thus the doctrine of general revelation is undermined. However, if Bavinck's affective theological anthropology and account of general revelation are true, then the locus of general revelation is not in cognition, but rather in the affections – in that pre-categorical intuition and everyday experience not reducible to beliefs, not even implicit beliefs.[41]

Here, I draw again from Dreyfus's discussion of Heideggerian phenomenology that seeks to overcome 'the myth of the mental'.[42] Dreyfus distinguishes Heidegger from the more recent views of Wilfred Sellars and John McDowell, according to which 'there couldn't be any such logos-free pure perception'.[43] Dreyfus argues that 'Heidegger could counter ... that in assuming that all intelligibility, even perception and skillful coping, *must be, at least implicitly, conceptual* – in effect, that intuitions without concepts must be blind, and that there is a maxim behind

---

40. Launonen and Mullins, 'Why Open Theism Is Natural and Classical Theism Is Not', p. 13.
41. For an alternative response to Mullins and Launonen, see Tyler McNabb and Michael DeVito, 'Cognitive Science of Religion and Classical Theism: A Synthesis', *Religions* 13 (2022): pp. 1–7. I would agree with their suggestion that 'it is not even clear to us that Romans 1 has propositional knowledge of God in mind' (6). It is also important to recall that Bavinck locates both affect (feeling) and cognition (reason) under the knowing faculty, as discussed in chapter two.
42. Dreyfus, *Skillful Coping*, pp. 105–24.
43. Dreyfus, *Skillful Coping*, p. 110. Emphasis original.

every action – Sellars and McDowell join Kant in endorsing what we might call the Myth of the Mental'.[44] As we shall see below, skillful coping is that fluid manner in which human bodies and perception respond to the world's affordances in ways that precede the formation of beliefs and conscious awareness. For Dreyfus, human mastery or skillfulness is not reducible to and often independent from the application of particular reasons, maxims, or propositions. For the Heideggerian phenomenologists: 'rules needn't play any role in *producing* skilled behavior.'[45] For Dreyfus, phenomenological and skilled behaviors – which are *nonconceptual yet meaningful* – are not reducible to the implicit believing of particular propositions. There is a kind of knowing without belief, a kind of skill that is submerged and which precedes the consciously mental: '*These features, although available to the perceptual system, needn't be available to the mind.*'[46] Dreyfus summarizes the difference between phenomenologists and conceptualists in this way: 'Phenomenologists therefore disagree with conceptualists in that phenomenologists claim that a study of expertise shows that nameable features are irrelevant to the current state of mind of the master when he acts …. *Nothing about the position need to be nameable and thinkable as a reason for acting.*'[47] One should resist the temptation to identify skilled coping with 'even *implicitly* rational' categories in terms of cognition, 'in the sense of being responsive to reasons that have become habitual but could be reconstructed'.[48] This account of skillful coping will be further elaborated below and it will prove important for our theological rendering of the phenomenology of the psychical effects of sin, but for now the key point is merely to note that, with Dreyfus's Heideggerian phenomenology in view, one is equipped with a distinction between phenomenological mastery (a kind of nonconceptual knowing) and implicit belief.

If this distinction is right, then what if the result of general revelation is a certain *affect*, giving rise to this phenomenological knowing that is irreducible to implicit beliefs that could be made explicit? As we have shown, this is exactly Herman Bavinck's position, as surveyed in the previous chapters in detail – prior to thinking and willing, one *feels* one's dependence on God, and this manifests itself in our unconscious psyche and the unconscious ways in which we function within the world. Though this position was evident in Bavinck's later writings in the Stone lectures and the essay on the unconscious, the roots of this were already found in the *Dogmatics*: 'The innate knowledge of God, *the moment it becomes cognition and hence not only cognitive ability but also cognitive action, never originated apart from the working of God's revelation from within and without, and is to that extent therefore acquired.*'[49] The knowledge of God and the locus of general revelation precede cognition entirely.

---

44. Dreyfus, *Skillful Coping*, p. 110. Emphasis original.
45. Dreyfus, *Skillful Coping*, p. 114.
46. Dreyfus, *Skillful Coping*, p. 114.
47. Dreyfus, *Skillful Coping* p. 115.
48. Dreyfus, *Skillful Coping*, p. 115.
49. Bavinck, *RD* 2: p. 73. Emphasis mine.

John Calvin also has a remarkable and often-quoted passage that gestures in this direction, and it is relevant to pay some attention to him here since interpreters who seek to bring together the findings of CSR with the deliverances of general revelation often identify Calvin's *sensus divinitatis* with a cognitive faculty that generates theistic beliefs.[50] Calvin claims:

> Men of sound judgment will always be sure that a sense of divinity which can never be effaced is engraved upon men's minds. Indeed the perversity of the impious, who though they struggle furiously are unable to extricate themselves from the fear of God, is abundant testimony that this conviction, namely, that there is some God, is naturally inborn in all, and is fixed deep within, as it were in the very marrow. ... I only say that though the stupid hardness in their minds, which the impious eagerly conjure up to reject God, wastes away, yet the sense of divinity, which they greatly wished to have extinguished, thrives and presently burgeons. From this we conclude that it is not a doctrine that must first be learned in school, but one which each of us is master from his mother's womb and which nature itself permits no one to forget, although many strive with every nerve to this end.[51]

Calvin identifies the sense of divinity not with the *cognitive capacity* to form beliefs about God (for infants in the mother's womb lack the cognitive capacity to form beliefs) but with the conviction itself that there is some God. The sense of divinity might be resisted, but it 'thrives and presently burgeons'. Most importantly, the sense of divinity 'is not a doctrine that must first be learned but one which each of us is master from his mother's womb and which nature itself permits no one to forget'. The claim that this is a 'doctrine' that even infants from the mother's womb possess has proven problematic for some who take a cognitivist rendering of the sense of the divine. Surely, some might say, infants do not *really* know God, for they have not formed the cognitive apparatus required to possess knowledge of God.[52] But I suggest this is to read into Calvin's text an exclusively cognitive/intellectual definition of knowledge, and we should take it at face value that Calvin, here offering theological reflections on the Scriptural witness, really means that infants do know God – perhaps akin to the way in which infants recognize facial

---

50. The genesis of such readings is Alvin Plantinga's *Warranted Christian Belief* (Oxford: Oxford University Press, 2000).

51. John Calvin, *Institutes of the Christian Religion*, John T. McNeill (ed.), Ford Lewis Battles (trans.), Library of Christian Classics (London: SCM, 1961), I: 3.3.

52. E.g., see the discussion in Kevin Diller, *Theology's Epistemological Dilemma: How Karl Barth and Alvin Plantinga Offer a Unified Response* (Downers Grove: IVP Academic, 2015), pp. 138–43.

movements pre-cognitively – while they do not have the cognitive developments necessary to form implicit or explicit beliefs.[53]

Observing the relevant texts in John Calvin about the human cognition of God, Jong et al. note that Calvin is remarkably pessimistic about whether human beings cognize the true God, 'Calvin is thus even more pessimistic than Aquinas about the deliverances of our *sensus divinitatis*: for him, the natural deliverances of the *sensus divinitatis* are almost certainly false, given our current moral and epistemic situation.'[54] Indeed, Jong et al. point to Calvin's famous passage on human nature as a 'factory of idols' to show that the natural cognition of humanity does not produce theism-tracking beliefs but rather idol-tracking ones.[55]

Jong et al. thus argue that the God of classical theism is not cognitively natural, and hence that the deliverances of CSR do not produce or vindicate classical theistic beliefs, for 'the tragedy of the classical theologian is precisely that idolatry is easier on the mind than orthodoxy'.[56] Jong et al., however, do not discuss explicitly the connection between this observation from Calvin that fallen humanity might be born idolaters and the doctrine of general revelation. For Launonen and Mullins, by contrast, that classical theism is not cognitively natural points to a possible compromising of one's doctrine of general revelation, unless one posits something akin to open theism as the correct model of God.

But what if the deliverances of our cognitive faculties on theism are not identifiable with the deliverances of general *revelation*? As Bavinck would often refrain, the human awareness of God is not credited to human reasoning or cognition: 'it is not humans who, by the natural light of reason, understand and know this revelation of God.'[57] Furthermore, if cognition arises from the heart, what if the locus of general revelation's impact is on that heart, and as such in ways that precede cognition altogether? As Bavinck wrote: 'God Himself has added to the external revelation in nature an internal revelation to man', and natural 'religion cannot be explained except on the basis of such an increated sense'.[58] Hence, to be clear, the veracity and efficacy of general revelation cannot be adjudicated by the results of surveys and polls. Even if no person professed to be cognitively aware of God, and even if every person professed belief in some form of atheism or

---

53. Katherine Sonderegger's recent reading of Calvin is consistent with the point made here, in her 'The Doctrine of God', in *The Oxford Handbook of Reformed Theology*, Michael Allen and Scott Swain (eds) (Oxford: Oxford University Press, 2021), pp. 389–404.

54. Jong, Kavanagh, and Visala, 'The Limits of the Philosophical Implications', p. 259.

55. Calvin, *Institutes*, I. 11. 8. As Jong et al. conclude, 'at best, Reformed Epistemology [e.g. Plantinga's, Barrett's, and Clark's] is inspired by and tenuously owes itself to the work of Thomas Aquinas and John Calvin, but to call it the Aquinas/Calvin model is almost certainly a misnomer' Jong, Kavanagh, and Visala, 'The Limits of the Philosophical Implications', p. 259.

56. Jong, Kavanagh, and Visala, 'The Limits of the Philosophical Implications', p. 265.

57. Bavinck, *RD* 2: p. 74.

58. Bavinck, *Wonderful Works of God*, p. 26. Bavinck reiterates this same point in *Bijbelsche en religieuze psychologie*, p. 205.

naturalism, the efficacy and veracity of general revelation would remain untouched. If human beings do profess true theistic beliefs, these representations would be in line with the phenomenological affections and knowledge of God – that increated sense in the embodied soul – but these affects and phenomenological knowledge are not identifiable with propositional awareness or cognition, whether implicit or explicit. Tersely, the product of general revelation is 'the feeling of absolute dependency'.[59]

The deliverances of the natural religion of the fallen person are also thus distinguished from the deliverances of general revelation – internal revelation is God's doing, whereas natural religion is the product of that human response to general revelation. The fallen human heart, not wanting to acknowledge God and our dependence on and accountability to him, always desires for this God not to exist, and in his place cognitively constructs an idol that is far less than the real God.[60]

Consider again some of the cognitive biases disclosed by CSR. We are prone to believe that we are far better than others; we overestimate our intelligence, moral behavior, and social status. It is no surprise, then, that the divinity we naturally believe in might also deem us to be better than others, to happen to like what we like, dislike what we dislike. This god might also be more forgiving when we have done something wrong, and more likely to be on our side when we hold a grudge against someone else, and so on. The real God that has implanted a sense of himself in us, however, as disclosed in Romans 1: 18-32, shows us that we would deserve death and his wrath, even as we are dependent on him at every point as he is our Creator. As Launonen and Mullins recognize: 'Most believers fashion God in the image of man, the Creator in the image of a creature.'[61] But this says much more about the fallen heart that drives the mind rather than general revelation. Classical theists within the Reformed tradition would not be surprised by this, and this is why many passages from Scripture teach that the gospel is considered an offense to the natural mind – a stumbling block, a stone of offense, and so on, and why the natural human religion is inclined to erect idols that can be contained in temples made by human hands, idols that can be gratified by our labors (e.g.,

---

59. Bavinck, *Wonderful Works of God*, pp. 26–7.

60. Though Bavinck affirms a historical fall that depicted a transition from an innocent state where humans professed beliefs about God that tracked with the affect of this absolute dependence to a state of corruption, such a phenomenological account of general revelation's affects would also be compatible with a Schleiermacherian account of the human that did not undergo such a fall. In such a scenario, one would be able to respond to De Cruz and De Smedt to the effect that humans were born idolaters all along, and, like Bavinck, one need not interpret the universal presence of false beliefs about God as if these were normative features of human existence. On Schleiermacher's account of humans nature and sinfulness, see Daniel Pedersen, *Schleiermacher's Theology of Sin and Nature: Agency, Value, and Modern Theology* (New York: Routledge, 2022).

61. Launonen and Mullins, 'Why Open Theism Is Natural and Classical Theism Is Not', p. 8.

consider Paul's speech in Acts 17). This is standard fare for those who are attuned to the tradition's discussion on the noetic effects of sin.

With the impact of general revelation located in pre-theoretical affection and phenomenology, then, how does one know what precisely God has disclosed about himself in nature? What propositional beliefs are consistent with the kinds of affections human beings have in relation to the real God? Bavinck would repeat an answer commonly found within the Reformed tradition: those beliefs which are in line with what special revelation discloses about general revelation. He writes, 'Our knowledge of revelation, *both the general and the special*, comes to us from the Holy Scriptures.'[62] Scripture is necessary such that even 'Christian believers would not be able to understand God's revelation in nature and reproduce it accurately had not God himself described in his word how he revealed himself and what he revealed of himself in the universe as a whole.'[63] As Bavinck observes in another oft-quoted passage, these convictions, in his view, come from the teachings of the Reformation:

> [T]he human mind was so darkened by sin that human beings could not rightly know and understand this revelation [from creation] either. Needed, therefore, were two things: (1) that God again included in special revelation those truths which in themselves are knowable from nature; and (2) that human beings, in order to again perceive God in nature, first had to be illumined by the Spirit of God. Objectively needed by human beings to understand the general revelation of God in nature was the special revelation of God in Holy Scripture, which, accordingly, was compared by Calvin to glasses. Subjectively needed by human beings was the eye of faith to see God also in the works of his hands.[64]

Equipped with the spectacles of Scripture, then, Christian theologians are in a position to interpret the data of affect theory and the CSR theologically, and thus to form the distinction between general revelation's efficacy and affect, on the one hand, and to recognize that, after the fall, humans are born idolaters. Thus, what humans tend to profess and to report in the polls do not conform to the deliverances of general revelation. The illumination of word and Spirit is required to conform our professed beliefs with the affect of general revelation.

Putting It All Together: Affect, Cognition, Religious Creatures, and the Psychical Effects of Sin

Let us take stock. Because CSR identifies the sense of the divine with a cognitive faculty, some have sought to explore the relationship between the theistic beliefs

---

62. Bavinck, *Wonderful Works of God*, p. 79.
63. Bavinck, *RD* 2: p. 74.
64. Bavinck, *RD* 1: p. 304. For a further discussion of this sort of passage within the neo-Calvinist tradition, see my 'Neocalvinism and General Revelation'.

produced by our cognitive output, general revelation and particular models of God. In exploring these issues, I showed that identifying the cognitive output of our faculties with the deliverances of general revelation is problematic, and that identifying the deliverances of general revelation instead with pre-theoretical affections in the unconscious (or, to use biblical language, the 'heart') yields particular benefits. One need no longer to identify the natural beliefs of the many with the deliverances of general revelation, and given the Scriptural witness on the noetic effects of sin, it is not surprising that, given the hardening of the fallen heart, the mind would be naturally inclined to believe in idols instead of the real God.[65]

The yields of CSR, then, should be read in light of a broader account of human beings as religious creatures, and also in light of the findings of affect theory and phenomenology. In what follows, I suggest that Hubert Dreyfus's work on skillful coping as the primordial context in which reasoning and willing occur fits well with the accounts offered by Bavinck above and complements well our discussion of affect theory and CSR. Furthermore, I show that his account (along with the yields of affect theory and CSR) can also be reinterpreted theologically in the context of the doctrine of sinful humanity's suppression of the truth, thus producing a phenomenologically granular description of the dynamic of 'knowing-yet-suppressing' God that takes place in everyday human existence. Though a discussion of the noetic effects of sin is indeed fruitful, given Bavinck's affective theological anthropology, focusing on cognition ignores the fact that the psyche – that unconscious depth of human personality that directs the faculties of the soul, which is the form of the body – is where God makes himself felt and where the tacit responses of the intransigent sinner take place. Theologically re-interpreting and deploying Dreyfus's phenomenology of skilful coping thus provides an affectively salient description of the *psychical* effects of sin.

Suppression as Skilful Coping: A Theological Re-interpretation of Dreyfus's Model

If those affective features correctly identify how we inhabit the world, how should one characterize human habituation, rationality, and expertise? Dreyfus's account of human expertise can be considered to arise from the implications of the para-cognitive, onto-phenomenological, and intransigent features of human life outlined in the previous chapter on affect theory. As such, my retrieval of Dreyffus's work in this section extends and elaborates on Bavinck's affective anthropology and fleshes out the way in which humans feel and response to God's creational revelation.

For Dreyfus, human expertise should not be couched in terms of the detached rationality of the modern philosophers, but rather by what Dreyfus calls a

---

65. I receive this point from Bonaventure, who argued that 'a joint capacity of will and reason [form] the principal faculties of the soul', such that 'the entire soul has a two-fold capacity: cognitive and affective'. *Breviloquium*, 2. 9. 1 and 2. 9. 6, respectively. This agrees with Bavinck's analysis in 'Primacy of the Intellect or the Will'.

phenomenology of *skillful coping*. An account of skillful coping contains at least these three related claims: first, conceptual reasoning and conscious acts of the will are not the primary ways in which human beings exhibit expertise; second, human skillfulness, instead, manifests itself in the intuitive, non- or pre-cognitive and non-volitionally responsive ways in which one copes with environmental affordances; and third, skillful coping not only marks expertise, but also everyday existence. Cognitive action and conceptual reflection, then, always take place in the context of 'everyday practice' that lies beneath 'our theoretical presuppositions and assumptions'.[66]

First, then, similar to the way in which religious affect theory rejects the linguistic fallacy, Dreyfus situates his argument against the backdrop of the Platonic and Western philosophical tradition that privileged the intellect. Human beings, intellectualists argued, act according to explicit or implicit conceptual rules, and practical knowledge itself could be extracted into a set of maxims one can then replicate and follow. Whether it was in the case of Plato himself, who argued that '[e]xperts had once known the rules they used ... but then they had forgotten them',[67] or, more recently, in John McDowell's model, according to which all human expertise and perception are always at least implicitly conceptual, the Western tradition prioritizes the conceptual over the phenomenological.[68]

This prioritization of the mental over the phenomenological, however, is mistaken. Two lines of argument are offered to support Dreyfus's thesis. The first line of argument observes that the hope that artificial intelligence can replace human expertise if only they had all of the same information and rules has been dashed. Current cognitive and technological research continues to produce evidence that artificial intelligence cannot replicate the simple ways in which children seem to be able to intuit stories, or sense the social climate of a relational interaction. Though human beings are often incapable of articulating how precisely they can sense the particular moves they ought to make, they are able to perform with fluid coping in ways that machines cannot.

The second line of evidence is also our second point: a human becomes skilled at something precisely when that 'skill has become so much a part of him that he need be no more aware of it than he is of his own body'.[69] Dreyfus's argument here explicates the relevant phenomenological data. Consider the chess master or driver:

> The expert chess player, classed as an international master or grandmaster, in most situations experiences a compelling sense of the issue and the best move. Excellent chess players can play at the rate of 5–10 seconds a move and even faster without any degradation in performance. At this speed they must depend almost entirely on intuition and hardly at all on analysis and comparison or

66. Dreyfus, *Skillful Coping*, p. 134.
67. Dreyfus, *Skillful Coping*, p. 27.
68. Dreyfus, *Skillful Coping*, pp. 105–11.
69. Dreyfus, *Skillful Coping*, p. 34.

alternatives .... The expert driver, generally without any awareness, not only knows by feel and familiarity when an action such as slowing is required, but he generally knows how to perform the act without evaluating and comparing alternatives. He shifts gears when appropriate with no conscious awareness of his acts .... [O]ur description of skill acquisition counters the traditional prejudice that expertise necessarily involves inference.[70]

Experts not only need no awareness to perform, they are also often incapable of describing all that they do, and they are not conscious of the particular steps within these acts. Crucially, this characterization of expertise does not just cover the professional technicality of specific tasks, but also *everyday practice*. Human beings require no conscious reflection or willing in most of their everyday decisions, and it is precisely when a disturbance occurs that our fluid coping is turned into conscious reflection. In Dreyfus's words, there is a kind of intentionality both in everyday coping and among experts that is *meaningful* yet *non-conceptual*:

> Thus, the pure perceiving of the chess master, as well as that of the *phronimos* [phenomenological appearance] and, indeed, the expert in any skill domain, even everyday coping, has a kind of *intentional* content; it isn't just conceptual content. A 'bare Given' and the 'thinkable' are not our only alternatives. We must accept the possibility that our ground-level coping opens up the world by opening us up to a *meaningful* Given – a Given that is *nonconceptual* but not *bare*.[71]

Everyday coping thus involves the intuitive ways in which one responds to the *affordances* of the world: features of our environment that elicit our responses. The chair is *for* sitting, the hammer is *for* hammering nails, and specific people *require* specific social interactions. Here, Dreyfus signals his indebtedness to Heidegger and Aristotle specifically: 'It is this necessary situational specificity of skillful coping that Aristotle and Heidegger noted in the case of the *phronimos*, and which led Heidegger to conclude that skillful coping is nonconceptual.'[72] The space of reasons and conscious reflection do have their place – they can help us reorient ourselves to the world – but everyday coping requires not the conscious use of reason, but the primordial instincts of the self, whether social, intuitive, or physical.

In this regard, Dreyfus's account finds an ally in that of Bavinck, who, as indicated above, argued that the soul and the knowledge of God lie underneath conscious willing and acting, and that knowing and acting themselves are moved by the unconscious self. As Bavinck wrote: 'Understanding and reason [indicate] so little

---

70. Dreyfus, *Skillful Coping*, p. 35.
71. Dreyfus, *Skillful Coping*, p. 116. Emphases original.
72. Dreyfus, *Skillful Coping*, p. 116.

of the essence of man and the whole of the content of the faculty of knowing; rather they are merely particular activities of the knowing faculty that first began their work as the fundamentals of human knowledge that lies broad and deep in the unconscious.'[73] The unconscious, in other words, is not merely that which characterizes technical expertise and skills that become second nature to us, but also that from which most of our everyday behavior stems.

The third point follows naturally from the previous two: reflection and conscious acts both always occur in a primordial context of skilful coping. We are always already skilfully coping with the world as we think and consciously will. Dreyfus draws on two Heidegerrian terms at this point: *Vorsicht* and *Vorhabe*. *Vorsicht*, the theoretical circle of human reflection and interpretation, always takes place in the context of *Vorhabe*, the 'background of practices'.[74] This background of practices is itself rooted in ontology, and ontology here does not refer to a *theory of being*, as commonly understood, but to the *way* humans are. Theoretical, conceptual reflection, 'is always already shaped by what might be called our implicit ontology, an "ontology" which is in our practices as ways of behaving toward things and people, not in our minds as background assumptions which we happen to take for granted'.[75] Intentions do indeed direct these practices, but they are neither conceptually nor consciously directed; they are moved 'by the *perceived conditions*, not by one's *volition*'.[76] The self is always moving within and toward particular horizons, even while conscious acts of the will or conceptual reflection lie elsewhere.[77]

The result of Dreyfus's analysis and affect theory, re-interpreted theologically for our purposes, is the following. Analyses of the noetic effects of sin that focus on whether the intellect is apprehending particular propositions about God, inferred from nature or Scripture, or on the rational and volitional acts of inference and suppression, do not go deep enough. Though they may be illuminating, focusing merely on the apprehension of the intellect or the conscious acts of the will does not yet penetrate to the soul's embodiment. In fact, the conscious reflection and acts of

73. Bavinck, *Beginselen der Psychologie*, p. 82.
74. Dreyfus, *Skillful Coping*, p. 134.
75. Dreyfus, *Skillful Coping*, p. 134.
76. Dreyfus, *Skillful Coping*, p. 148. Emphases original.
77. Andrew Inkpin notes that at times Dreyfus's polemic against the intellectualist tradition risks emphasizing the mindlessness of embodied activity too much. As a remedy, Inkpin argues (rightly, in my judgment) that coping can be theorized, though absorbed coping is irreducible to the latter: 'whereas Dreyfus reads it as a switch from a nonconceptual "ground floor" to conceptual "upper stories" of experience, I have presented it as the transition from prepredicative to predicative forms of understanding.' *Disclosing the World*, p. 279. In line with the emphasis laid on para-cognition, the movement from non-cognitive to explicitly cognitive forms of functioning is porous rather than categorical.

the sinner are always already being performed within the context of unconscious, skilled, behavior in response to the affordances of the world.[78]

Theologically, we have observed in Chapter 2 that, for Bavinck, the primordial context in which humanity lives is *precisely God's self-revelation*. That is, in a manner more pervasive than any social or physical environment that we inhabit, the human self is always living in the context of divine action. In God we live and move and have our being. Since that is the case, the human self is always already skillfully coping with this primordial environment. God's creational revelation is the primary *affordance* that elicits our fluid coping, and it is the context out of which we reflect and make conscious decisions.[79]

Skillful coping is not just the assimilation of learned techniques that then become second nature, but also the very way in which human beings live in the everyday. Suppressing this primordial environment, then, is not something we need to learn. It is *not* a second-nature skill that we have learned to master in a progression that moves from explicit learning to implicit expertise. Rather, Scripture attests that we are 'by nature children of wrath', for we come into the world walking in trespasses and sins (Eph. 2:1-3). Sinfully suppressing God's self-revelation is our nature's fallen skill. It need not be taught, for in sin we were conceived (Ps. 51).

In the language of affect theory, this is the *onto-phenomenological* mode of daily human existence – prior to our conscious awareness, our bodies are fluidly engaged with creation and are hard-wired to respond to it in particular ways. Our lives are marked by the ruptured relationship that we have with God, and sinners come forth already, by nature, suppressing their relationship with God. Due to the *para-cognitive* emergence of our explicit beliefs, they are conditioned by the direction of the unconscious self, and that unconscious self involves resisting the awareness of God and our accountability to him that is disclosed by those affordances. The self's *intransigence* resists easy redirection and behavior modification. Such a reading allows one to revisit Romans 1 with several benefits. First, we can affirm that the knowledge of God is ever-present without denigrating the effects of sin that cause us to fail to apprehend God properly. Second, following from the first, we can maintain the paradox of knowing-yet-not-knowing that we articulated is the

---

78. As sinners suppress the truth and lack a personal relationship with God, sinners are deprived and are in that sense 'harmed', though without explicit cognition of that deprivation: 'one could be in a state of harm without knowing it.' McKirland, *God's Provision, Humanity's Need*, p. 30.

79. In this sense, my argument here complements James K. A. Smith, especially in his *Imagining the Kingdom: How Worship Works* (Grand Rapids: Baker Academic, 2013).

condition of sinners living in God's good world. Third, we capture a deeper sense of sin's pervasiveness that goes beyond mere analyses of the intellect or the will.[80]

Common Grace, Consciousness, and Acts of Disruption

The bleak picture of the pervasiveness of sin's effect on the psyche sketched above should not be taken to imply that humans will therefore never recognize the divine or be virtuous. God did not leave creation to corruption, but preserves it such that remnants of the intrinsic goodness of creation remain. In Bavinck's 1914 treatment of religious psychology, he returns to common grace precisely after an extended discussion of Scriptural teaching on sin's impact on the consciousness (which manifests itself precisely in the sin of deception).[81] He writes that common grace 'serves to preserve and strengthen these little remnants of the image of God against the destructive powers of iniquity …. [I]f sin had not been curbed, it would have destroyed everything that reminded us of God's original creation, both outside and within mankind.'[82] Those preserved aspects that are 'within' humanity involve both cognition and affects, and Bavinck identifies five such aspects. First, fallen humanity continue to feel shame for their wrongdoing, and do not devolve into bold debauchery. Second, they feel fear for the consequences of their misdeeds. Third, they still possess rationality. Fourth, they have the 'need, the propensity, the compulsion' (*de behoefte, de neiging, den drang bezit*) to honor God as religious creatures. And fifth, they feel the weight of the conscience weighing down on them as moral beings.[83] Appealing to Calvin, Bavinck argues that these remnants are not explained 'from a principle that remains in nature itself, but from a power of God, which, in spite of sin and precisely to curb its influence, remains at work within creation'.[84] Indeed, much of what he writes here on the inner consciousness of humanity is an application of the general teaching on common grace that he has taught elsewhere:

> God did not leave sin alone to do its destructive work. He had and, after the fall, continued to have a purpose for his creation; he interposed common grace between sin and the creation – a grace that, while it does not inwardly renew,

---

80. Though beyond the scope of this current chapter, Johan Bavinck's reading of Romans 1 fleshes out Herman Bavinck's affective anthropology and applies it to his exegesis to good effect. See Johan Bavinck, 'Religious Consciousness and Christian Faith', in *The J.H. Bavinck Reader*, John Bolt, James Bratt, and Paul J. Visser (eds), James A. De Jong (trans.) (Grand Rapids: Eerdmans, 2013), pp. 284–5. For an elaboration, see my 'On Revelation and the Psychical Effects of Sin: Toward a Constructive Proposal', in *Ruined Sinners to Reclaim: Sin and Depravity in Historical, Biblical, Theological, and Pastoral Perspective*, David Gibson and Jonathan Gibson (eds) (Crossway: Wheaton, 2024), pp. 669–99.
81. Bavinck, *Bijbelsche en religieuze psychologie*, p. 177.
82. Bavinck, *Bijbelsche en religieuze psychologie*, p. 186.
83. Bavinck, *Bijbelsche en religieuze psychologie*, p. 198.
84. Bavinck, *Bijbelsche en religieuze psychologie*, p. 203.

nevertheless restrains and compels. All that is good and true has its origin in this grace, including the good we see in fallen man ... *Consequently*, traces of the image of God continued in mankind.[85]

In this era of redemptive history before Christ's second coming, God continues to uphold creation for the purposes of the Gospel. Bavinck's application of common grace, however, does not merely emphasize the cosmic and universal gifts of the preservation of the world. Common grace extends itself also in the inner life of the religious self, in the deepest core of every human heart. God gifts common grace to the created order, restraining unregenerate hearts such that the evil within is curbed. The unconscious and conscious acts of rebellion do not yet emerge to eschatological fruition.

Johan H. Bavinck, Herman's nephew, extends these insights on sin's psychical effects and common grace in his discussion on their affective and dynamic relation. He argues that there are 'moments' where fallen human beings are confronted viscerally by how they have been suppressing the very ground of their being.[86] These moments could also be elicited when one encounters the gospel itself, prompting an existential crisis in which they are called truly to see themselves, becoming 'aware of the horror of this suppressing process and realize that they have always known but have never wanted to know'.[87] The suppression, in God's providence, never takes place equally in all people. In some, the suppression is so skilled and unconscious that it never enters into their consciousness; in others, the suppression easily rises up to the surface, prompting people to ask questions about their existence. Others are overwhelmed by God's presence such that they cannot but see that they have been unconsciously suppressing, triggering them to enter into times of crises – for this 'suppressing only takes place accompanied by a great deal of unsettledness'.[88]

Furthermore, Christian evangelization is possible because God never leaves himself without a witness, and his sheep will ultimately recognize his voice. Common grace exists for the purposes of redemptive grace. As J.H. Bavinck continues to emphasize, these 'moments' of recognition and consciousness are due to God, and not human creatures themselves: 'This is due to no human virtue. It proves nothing about the nobility of human nature. It is only due to God's personal involvement with people and to the overpowering force with which he has clearly made himself known to people.'[89] Hence, 'deep within the hidden recesses of

---

85. Herman Bavinck, 'Common Grace', Raymond C. Van Leeuwen (trans.), *Calvin Theological Journal* 24 (1989): p. 64. Emphasis mine.
86. Bavinck, 'Religious Consciousness and Christian Faith', p. 285.
87. Bavinck, 'Religious Consciousness and Christian Faith', p. 285.
88. Bavinck, 'Religious Consciousness and Christian Faith', p. 286. Here, J. H. Bavinck cites Calvin's doctrine of the *semen religionis*.
89. Bavinck, 'Religious Consciousness and Christian Faith', p. 286.

people's beings, that repressed and suppressed truth is still present. It has never simply disappeared but has always been alive and active.'[90]

Common grace, therefore, prevents humanity from totally nourishing their deep suppression of God's general revelation, and allows for sinners to recognize disruptions to that skilled coping underneath all of their thinking and willing.

Conclusion: Bavinck and the Structural Image of God

This chapter offered a constructive account of the ways in which Bavinck's affective anthropology can include fruitfully insights from affect theory, and resists a conflation between the deliverances of cognition and the creational revelation of God. It then shows how Hubert Dreyfus's Heidegerrian phenomenology can be theologically deployed in order to provide Bavinck's account with empirical granularity, thus providing a concrete depiction of the way in which sinners are always skillfully coping with the affordances of God's revelation. This sketch of the primordial human condition will prove fruitful in the coming chapters on human diversity and race.

With this sketch of Bavinck's affective theological anthropology, its generative connections with contemporary trajectories in affective theory and the cognitive science of religion, and its implications in view, it is worth asking where Bavinck might fit in the current conversations on the 'structural' view of the image of God.

Despite some recent challenges to this position in recent years in favor for a relational, Christological, or vocational view of the image of God, some recent defenders have argued that all of these alternatives actually presuppose some account of the structural/substantial capacities of the human being in order to function relationally, vocationally, and to point to Christ.[91] Matthew Levering, for example, points to Aquinas in order to argue that 'the (embodied) soul and its powers also accords with Genesis's depiction of the first humans as distinguished from the other animals solely by rationality and linguistic communication', and that the relational, vocational, and Christological dimensions of the image require 'the right embodied exercise of the powers that sustain our communion with God and each other that enable us to be good stewards of the earth'.[92] Aku Visala summarizes Levering's position well when he argues that 'the cognitive capacities for Godlike dominion thus include reason, freedom, and morality,

---

90. Bavinck, 'Religious Consciousness and Christian Faith', p. 286.

91. For an introduction to these issues and the turn toward vocational or Christological and relation accounts of the image of God, see Joshua Ryan Farris, *An Introduction to Theological Anthropology: Humans, Both Creaturely and Divine* (Grand Rapids: Baker Academic, 2020), Marc Cortez, *Theological Anthropology: A Guide for the Perplexed* (London: Bloomsbury T&T Clark, 2010), and Peppiatt, *Imago Dei*.

92. Matthew Levering, *Engaging the Doctrine of Creation: Cosmos, Creatures, and the Wise and Good Creator* (Grand Rapids: Baker Academic, 2017), p. 190.

which together make loving and caring stewardship possible'.[93] Those capacities (or active potencies) may not be actualized in the right way, and that actualization might well be hampered by physical and fallen conditions in the present life, but, as Harriet Harris puts it, 'to be a person is to have certain capacities whether or not these are realized'.[94] Indeed, human beings are the sorts of beings with the active potencies of intellect and will that are presupposed for a relation with God.[95]

Bavinck, as we have seen, affirms this basic structural view of the image of God: the psychosomatic unit with its faculties/capacities itself is the image of God. However, in Bavinck's phenomenologically attuned description of those capacities, one sees a deeper account of the ways in which personality precedes cognition and linguistic awareness or development. In other words, an affirmation of a structural account of the image of God does not necessarily mean identifying the capacity for conscious rationality as that by which the person is uniquely identified in God's image, but can instead refer to the very notion of a gifted *personality* itself. This personality, to be sure, manifests itself in the embodied soul's explicit exercising of its intellectual and volitional faculties, but also in the ways in which it precedes that exercise, with all of its mysterious and phenomenological depths. In other words, one cannot exhaust *who* a person is by a description of their use of reason or what they desire. The image of God may include the capacities of reasoning and desiring, but it involves much more – human beings are persons in ways that other creatures are not. This affective theological anthropology allows one to appreciate the unique cognitive abilities of human beings (as witnessed in the natural ways in which our cognitive apparatus allows us to form a highly developed theory of mind and agency-detecting device), without solely isolating these abilities from its broader unconscious origins: 'human beings do not live only a cognitive life'.[96]

Furthermore, in Bavinck's affective account and through the deployment of affect theory above, one is provided with some generative resources by which to respond to the common charge that a structural view of the image of God compromises the embodied and social character of human beings: 'a move that inevitably leads to abstract, remote notions of the *imago dei*'.[97] Visala has responded well to this charge by affirming that cognition and soul maintain a close relationship to the body: '[these are] closely tied to the workings of our

---

93. Visala, 'Human Cognition and the Image of God', p. 97.
94. Harriet A. Harris, 'Should We Say That Personhood Is Relational?' *Scottish Journal of Theology* 51 (1998): p. 234.
95. Edward Feser, *Scholastic Metaphysics: A Contemporary Introduction* (Piscataway: Editiones Scholasticae, 2014), pp. 43–6.
96. Williams, *On Augustine*, p. 43.
97. J. Wentzel van Huyssteen, *Alone in the World? Human Uniqueness in Science and Theology* (Grand Rapids: Eerdmans, 2006), p. 134.

brain, bodies, environments, and social contexts'.[98] The phenomenological depth of Bavinck's affective theological anthropology shows that a structural account can indeed give a more substantive construal of the ways in which the body influences the mind and vice versa, and demonstrates that mentioning the body need not be mere lip service. Furthermore, the emphases on para-cognition, intransigence, affordances, and skillful coping I provided above enrich a structural account of the image.

---

98. Visala, 'Human Cognition and the Image of God', p. 98. So, Levering, 'Even if the powers of the soul are not in act or unable in this life ever to be in act due to a bodily defect, the grace of the Holy Spirit can still transform the soul and elevate the person relationally to union with the persons of the Trinity.' *Engaging the Doctrine of Creation*, p. 174.

Chapter 5

ORGANIC HUMANITY AND SIN

This monograph has advanced the implications of Bavinck's religious account of the human individual. However, as noted in the introduction, that is merely one side of the equation when it comes to developing a holistic theological anthropology. In Bavinck's account one also finds an emphasis on humanity as a single organism that is bound together as diverse individuals represented by a federal head. What comes to the fore in this account are the ethical bonds that tie each individual with one another and the corporate responsibilities that humanity shares. The next few chapters thus explore these two dimensions. Precisely because Bavinck envisions humanity as an organic and religious whole, and thus as comprising a unity-in-diversity, his theological outlook holds resources for upholding humanity in all of its diversity, without sacrificing its common destiny under the headship of Christ.

This chapter therefore proceeds in three steps. First, I show how Bavinck consistently develops a corporate and organic account of the image of God and original sin across his *Reformed Dogmatics* and the *Reformed Ethics*, and I pay attention to the way in which he tethers a divinely instituted federalism to a corporate ontology of humanity. Second, I home in on his identification of egocentricity as the organizing principle of actual sins, and relate this identification to his organic anthropology. More precisely, I argue that his identification of egocentricity with the organizing principle of sin fits well with his account of the image of God and of the dissecting or loosening power of sin. Sin loosens that which is supposed to be together, and egocentricity thus separates and creates division within the organism of humanity and its relationship to God. Egocentricity is not just a violation of our ethical obligations but also of our metaphysical make-up. Precisely because the organism of humanity is tied together by way of ethical bonds, egocentricity has ontological implications: it is the means by which the organism of humanity is torn asunder. Third, I argue that Bavinck's organic anthropology, along with his identification of egocentricity as a principle of actual sin, leads him to eschew an ethical account that focuses on individualist marks of piety and action and to move toward an account that centers on the free reformation of ethical relations for the task of forming humanity. The Spirit's work is that of renewing individuals for the sake of binding them together, thus refashioning state, society, culture, and ultimately humanity as a whole. Hence, this chapter further supports Philip Ziegler's comment that 'there is a holism' to Bavinck's understanding of the image of God.[1] The Spirit does not cause renewed humanity to separate itself from the world, but restores its shape as a unity-in-diversity of free personalities as part and parcel of God's redemption of the entire cosmos – consistent with the neo-Calvinistic principle of grace renewing nature and of the Gospel as a leavening, transformative agent. As we shall see, Bavinck would call this nothing short of an 'organic reformation'. Having expounded on Bavinck's organic account of corporate humanity, I then illumine further his account by comparing it with two contemporary discussions in theological ethics in the final section, particularly, within Jonathan Edwards studies and Jennifer Herdt's recent critical retrieval of the *Bildung* tradition in post-Enlightenment German thought.

Humanity and Original Sin in the Dogmatics and Ethics

The dogmatic logic of Bavinck's theological anthropology in his *Dogmatics* displays the concreated responsibilities that each human being has. For Bavinck, the image of God is not just found in the organic unity of individual persons, but encompasses all of humanity precisely because human beings are image-bearers of a triune God. We are not a collection of atomistic individuals but are united together as an organism. Human beings make up a unity-in-diversity, and what binds them together is a common human nature and the *ethical* relations they share.[2] Each human being is bound to another by layers of relational and ethical ties. This ethical unity that binds the diversity of individuals into a single organism is precisely why the covenantal representations of Adam and Christ are fitting: their federal representations are proper to the organic shape of the human race. Adam was appointed as the federal representative of the human race. Whether he obeyed or disobeyed God at the point of creation would determine the fate of his progeny. Adam, of course, failed, and Christ came precisely to accomplish what Adam could not. Because Christ was the obedient second federal head, it is through him that all of humanity would be blessed. A key passage from Bavinck's *Dogmatics*:

> The covenant of works and the covenant of grace stand and fall together. The same law applies to both. On the basis of a common descent an ethical unity [*etische eenheid*] has been built that causes humanity – in keeping with its nature – to manifest itself as one organism and to unite its members in the closest possible way, not only by ties of blood but also by common participation in blessing and curse, sin and righteousness, death and life.[3]

---

1. Philip Ziegler, 'Those he also glorified', p. 169.
2. A more comprehensive sketch of Bavinck's doctrine of the image of God and original sin can be found in Sutanto, 'Herman Bavinck on the Image of God and Original Sin.'
3. Bavinck, *RD* 2: p. 579; Herman Bavinck, *Gereformeerde dogmatiek*, 3rd ed., 4 vols (Kampen: Kok, 1918), 2: p. 624. Hereafter, *GD*. Cf. Bavinck, *Guidebook*, pp. 91–2.

In other words, if human beings are made in the image of a triune God, then humanity too will be shaped by an ectypal unity-in-diversity. The covenantal representations of Adam and Christ form the central core of that unity, as the one represents the many. Bavinck thus imbued an ontological significance to ethical relations. Human beings are those for whom ethical relations are ontologically constitutive, and to be ethically related is essential to human being:

> [the *Imago Dei*] can only be somewhat unfolded in its depth and riches in a humanity counting billions of members. Just as the traces of God (*vestigia Dei*) are spread over many, many works, in both space and time, so also the image of God can only be displayed in all its dimensions and characteristic features in a humanity whose members exist both successively ... and contemporaneously side by side.[4]

The human individual is thus a 'compendium, the epitome of all of nature, a microcosm, and, precisely on that account, also the image and likeness of God, his son and heir, a micro-divine-being (*mikrotheos*)'.[5] Human beings are connected to one another in such a manner that the individual is not comprehensible without the whole, and the whole is illumined by the individual. Bavinck thus envisions that human beings will spread out across the earth as it develops over time, creating geographically sustained cultures and identities and thus exhibiting distinct ethnic and national expressions that ultimately conflict only due to sin's entrance.[6]

The unity of the image of God in the human race, then, explains why sin inflicts the entirety of Adam's race. The parts are affected because they are comprehended in the whole, and the diversity of individuals is compromised by the corruption due

---

4. Bavinck, *RD* 2: p. 577.
5. Bavinck, *RD* 2: p. 562. One hears an echo of the early Schleiermacher: 'You are a compendium of humanity. In a certain sense your single nature embraces all human nature.' *On Religion: Speeches to Its Cultured Despisers*, 3rd ed., John Oman (trans.) (London: Paul, Trench, Trubner, 1893), p. 79.
6. The biological distinction between male and female, along with the qualities of temperament that are usually termed as 'masculine' or 'feminine', also exhibits for Bavinck the unity-in-diversity of humanity's organic shape: 'Together in mutual fellowship they bear the divine image. God himself is the creator of duality in unity'. *The Christian Family*, p. 5 (see also, 'Herman Bavinck on the Image of God and Original Sin', pp. 182–3). While this is an important feature of Bavinck's theological anthropology and fills out his understanding of the image as referring to something greater than the individual, one would have to attend to the development of Bavinck's thought on the idea of 'womanhood'. For Bavinck's more mature view, see his *De vrouw in de hedendaagsche maatschappij* (Kampen: Kok, 1918); for the occasions that elicited his reconsideration of 'womanhood', which in turn led him to affirm universal suffrage and to allow for the entrance of women into the Free University, see Eglinton, *Bavinck*, pp. 234–8, 277–80.

to Adam's sin. The imputation of Adam's sin is not based on an arbitrary decision of God, but fits the created design of the human race.[7] As Bavinck elaborates:

> If humanity, both in a physical and an ethical [*ethischen*] sense, were to remain a unity, as it was intended to be .... [I]f in that human race there were to exist, not just community of blood, as in the case of the animals, but on that basis also community of all material, moral [*zedelijke*], and spiritual goods, then that could be brought about and maintained only by judging all in one person. As things went with that person, so they would go with the whole human race. If Adam fell, humanity would fall; if Christ remained standing, humanity would be raised up in him. The covenant of works and the covenant of grace are the forms by which the organism of humanity is maintained also in a religious and an ethical [*ethischen*] sense. Because God is interested, not in a handful of individuals, *but in humanity as his image and likeness*, it *had* [*moest*] to fall and be raised up again in one person.[8]

An organic anthropology provides resources for Bavinck to combine the instincts of both realist and federalist accounts of the transmission of original sin. In brief, a realist account argues that sin is transmitted from Adam to humanity because it was, somehow, *really* present in Adam. A federal account, however, argues that Adam's sin is transmitted to his progeny by way of divine imputation, as Adam was chosen to be their representative by God's will. In this important passage, Bavinck is effectively arguing that Adam's federal representation is no legal fiction, but is that which conforms to humanity's organic shape. The representation of Adam, therefore, is in keeping with the metaphysics of human nature, due to its creation in the image of the triune God. This explains the language above that humanity 'had' to fall and be raised up again in one person – not that God was 'bound' against his will to impute Adam's sin to the rest of his progeny, but that this federal representation is *fitting*, given that humanity is created in the image of

---

7. Bavinck argued that the covenant of works accommodated the basic insights of Schleiermacher and Kant, in the sense that a covenantal arrangement maintained both the dependence of humankind on the God who establishes the covenant and the freedom of the human personality in relative self-determination: 'The covenant of works, accordingly, does justice to both the sovereignty of God – which implies the dependence of creatures and the nonmeritoriousness of all their works – and to the grace and generosity of God, who nevertheless wants to give the creature a higher-than-earthly blessedness. It maintains both the dependence as well as the freedom of mankind. It combines Schleiermacher [dependence] and Kant [freedom]. The probationary command relates to the moral law as the covenant of works relates to man's creation in God's image. The moral law stands or falls in its entirety with the probationary command, and the image of God in mankind in its entirety stands or falls with the covenant of works.' *RD* 2: p. 572.

8. Bavinck, *RD* 3: p. 106; *GD* 2: p. 96. Emphasis mine. The language implies that the modality of necessity, however weakly or strongly interpreted, is invoked.

the triune God. Covenantal representation is fittingly in keeping with humanity's organic shape.

To be sure, Bavinck's organic construal of the image of God is not reducible to a realist one, as is often expected of organic theories. According to Thomas McCall, an organic whole theory of theological anthropology is typically also an 'organic whole realist' account according to which humanity is somehow a single entity.[9] Tied to the doctrine of original sin, a realist account argues that human beings inherit Adam's guilt or corruption because humanity really was, in some way, *in* Adam. Bavinck, however, was critical of a thick realist account, so long as it was untethered to federalist covenant theology. Bavinck argued that pushing realism to its logical consequences (without adhering to federalism) would render imputation (mediate or otherwise) wholly unnecessary to account for the transmission of sin and guilt. Realism would hold that we inherited a corrupted nature from Adam (as we are somehow metaphysically one with him), and consequently we would then inevitably sin, thus incurring guilt for our own sin.[10] To the contrary, Bavinck argues that while we are 'seminally ... comprehended' in Adam, 'it was he who broke the probationary command, and not we.'[11] Though humanity now stems physically from the first humans, they do not form a single metaphysical entity. Imputation accounts for why the first sin is thus imputed, but not every other sin Adam commits. On the other hand, federalism respects the created ontology of the human race and the unity of our shared human nature, and federalism would be crassly voluntaristic without this grounding in humanity's created nature. Federalism 'certainly does not rule out the truth contained in realism; on the contrary, it fully accepts it.'[12] As we have seen, federalism comports with the triune and organic make-up of humanity.

If Bavinck is right, then, realism and federalism complement one another and need not be presented as a binary. Ian McFarland's critique, that Bavinck failed to provide a 'rationale' by which '*Adam* can be described' as a federal head, then, does not take into sufficient account the Trinitarian and realist underpinnings of Bavinck's theological anthropology.[13] Bavinck did not merely ground Adam's representative status on his being a '*first* in a series', but on the organic make-up of humanity as an ectypal image of God's own unity-in-diversity. When Adam failed, Christ is the second Adam that undergirds the diversity of renewed humanity.[14]

---

9. Thomas McCall, *Against God and Nature: The Doctrine of Sin* (Wheaton: Crossway, 2019), p. 185. McCall identifies specifically the views of Jonathan Edwards with this organic realist model.

10. For more discussion on Bavinck's critique of realism as a way of accounting for original guilt and corruption, see Sutanto, 'Herman Bavinck on the Image of God and Original Sin', especially pp. 184–7, and McCall, *Against God and Nature*, pp. 168–70.

11. Bavinck, *RD* 3: p. 102.

12. Bavinck, *RD* 3: p. 104.

13. McFarland, *In Adam's Fall: A Meditation on the Christian Doctrine of Original Sin* (Oxford: Blackwell, 2010), p. 153. Emphasis original.

14. McFarland, *In Adam's Fall*, p. 153.

Hence Bavinck cannot be charged with presenting a legal fiction account of original sin or the atonement, since the imputation of Adam's sin (or Christ's righteousness) corresponds to humanity's organic shape.[15] Without federal representation and the ethical tie between the one and the many, humanity would be a mere aggregate of individuals, not a corporate organic whole. Bavinck had opened the way forward to be *organic whole federalists*, where the covenantal administration represents not legal fictions but the triune design of human beings, for Bavinck held that the *imago Dei* referred not merely to human individuals but to the entirety of the human race.

The ethical bonds that unite humanity render responsibility an inherently communal affair. After Bavinck's presentation of his organic account of the imputation of Adam's sin, he was keen to maintain the balance between communal guilt – which acknowledges the reality of inherited sin as a law and reality – and the individual guilt that accrues from actual sin. Here, Bavinck appealed to Schleiermacher, agreeing that humanity is caught up in one another's guilt:

> It is ... completely true that we can never with complete accuracy indicate the boundaries that separate personal guilt from communal guilt. What Schleiermacher says of original sin is something very different from what Scripture and the church say concerning it, but by itself is completely true of sin in general that it is the collective deed and collective guilt of the human race as a whole. In other words, the sinful state and sinful deeds of each individual are, on the one hand, conditioned by those of the previous generation, and, on the other, they in turn condition the sinful state and acts of later descendants. Sin is "in each the work of all and in all the work of each".[16]

In accommodating Schleiermacher's insight at this point, what emerges is a nuanced account of sin that does not reduce it merely into individual actions. A social and corporate account of the image of God leads to an acknowledgment of the systemic and generational character of sin that develops over time. This emphasis on the social and the corporate leads us to Bavinck's comments on the matter in the *Ethics*. Under the section on essential human nature, Bavinck

---

15. It is worth mentioning here that Bavinck remained a staunch creationist (the view according to which God immediately creates souls at the moment of conception) despite holding to some central tenets of realism: 'Creationism preserves the organic – both physical and moral [*beide physische en moreele*] – unity of humanity and at the same time it respects the mystery of the individual personality.' Bavinck, *RD* 2: p. 587; *GD* 2: p. 634. Creationism is usually set as the opposite of traducianism, according to which souls are somehow transmitted from parents to children.

16. Bavinck, *RD* 3: p. 116, quoting Friedrich Schleiermacher, *Christian Faith: A New Translation and Critical Edition*, Catherine L. Kelsey and Terrence N. Tice (eds), Terrence N. Tice, Catherine L. Kelsey, and Edwina Lawler (trans.) (Louisville: Westminster John Knox, 2016), §71.1 Hereafter, *CF*.

emphasizes that though image-bearers are individuals in relationship with God, they cannot be divided up and merely considered individualistically as 'atoms or numbers',[17] but must be conceived collectively as a unity. Though individuals truly are made in God's image, individual*ism*, Bavinck argues, is a product of 'revolutionary' and anti-theistic thought:

> This atomistic view was the error of the French philosophers like Rousseau and is the fundamental error of revolutionary thought. The term "individual" belonged to the revolution and expressed its all-consuming character. Our fathers did not know the word "individualism" because for them there were no more individuals; to be human was always to be the image of God, a member of the human race. For the revolution, humanity is an aggregate mass of individuals who can be arbitrarily combined, like the random collision of Epicurus's atoms, into state, society, etc. The revolutionary view is false. We have to be understood in the *relations* in which we stand, naturally and historically.[18]

Consequently, humanity's eschatological perfection is not displayed by exhibiting virtues or good works individually, as if one's character can be properly developed or adjudicated in isolation. As Bavinck observes instead, 'The highest good is not individual moral perfection but the moral perfection of humanity. In fact, the one cannot be achieved without the other.'[19]

What, precisely, ties the organism of humanity together? Crucially, and in accord with his *Dogmatics*, Bavinck unites the diversity of individuals together not merely by the physical connectedness that binds them but also in the *ethical relations* that obtain between them. In distinction from animals, human beings have ethical responsibilities, ties, and obligations, and these consist precisely in, with, and toward relationships. 'Animals form no family, society or state', Bavinck wrote.[20] By way of contrast:

> For people, the physical, natural relation is also the first, and also passes away; but *ethical* [*ethische*] relationships develop out of and on the basis of the physical. Although the natural relationship is first, the moral and spiritual relationships follow. People remain in relationship to each other until the end of their lives. Those ethical ties are many and manifold.[21]

We are created as social and ethical creatures, made dependent upon the families, societies, and cultures from which we come, and hence we have responsibilities

---

17. Bavinck, *RE* 1: p. 49.
18. Bavinck, *RE* 1: p. 49–50. Emphasis mine. See also James Eglinton and George Harinck (eds), *Neo-Calvinism and the French Revolution* (London: Bloomsbury T&T Clark, 2015).
19. Bavinck, *RE* 1: p. 230.
20. Bavinck, *RE* 1: p. 60.
21. Bavinck, *RE* 1: p. 60; *GE* 1: p. 71. Emphasis original.

toward one another. Human life is thus an essentially '*moral* life'.[22] To be moral is never an issue of mere individual piety but requires living in accordance with this corporate reality. Bavinck writes in no uncertain terms: 'people are moral when they live according to the human standard – or, somewhat more profoundly, according to the notion of humanity – in all these relations.'[23]

After sketching the essence of humanity – as whole individuals and as a corporate unity – Bavinck turns to humanity under sin. At the outset of his discussion, he reminds readers that it would be a mistake to include the entire doctrine of sin under ethics.[24] He presupposes his discussion of the 'origin, essence, and nature of sin … [and the] guilt and punishment of sin' in the *Dogmatics*, and he notes that what must be discussed under ethics is 'what we have become because of that sin', that is, the 'the effect of sin on humanity in all areas of life'.[25] Here, I suggest that Bavinck is drawing upon the classical distinction between originating sin and the sin originated as the twin aspects of original sin.[26] Originating sin refers to that first sin by the first human beings, while originated sin refers to the impact or effects of that first sin upon the rest of humanity. Under *Ethics*, then, Bavinck argues that what needs to be discussed primarily is *the sin originated* rather than originating sin.

For Bavinck, the sin originated is nothing short of pervasive. It impacts every faculty of the human being. It signifies not merely the loss of original righteousness (contra Roman Catholic teaching) but the distorting of human nature. It is an animating principle that turns the whole self against God and neighbor. The heart, the *I*, the 'very core' of our being is 'corrupt', and 'this is why all human capabilities are also corrupt'.[27] The sin originated thus impacts not merely the human's 'spiritual

---

22. Bavinck, *RE* 1: p. 61. Emphasis original.

23. Bavinck, *RE* 1: p. 61. This makes logical sense of Bavinck's comments concerning the relationship between religion and morality: love of God and love of neighbor are distinct but never divorced: *RE* 1: pp. 70–5.

24. Bavinck writes: 'Vilmar includes the entire doctrine of sin in his *Ethics*, which is incorrect.' *RE* 1: p. 79. Bavinck is referring to August Vilmar, *Theologische Moral: Akademische Vorlesungen* (Gütersloh: Bertelsmann, 1871), 1: pp. 119–392.

25. Bavinck, *RE* 1: p. 79. Later on, before classifying sins and identifying the organizing principle of sins, Bavinck writes this: 'Here we are not discussing what sin is – that is, in relation to God, which is how we can first determine the nature of sin. Here, that issue is being assumed from dogmatics.' *RE* 1: p. 100.

26. See Bavinck, *RD* 3: p. 101. Despite redefining these terms considerably, Schleiermacher's comment on originated sin is also helpful because it recognizes the social pre-conditions of acts of sin. If originating sin has its origin within the human person, originated sin focuses on the entrance of sin into an individual from an extrinsic source: 'Until then, and only to that degree, original sin is rightly called "originated" because it has its cause outside the individual.' *CF*, §71.1.

27. Bavinck, *RE* 1: p. 88.

life, our fellowship with God (Rome's view). But precisely because of that loss, the natural life in all its forms and dimensions is corrupted as well'.[28]

This corruption takes the form of a division within one's internal life, as the faculties now war against each other instead of working together in harmony. 'The mind has been loosened from the will through sin; it has become immoral, one capability alongside others rather than within them. It is torn loose from life; the heart that is dead also kills the mind.'[29] Sin is an atomizing force; it detaches the faculties from one another.[30] Analogously, and as a consequence, sin blinds us such that we now grasp only partial, isolated truths rather than the whole: 'Thus, we do have some knowledge of individual verities, but we do not know *the* truth, the system, the unity of all truth in God.'[31]

Egocentricity and Organism

With the basic framework now established, we can now turn to Bavinck's identification of the organizing principle (*beginsel*) behind every sin. With some qualifications, he argues that the 'organizing principle [*beginsel*] of sin is self-glorification, self-divination; stated more broadly, ego-centricity [*zelfzucht*]'.[32] This does not mean, he later clarifies, that all sins '*subjectively* proceed … from egocentric motives'.[33] But it does mean that '*objectively* all sins may be traced back to egocentricity'.[34] To be more precise, there is a subjective and objective organizing principle for sins: while the former is as diverse as the circumstances at hand and the individuals responsible, the latter is egocentricity. Furthermore, this egocentricity is identified with 'covetousness or concupiscence and accompanies our birth … and is itself sin and the root of sin'.[35] Bavinck emphasizes once again

---

28. Bavinck, *RE* 1: p. 93.
29. Bavinck, *RE* 1: p. 100.
30. This view is consistent throughout Bavinck's corpus. Crisply stated in his early essay, 'The Kingdom of God, the Highest Good', he wrote this: 'Understanding and heart, consciousness and will, inclination and power, feeling and imagination, flesh and spirit, these are all opposed to each other at the moment, and they compete with each other for primacy.' 'The Kingdom of God, the Highest Good', p. 143.
31. Bavinck, *RE* 1: p. 100. Emphasis in original. See also my discussion of the distinction between mechanical and organic knowing in *God and Knowledge*.
32. Bavinck, *RE* 1: p. 105; *GE* 1: p. 97. Interestingly, the original Dutch text only mentions egocentricity, thus omitting 'self-love', which is in the English edition.
33. Bavinck, *RE* 1: p. 110. Emphasis original.
34. Bavinck, *RE* 1: p. 110. Emphasis original.
35. Bavinck, *RE* 1: p. 110.

that this identification is '[c]ontrary to Rome'.³⁶ Egocentricity manifests itself in both spiritual and sensuous sins, sins directed against God and neighbor.

Right after he first identifies egocentricity as the organizing principle of actual sin, however, Bavinck strikes a familiar note concerning the dissecting and atomizing power of sin. Sin does not just create divisions within the individual self, nor does it just mean a turning away from God and toward the self. More comprehensively, sin affects the order of humanity as a whole by '*loosening*' it. Thus

> Humanity not only surrendered its true center but also replaced it with a false center. On the one hand, sin is a *de*centralization of all things away from God, a loosening, an undoing of bonds with God – atomism, individualism. On the other hand, it is at the same time also a concentration of everything around the human self, an attempt to subjugate everything to an individual 'ego.' Thus sin is not only a matter of turning away from the existing order – in effect, undermining order – but also an establishing of another order, which actually is a *dis*order. Sin produces not only an alternative or counterorder but an antiorder; in a word: *revolution*.³⁷

This significant passage merits a few reflections. It is worth noting that sin replaces the center not of mere individuals but of the entirety of humanity: 'Prior to this, God was the center of all human thought and action; now it is the person's "I".'³⁸ Every individual's ego is now that substitute. But the ego cannot carry the weight of humanity's center; it is a 'false' center that does not produce unity within the human race but rather 'disorder'. God is not only the appropriate ethical center of the human race; God is the only one with the metaphysical essence that can bear the weight of humanity, uniting it into a single ordered organism.³⁹ An undoing of the bonds with God, therefore, and a substituting of the center of humanity by the countless egos of each individual human self is nothing short of catastrophic. It is nothing short of a revolution that creates not an alternative reality but an unstable anti-order that is bound to collapse under its own weight. As Bavinck puts it in an earlier essay: 'Sin dissolves .... [S]in propagates atomism and individualism to the extreme. Sin is a disorganizing power possessing no reason for existence and thus no purpose in itself.'⁴⁰ Furthermore, if sin is not only a disorder within the self but the breaking apart of the organism of the image of God as a singular unity, then it follows that redemption demands the renewal of 'not only individual, isolated

---

36. Bavinck, *RE* 1: p. 110. One should also bear in mind his clarification a few pages earlier on page 97: '*The basic principle, the driving force* of such a life is thus not faith, [or] love for God, but concupiscent desire. These desires, inclinations, and passions are not sinful as such, but the distinction in which they move makes them sinful; they do not focus on God, but on the *I* (selfishness), on the world.' Emphases original.
37. Bavinck, *RE* 1: p. 105.
38. Bavinck, *RE* 1: p. 105.
39. *RD* 2: pp. 577–8.
40. Bavinck, 'Kingdom of God, the Highest Good', p. 141.

human beings but humanity as an organic whole'. There must be a redemption of 'the whole world in its organic connectedness' from 'the power of sin'.[41]

Where, however, does egocentricity fit in all this? What is the relationship, in other words, between egocentricity as the organizing principle of actual sin and the inherently atomizing character of sin that tears apart humanity as an organism? Bavinck does not render this relationship explicitly, but we can draw out the implicit logic that underlies Bavinck's thought. Egocentricity is not just a distortion of the self, nor is it merely an ethical violation that breaks a command. Precisely because humanity is a single organism, and ethical ties are the means by which human individuals are united as a unity-in-diversity, egocentricity is an ethical misdirection with strongly *ontological* connotations. Egocentricity is precisely the misdirection through which the organism of humanity is torn asunder. If sin is a dissolving and loosening power, egocentricity is the instrument that dissolves and loosens the bonds that bind humanity together and the precise and concrete manifestation of that dissolution and loosening. Egocentricity destroys the ethical ties that bind together marriages, families, states, and cultures. It is the catalyst of atomization and thus the means of revolution.

An 'Organic Reformation': Organism and Ethics

We now turn to the second question: how does Bavinck's organic vision of humanity inform his ethical outlook? His discussion of the spiritual life addresses the sinful life that the Spirit renews. Fittingly, regeneration produces a reuniting of one's self into a harmonious whole and a renewal of one's fellowship with God and others. It produces a life force that redeems the self and necessarily turns us *toward* others, thereby restoring the spheres of state, science, art, culture, and family. The human individual is filled with gaps and disharmony – our wills conflict with our minds, our deeds with our conscience, and so on – but the spiritual life gives us a new, organizing principle. Bavinck writes:

> [T]he foundational principle of the spiritual life is the love of God in Christ poured out through the Holy Spirit ... and this principle now flows into all of life, into all the thoughts and deeds of the spiritual person. Love of God gives stature and form to the spiritual life; it organizes and inspires it, turning it into one beautiful organic whole which functions as the foundational *life-force*.[42]

If sin loosens and atomizes, then the Spirit renews and rebinds. This Spiritual life force, crucially, is relationally disposed. It drives one's self into fellowship with others and thus reverses the atomizing powers of egocentricity. The spiritual life manifests itself precisely in the new bonds that are recreated precisely as believers

---

41. Bavinck, *RD* 1: p. 346.
42. Bavinck, *RE* 1: p. 248.

are drawn toward God: 'Because love for God is its foundation, spiritual life itself consists of fellowship with God, with Christ, and with fellow believers. Love strives after and *is* fellowship, a fellowship that is only possible through and in love. Hatred separates; love binds.'[43]

Fellowship, then, has ontological significance. When Christians reconcile and bind ourselves in ethical ties with one another, we are not only obeying God's commands; we are becoming *whole* once again. And in doing so, we are witnessing the work of God which renews and reconnects together the organism of humanity. Love of God binds the organism of redeemed humanity together, uniting them under a single head, and leading them toward an eschatological telos. Crucially, Bavinck specifies egoism and isolation as twin dangers that threaten the organism of spiritual life, and lauds cooperation as an essential part of it:

> The genuine, normal condition – that is, the health, of an organism consists in the following: (a) A vital principle animates from its center and controls and regulates everything. (b) No organs, parts, or members of an organism, animated from that center, isolate themselves from each other; rather, they cooperate with each other. This should happen in such a way that each member confines itself to being what it is supposed to be and actually is what it is supposed to be, arrogating nothing to itself (egotistically) [*egoïstisch*] but also not withdrawing itself (isolation) [*isolement*], such that the hand is the hand and nothing more, the foot is the foot, etc. (c) All members together, through the one vital principle, work toward one goal and consider themselves instruments for achieving the one task of life.[44]

More precisely, the organism of humanity does not deny the individuality of each person, but rather recognizes that renewed humanity is a unity of diverse individuals and personalities. It embraces diversity and rejects one-sidedness, refusing to privilege one temperament, faculty, or attribute over another. Bavinck

---

43. Bavinck, *RE* 1: p. 248. As Ziegler also notes, fellowship with God and with other believers go together: 'Reformed sources will regularly speak in related terms of a "glorious and perfected *fellowship*" of believers with God and one another: when this tradition comments on the eschatological *state* of human being it does so chiefly with affective terms befitting this relational scenario, speaking of joy, blessedness, glory, and a "full and pleasant sense of God's favor."' 'Those He Also Glorified', p. 173.

44. Bavinck, *RE* 1: p. 417; *GE* 2: p. 279. This understanding of the spiritual life as *organic* life applies not only to renewed humanity as a whole but also to the individual Christian: 'The very *I* of a new person dies and lives with Christ (Gal. 2:20); in the regenerated person there arises immediately a new consciousness, will, feeling, spirit, soul, and body; albeit all of these in principle. The spiritual life is an organism. But the new person is not one perfected in stages; we are perfected, but never perfect here on earth. The new life thus reveals itself like all organic life on earth, as a "formative drive," "a creative drive." For the Reformed, the organic life of those who are born again cannot be terminated, contrary to the Lutherans, who deny the doctrine of perseverance.' *RE* 1: pp. 346–7. Emphasis original.

argues that this is already signified by the personalities of the apostles: John, Peter, Paul, and James each has differing modes of expressions, emphases, and strengths, yet no one overrules the others and they work complementarily. Bavinck writes: 'Indeed, variety must continue so that humanity may be a single organism in which one member is different from and complements the other.'[45] The imitation of Christ, consequently, means following Jesus with our own uniqueness intact: 'we must imitate him in everything, albeit in our own way, with our own individual personality, status, social class, and calling.'[46]

Here Bavinck would concur with Jennifer Herdt's criteria concerning a proper Christian humanism that seeks to preserve the individual personality's self-expressiveness even while its goal is the spiritual renewal of all of humanity, 'the realization of humanity as a way of participating in a cosmic process of diversification and harmonization, the finite expression of the image of God.'[47] The concern to preserve personality is expressed with great clarity in Bavinck's essay on the Kingdom of God, in which one finds a 'noncontrastive' relation between the one and the many according to which human self-realization does not compete with the unity of the kingdom of God:[48]

> [I]n the Kingdom of God all of those [faculties of the self] are once again pure instruments of the personality, arranged in perfect order around the personality as its center .... Everything moves outward from the center of the personality and returns there. All powers exist in the full light of consciousness and are fully included in the will. All compulsion is excluded since it is a kingdom of the spirit and thus of freedom. In this kingdom the natural and the visible are placed completely under the perspective of the spiritual and eternal; the physical is a pure instrument of the ethical even as everything, including our own body, which belongs to our persons and yet is not identical to our persons, stands completely in the service of our personality and is glorified precisely as an instrument of the dominion of the Spirit.[49]

This complementary relation between the self's fulfillment and the pursuit of the kingdom of God is reiterated in Bavinck's *Ethics*: 'Everything becomes the agent of the believer's *I*, of the spiritual life as it finds its goal again in the glory of God.'[50] The organism of renewed humanity, then, does not come at the cost of the free personality nor of its absorption into passivity by way of divine formation, but is

---

45. Bavinck, *RE* 1: p. 420.
46. Bavinck, *RE* 1: p. 339. Bavinck writes, 'Every human being, while a member of the body of humanity as a whole, is at the same time a unique idea of God, with a significance and destiny that is eternal!' Bavinck, *RD* 2: p. 587.
47. Jennifer Herdt, *Forming Humanity: Redeeming the German Bildung Tradition* (Chicago: University of Chicago Press, 2019), p. 83.
48. Herdt, *Forming Humanity*, pp. 187, 239.
49. Bavinck, 'Kingdom of God, the Highest Good', p. 143.
50. Bavinck, *RE* 1: p. 253.

rather realized by its organic, voluntary expression and creative actualization by the Spirit. Bavinck observes that the glory of redeemed humanity is manifested in part by the way in which it incorporates the free human personality:

> [T]he Kingdom is a kingdom of free personalities where each personality has reached its full development. But it is a *kingdom* of free personalities who do not live separated from each other, like individuals, but who together constitute a kingdom and are bound to each other in the most complete and purest community. The Kingdom of God is not an aggregate of disparate components, not even an entity bound together accidentally by a communal interest.[51]

This focus on the freeing and horizontalizing effects of the Spirit's renewing work, I would suggest, informs and undergirds Bavinck's critiques of various ethical schools in the history of Christian thought. Surveying Bavinck's analyses of these ethical movements, one comes to the impression that he was most critical of those Christian traditions that identify progress in the Christian life narrowly with self-cultivation, self-introspection, or marks of individualistic virtue. By contrast, a Bavinckian ethic pushes toward a reformation of every sphere of relationship. This is signaled in his criticisms, for example, of pietism, Methodism, and asceticism, all of which revolve around the claim that these movements end up compromising a holistic anthropology according to which unity and diversity are to be found in equipoise and every sphere of interconnected human life is to be renewed. To be sure, Bavinck's critique of these various movements is doubtless not wholly fair – moreover, his critiques here seem oddly out of place with his usually ecumenical tone.[52] However, the point here is not to vindicate Bavinck's critiques themselves but to grasp Bavinck's understanding of humanity as a singular whole and how this informs his account of the shape of the Christian life.

Each of these three criticisms deserves further exploration in turn. 'Mysticism and Pietism', Bavinck writes, 'put the seat of faith in feeling and thus do not embrace the fullness of our humanity'.[53] As such, pietism emphasizes that true conversion requires walking through specific experiences and stages of internal growth, creating a division within the church between those who are truly converted and those who lack the internal marks:

---

51. Bavinck, 'Kingdom of God, the Highest Good', p. 143.

52. One ought to keep in mind as one attends to his criticisms of the various ethical movements below that Bavinck's *Ethics* has a complicated manuscript history. As an unpublished manuscript based on lecture material, his criticisms here appear with less caution and restraint, especially when compared with his usual balanced tone in the *Dogmatics*. See, in this regard, Michael Allen, 'Review of Herman Bavinck, *Reformed Ethics*, vol. 1: *Created, Fallen, and Redeemed Humanity*', *Reformed Faith and Practice* 4, no. 2 (2019): pp. 69–72.

53. Bavinck, *RE* 1: p. 309.

Pietists want to express the divine in their lives always and everywhere; pietism sinks away into the self and does not rest in God but pays attention to the subject, who has to appropriate the divine and has to display this in his daily walk ... Mystics lose themselves in God and become quietists; pietists lose God in themselves, always consider themselves, but are also active, engage in mission work, in teaching, in education of the people; in one word: philanthropy.[54]

As such, despite bringing some necessary corrections to rationalist and intellectualist tendencies within the church, pietism loses sight of the covenant idea that brings together the corporate reality of the church, giving way to a 'pernicious group (club) mentality. The converted separate themselves, live apart, and leave family and world to fend for themselves. They are salt not within but alongside the world'.[55] Assuming that the standard of piety is precisely *this* kind of walk, the pietist lacks an appreciation for the individuality of each person: 'By constantly attending to self-contemplation, people make their experience the norm for everyone else' – a pathology hence enters the organism.[56] Pietism, in effect, pushes Christians to separate from others in isolation, and fails to appreciate the diversity of the members of renewed humanity by making specific character traits and practices the norm for every Christian.

Bavinck continues his critique of pietism under the section on the pathologies of the Christian life. There, he argues that that pietism's separatist character lacks a sense of holism:

[T]he Pietist is always a separatist. Whatever lies outside is "the world." It follows that such a person has no eye for the whole, for history, not even for the history of Christianity, whose history of dogma the Pietist rejects entirely or fails to appreciate, nor even an eye for the church, whose value the Pietist does not see .... Next, having no eye for the whole, they set their hope on converting single individuals, through direct contact.[57]

Methodism, locating the seat of faith in the will rather than in the emotions, likewise, ironically falls into similar pitfalls:

Methodism has an aggressive character, seeks only conversion, and looks for the seat of faith in the will (pietism in feelings, rationalism in the intellect). But

---

54. Bavinck, *RE* 1: pp. 289–90. See also the critical observations on pietism in Herdt, *Forming Humanity*, especially chapter 2.

55. Bavinck, *RE* 1: p. 309. On the same page, Bavinck continues: 'Religion is limited to being busy with the things of God (reading, praying). Daily work becomes a matter of necessity alone rather than a holy calling. Sunday stays disconnected from the rest of the week; faith is not tested *in* the world. Christians become passive, quietistic.' Emphasis original.

56. Bavinck, *RE* 1: p. 309.

57. Bavinck, *RE* 1: p. 432.

it regards conversion as a sudden, momentary, and immediate act. Therefore, it also misunderstands the church, baptism, and Christian nurture. In addition, it runs the risk of allowing sanctification to be absorbed entirely in the task of converting others. This is the reason for blind zeal without understanding, for all those committees, and for penitential sermons. Everything must be geared toward missions; children, young men and women, must establish societies, evangelize, and mobilize all efforts to make converts, and with tracts and Bibles to conquer the world by storm. The natural consequence of all this is the Salvation Army. The result is that all secular areas, science, art, literature, politics, are abandoned to the world. It is important to abstain from smoking and drinking, among other activities, because they all belong to the world. By putting the *will* in the foreground in order to oppose quietism and predestination, Methodism lacks a harmonious anthropology of the whole person.[58]

Methodism's focus on exclusively spiritual matters, revivalism, and conversion, while initially seeming like an emphasis on corporate humanity, is actually individualistic and non-holistic. It focuses on mission work to bring about conversions rooted in a decision of the will, and leaves the large nexus of natural human social relations to themselves. It does not see the renewal of humanity as involving the reworking of all human connections in state, science, society, and so on.

These concerns come into an even sharper focus in Bavinck's rather scathing critique of asceticism – a form of Christian piety that claims to be most like Christ but actually – according to Bavinck – is inwardly far from him. For Bavinck, while Jesus lived *for humanity*, the ascetics live inwardly for themselves. He observes:

After all, Jesus lived *for humanity*, suffered and died for them; the monk and the martyr who seek death live *for themselves*, are *preoccupied with themselves*. This view thus leads to externalism, to superficiality, to outward conformity without inner relationship. The imitation of Christ is not limited to the religious even through during his travels on earth it often consisted of a specific forsaking of family and occupation, following and preaching Jesus; this cannot be everyone's calling. Christ wants not only renunciation of the world but also to conserve the world, to save the world (John 3:17). Asceticism is only one exercise of virtue, an exercise that has no content other than the exercise itself.[59]

Consistently, his account eschews individualistic and one-sided moral piety for the holistic renewal of all human relations. The imitation of Christ is reflected differently in every person according to their various personalities, social locations, and cultures, and the Gospel renews and leavens their relationship to God and all of natural life. Humanity in all of its relational connectedness is the object of God's rebinding power. In short, the Gospel's transformative effects are both vertical and

---

58. Bavinck, *RE* 1: p. 314. Emphasis original.
59. Bavinck, *RE* 1: p. 338. Emphases mine.

horizontal, and Bavinck's critique of these movements indicates that he thought they lacked precisely this horizontal dimension: '[T]here is never a methodic, organic reformation of the whole cosmos, of nation and country.'[60]

The upshot is clear: an organic anthropology and thus an organic soteriology require a rejection of any ethics that focuses on inward-focused piety, individualist conversion, and separatism. The renewal of the Spirit is a *binding* power, and as such binds societies, nations, and humanity together once again. As such, Bavinck's call for an organic spiritual reformation of humanity does not result in the valorization of any particular nation, but rather looks toward a single kingdom of God which unites a diversity of nations in a way finally achievable only in the eschaton. This conviction led him presciently to critique the rising German nationalism in the early twentieth century as being woefully inattentive to the unity of humanity.[61] It is thus no surprise that Bavinck was planning to devote his unfinished fourth volume of the *Ethics* to the spheres of the family, society, the state, and so on.[62]

Conclusion

With Bavinck's organic ethical outlook in view, it is useful to conclude by relating the exposition to the two contemporary discussions in theological ethics and to suggest the ways in which Bavinck could be a fruitful conversation partner in current ethical discourse.

First, then, Bavinck's work contributes in interesting ways to the conceptual trajectories that arise from the recent retrieval of Edwards's moral theology, especially on the relationship between divine commands and ontology as a way of grounding theological ethics. This is seen, for example, in the tension between Elizabeth Cochran's emphasis on Edwards's rejection of grounding morality in 'an arbitrary divine fiat' and Oliver Crisp's rejoinder that Edwards's account in *Original Sin* bears a distinctly voluntarist character.[63] Bavinck interestingly offers a third way through this tension. While Bavinck places a heavy emphasis on the divine love commands, these commands arise out of the organic ontology of human nature as a singular unit. Bavinck suggests that ethical relations are no mere legal fictions that lack a basis in the metaphysics of human nature, thus resisting

---

60. Herman Bavinck, 'Catholicity of Christianity and the Church', John Bolt (trans.), *Calvin Theological Journal* 27 (1992): p. 246.

61. Bavinck's critiques of German nationalism can be found in *Christian Worldview*, chapter 3, and *PoR*, chapters 9–10.

62. Dirk van Keulen, 'Herman Bavinck's *Reformed Ethics*: Some Remarks about Unpublished Manuscripts in the Libraries of Amsterdam and Kampen', *The Bavinck Review* 1 (2010): p. 42. n. 57.

63. Elizabeth Agnew Cochran, *Receptive Human Virtues: A New Reading of Jonathan Edwards' Ethics* (University Park: Pennsylvania State University Press, 2011), p. 23 and Oliver Crisp, 'Moral Character, Reformed Theology, and Jonathan Edwards', *Studies in Christian Ethics* 30 (2017): p. 276.

narratives that locate Protestantism as a source of metaphysical suspicion.[64] In contrast, precisely because humanity analogically mirrors the nature of the triune God, ethical relations are ontologically constitutive for us: we were created in, for, and toward relationships. This organic *federalism*, I argue, pushes toward a reconciliation of metaphysical commitments and a socio-ethical vision, and of realistic and federalist accounts of humanity's unity.

Hence, one might also begin to relate Bavinck's account here more explicitly to Oliver Crisp's claim concerning Edwards and Augustine: 'The beauty or excellency that is true virtue is, according to Edwards, benevolence to Being in general .... In Edwards's nomenclature, benevolence to "Being in general" has to do with all existing beings .... Like Augustine, Edwards regards love to God and to all existing beings, as the heart of true virtue.'[65] While Edwards was concerned to characterize true virtue as love of God and thus a source of unification between the moral agent and other beings, this trajectory of reasoning leads Edwardsean ethics not to discussions of those corporate relationships themselves, but rather to explications of the habits and dispositions of the self that lead toward corporate unity. In distinction, Bavinck gives a more thoroughgoing account of corporate solidarity and social relationships themselves, while remaining rooted in an organic metaphysic. In my view, this distinctive need not be set in opposition to the virtue ethics of Edwards, but rather as a complement, for both seek to give an account of how human beings can grow in love of the other in order to forge a greater bond within humanity as a single organic unit.

Secondly, we have seen that Bavinck's view theologically overlaps with Jennifer Herdt's recent description of the *Bildung* tradition as a partial recovery of a Christian humanism that depicts corporate humanity as 'those creatures made to the divine image, capable of responsibility, of responding to God on behalf of creation, of accepting God's offer of friendship and extending it to others, to strangers and enemies. Human beings do not execute this task in a space evacuated of divine

---

64. See, for example, Alasdair MacIntyre, *After Virtue: A Study of Moral Theory*, 3rd ed. (Notre Dame: University of Notre Dame Press, 2007), p. 54. Pieter Vos thus focuses on the formation of virtue among the Reformed: 'Calvinists Among the Virtues: Reformed Theological Contributions to Contemporary Virtue Ethics', *Studies in Christian Ethics* 28 (2015): pp. 201–12. One may connect this recognition with the recent surge of interest on Christian metaphysics within Protestantism especially in relation to the doctrine of God. See, in this regard, Steven Duby, *God in Himself: Scripture, Metaphysics, and the Task of Christian Theology* (Downers Grove: IVP Academic, 2020); Steven Duby, *Jesus and the God of Classical Theism* (Grand Rapids: Baker Academic, 2022).

65. Crisp, 'Moral Character, Reformed Theology, and Jonathan Edwards', 272. Cochran observes the same point: 'Edwardsean true virtue is "benevolence" to God and to the created order; Edwards speaks of this virtue as a "consent" to God and the universe that unifies the moral agent with all other being. Love is likewise central to Edwards's account of the religious affections.' Elizabeth Agnew Cochran, 'The Moral Significance of Religious Affections: A Reformed Perspective on Emotions and Moral Formation', *Studies in Christian Ethics* 28 (2015): p. 154.

agency but as empowered by grace.'[66] Like this tradition, Bavinck sketched a non-competitive relationship between the individual and society, and between the human and the divine. Bavinck argued that the renewal of the Spirit brings about the awakening of the ego from self-love and the emergence of a free, willing personality who seeks fellowship with God, thus becoming a part of the organism of redeemed humanity as a whole. One sees in Bavinck the same desire not to contrast human agency and corporate formation, or to conceive 'divine agency as competing with human agency'.[67] Hence, though Pieter Vos notes that 'neo-Calvinists' often regard virtues with a 'hostile attitude',[68] one shall see that Bavinck's organicism shares the same goal as the work of the virtue ethicist: 'Searching for the good for one's own life, one asks at the same time: what is the good for humanity as such?'[69] The individual's responsibilities before God thus cannot be separated from their social responsibility for human flourishing as a whole.

This does not mean, however, that the *Bildung* tradition could be appropriated without critique. Its particular manifestation within the German intellectual milieu, as Herdt shows, is tethered to strands of nationalism and triumphalism that easily fed into the racist horrors of the twentieth century. Here, Herdt finds an ally in Karl Barth's critique of Kant and the *Bildung* tradition as 'fundamentally monological'.[70] With Barth, Herdt argues that discerning what is salvageable from the *Bildung* tradition must involve a proper account of humanity's need to *listen* to the Word of God in an encounter, ever aware of humanity's limitation and tendency to see itself as self-sufficient. This dialogical focus aids the task of cultivating humanity not as a *nationalist* endeavor but as an invitation of grace that allows us to attend to those in the margins. One possible fruit of the exposition of Bavinck's ethics above is to suggest that he, too, might be invoked as a fruitful dialogue partner in this aim, as he shared in the vision of conceiving humanity as a corporate task, undergirded by the summons and renewal of the Spirit, and as he evades, within his own Dutch and late nineteenth-century context, the dark and imperialist overtones of the *Bildung* tradition by attending to the organic and cosmological dimensions of the Kingdom of God. Precisely against the emerging

---

66. Herdt, *Forming Humanity*, p. 239.
67. Herdt, *Forming Humanity*, p. 9.
68. Vos, 'Calvinists among the Virtues', p. 203.
69. Vos, 'Calvinists among the Virtues', p. 205, building on MacIntyre, *After Virtue*. See also the neo-Calvinist work of Henk Jochemsen and Gerrit Glas, *Verantwoord medisch handelen: Proeve van een christelijke medische ethiek* (Amsterdam: Buijten and Schipperheijn, 1997), pp. 64–99. This is not surprising, as Bavinck's distinction between good works and virtues does not go without acknowledging the latter's merits, especially within the unregenerate: '[The Reformed] fully acknowledged the virtues of pagans and affirmed their validity.' Bavinck, *RE* 1: p. 158. See also Herman Bavinck, *RD* 4: p. 257: '[Good works] are therefore distinct from the virtues of the pagans and the virtues of all who do not have such saving faith. The Reformed have always fully acknowledged the existence and moral value of such virtues.'
70. Herdt, *Forming Humanity*, p. 245.

nationalism of twentieth-century German social thought, Bavinck argued that it is by attending to divine revelation that one can begin to appreciate a greater unity than nationhood that underlies humanity, and thus begin to pursue the strengthening of those ethical bonds by which we are united: 'This revelation is the starting point (*uitgangspunt*) of the unity of nature, the unity of the human race, the unity of history, and is also the source of all laws – the laws of nature, of history, of all development.'[71]

Contemplating the unity of the human race and the necessity of divine revelation to construe that unity leads us to a consideration of Bavinck's alternative to the German trajectory he predicted. It is to this subject of race and Euro-centricism that the next chapter turns.

---

71. Bavinck, *Philosophy of Revelation*, p. 240.

Chapter 6

RACE AND HISTORY

Embedded within Bavinck's holistic and corporate account of humanity is a powerful affirmation of the inherent good of ethnic and cultural diversity. As human beings were originally intended to be 'fruitful and multiply', Bavinck (along with other thinkers in the broader Dutch neo-Calvinist tradition) envisioned an organically unfolding human race that would take up distinct cultures as it spreads naturally around the globe. Consistent with Willie James Jennings' argument that race develops along the lines of 'geographically sustained identities', Bavinck envisioned human beings as made for diversity across place and time, such that the kingdom of God is irreducible to a single culture. Consummate human culture is not uniform, but pluriform.[1] Despite the potential fruitfulness of Bavinck's thought on race, diversity, and the corporate unity of humanity, however, the legacy of broader neo-Calvinism, and especially that of Abraham Kuyper, has muted investigation into Bavinck's own contributions. Other than a few acknowledgments that Bavinck may offer a more developed and consistent account of humanity than Kuyper, a fuller exploration of that account has not yet been produced. The next two chapters serve to remedy this lack.

This chapter first surveys the current scholarship on neo-Calvinism on race, acknowledging that it has focused almost exclusively on the reception of Kuyper and recognizing that neo-Calvinism has had a checkered legacy. The chapter then begins to explore Bavinck's identification of the origins of racism, in the form of Euro-centrism, and his critique of it, with some critical supplementation from contemporary theological work. As will become clear, Bavinck argues that racism emerged from two mutually confirming directions, based on the construct of a tiered existence and an evolutionary account of human civilization, with particular European cultures at the top of this constructed scale. The following chapter

---

1. Willie James Jennings, *The Christian Imagination: Theology and the Origins of Race* (New Haven: Yale University Press, 2010), p. 63. See also Vincent Bacote, 'Erasing Race: Racial Identity and Theological Anthropology', in Anthony Bradley (ed.), *Black Scholars in White Space: New Vistas in African American Studies from the Christian Academy* (Eugene: Pickwick, 2015), pp. 123–38, and Elizabeth Sung, '"Racial Realism" in Biblical Interpretation and Theological Anthropology: A Systematic-Theological Evaluation of Recent Accounts', *Ex Auditu* 31 (2015): pp. 3–21.

will continue his genealogical diagnosis of racism in relation to the emergence of the science of religion, while connecting this diagnostic to his insistence on the intrinsically religious character of human natures to race. The result of these efforts will be to show that Bavinck's position and his critiques of the racializing tendencies of the nineteenth century are indeed prescient and a great improvement upon Kuyper, and that contemporary thinkers might well find in Bavinck a fecund ally for contemporary reflections on race, even as some of his claims call for further critical reflection and development.

Neo-Calvinism and Race: Bavinck among the Neo-Kuyperians

As mentioned above, studies of the relationship between neo-Calvinism and race have centered on the complicated reception of Bavinck's contemporary, Abraham Kuyper. Commentators have noted that they were deeply moved, even inspired, by the inherent relevance of Kuyper's thoughts on creation, common grace, and theological anthropology for contemporary discussion. Kuyper, after all, shared Bavinck's vision of the *imago Dei* as referring to corporate humanity. The divine essence is so rich, for Kuyper, that if human beings are images of this 'eternal being', then that image must be 'much too full and rich to be reproduced in one individual'.[2] And the individual is not devalued by the appeal to the corporate, as Kuyper also points to the principle of organicism to describe humanity:

> Just as every tiny part of the root, stem, bark, bloom, and fruit exists organically in the whole of a tree, so it has to be that in the great organism of our human race which mirrors the image of God, every individual, every separate human specimen has to be created in conformity to that type of God's image and even in its sinful degradation has to exhibit the inverted outline of that image.[3]

This account of humanity attunes Kuyper to the social dimensions of human existence and sin's transmission. Observing Kuyper's sensitivity to the ways in which sinful principles can produce 'systems' which 'varnished over injustice and stamped as normal that which is actually opposed to the requirements of life' in *The Problem of Poverty*, Jeff Liou argues that 'the neo-Calvinist doctrine of sin displayed here is profoundly structural and systemic in its scope. Evil is understood, not simply as an individual action or disposition of the heart, but as an institutional and cultural virus that is pervasive.'[4] This sensitivity to the corporate

---

2. Abraham Kuyper, 'Common Grace', in *Abraham Kuyper: A Centennial Reader*, James Bratt (ed.) (Grand Rapids: Eerdmans, 1998), p. 177.
3. Kuyper, 'Common Grace', pp. 177–8.
4. Jeff Liou, 'Critical Race Theory, Campus Culture, and the Reformed Tradition', in *Reformed Public Theology: A Global Vision for Life in the World*, Matthew Kaemingk (ed.) (Grand Rapids: Baker Academic, 2021), p. 245, discussing Abraham Kuyper, *The Problem of Poverty*, James Skillen (trans.) (Sioux Center: Dordt College Press, 2011), p. 31.

and institutional expressions of sin thus provides a point of contact between Dutch neo-Calvinism and the observations of critical race theorists.[5] As Liou shows:

> [Neo-Calvinism] is extremely critical of Western modernity and its oppressive claims of neutrality and universality. In contrast, neo-Calvinism emphasizes a sensitivity to the perspectival diversity and particularity of different human communities. It resists attempts to assimilate deep difference through societal systems of power (political, cultural, or institutional). Both CRT [Critical Race Theorists] and neo-Calvinism argue for the liberation of diverse perspectives from under the oppressive universal claims and systems of Western modernity.[6]

Jeff Liou's argument recalls Allan Boesak's exhortation to Black South African theologians to reclaim the Dutch Reformed tradition's own resources for a theology of liberation. While Boesak acknowledges that the sin of apartheid was perpetuated by white Reformed churches, this decline marks a departure from the principles of the historic Reformed tradition. Indeed, Boesak appeals specifically to Kuyper's thought in 'the area of social justice': 'Unlike so many rich Calvinists and other Christians who keep on telling the poor that [their] poverty is the will of God, Kuyper refused to believe it.'[7] Boesak further appeals to Kuyper's call to follow the Lordship of Christ in every area of life to reject double-mindedness, as if one's theological confession could be siloed from the public area:

> Confessional subscription should lead to concrete manifestation in unity of worship and cooperation in the common tasks of the church. In South Africa adherence to the Reformed tradition should be a commitment to combat the evil of apartheid in every area of our lives and to seek liberation, peace, justice,

---

5. See Robert Chao Romero and Jeff Liou, *Christianity and Critical Race Theory: A Faithful and Constructive Conversation* (Grand Rapids: Baker Academic, 2023). Critical race theorists are also sensitive to the ways in which the intersectionality of race, embodiment, class, and gender affects, filters, and diversifies human experience and one's social imagination. See Kimberlé Crenshaw, 'Demarginalizing the Intersection of Race and Sex: A Black Feminist Critique of Antidiscrimination Doctrine, Feminist Theory and Antiracist Politics', *University of Chicago Legal Forum* 8 (1989): pp. 139–67; Lisa Bowleg, 'Intersectionality: An Underutilized but Essential Theoretical Framework for Social Psychology', in *The Palgrave Handbook of Critical Social Psychology*, Brendan Gough (ed.) (London: Palgrave Macmillan, 2017), pp. 507–29. Helen De Cruz adopts intersectionality as a 'guiding methodological principle' and applies it to the philosophy of religion in: 'Philosophy of Religion from the Margins: A Theoretical Analysis and Focus Group Study', in *The Lost Sheep in Philosophy of Religion: New Perspectives on Disability, Gender, Race, and Animals*, Blake Hereth and Kevin Timpe (eds) (New York: Routledge, 2020), pp. 31–54. See also Jonathan Tran, *Asian Americans and the Spirit of Racial Capitalism* (Oxford: Oxford University Press, 2021).
6. Liou, 'Critical Race Theory', p. 244.
7. Allan Boesak, *Black and Reformed: Apartheid, Liberation, and the Calvinist Tradition* (Eugene: Wipf & Stock, 1984), p. 91.

reconciliation, and wholeness for all of God's children in this torn and loved land.[8]

In a similar vein, Nico Vorster argues that Reformed theologians can and '*must* affirm' several insights from the theology of 'decolonization', especially in its emphases on alleviating the sufferings of the oppressed.[9] Vorster points to three themes in neo-Calvinism that dovetail well with the concerns of decolonization theology: the noetic effects of sin, such that sinful patterns of thought have contributed to injustice; the Reformed commitment to 'defending and restoring the dignity of the oppressed'; the concomitant goal of respecting the preservation of indigenous languages and 'cultural pluriformity'.[10] As such, decolonization theology calls Reformed theologians to remember that the tradition provides tools to support criticism of unjust structures and actions and critically reflect on their own complicity in perpetuating those structures in the past.[11]

Yet, when many of these same commentators encounter Kuyper's profoundly problematic racist claims, an existential crisis occurs – one that demands a decision as to whether to remain within the Kuyperian tradition. Vincent Bacote's description identifies this experience as a process of delight, dissonance, distress, and decision. It is first an experience of delight, due to the profound attractiveness of Kuyper's overall thought and its culture-embracing yet theologically grounded direction, followed by dissonance, due to Kuyper's racist rhetoric, leading to a distress that forces a decision on whether to stay within Kuyperian lines. In his words:

> [M]y experience with Abraham Kuyper has walked through the phases of delight, dissonance, distress, and decision. My encounter with Kuyper via his *Lectures on Calvinism* was at first wonderful, because in him I found a figure who gave me theological language for my interests in a theology of public engagement, particularly his language of common grace. Before I finished the book, however, I encountered the remaining three phases because of Kuyper's terrible views on race.[12]

---

8. Boesak, *Black and Reformed*, p. 96.
9. Nico Vorster, 'African Decolonization and Reformed Theology', in *Reformed Public Theology: A Global Vision for Life in the World*, Matthew Kaemingk (ed.) (Grand Rapids: Baker Academic, 2021), p. 54. Emphasis original.
10. Vorster, 'African Decolonization', pp. 54–5.
11. Vorster, 'African Decolonization', pp. 55–6.
12. Vincent Bacote, *Reckoning with Race and Performing the Good News: In Search of a Better Evangelical Theology* (Leiden: Brill, 2021), p. 48. See also Vincent Bacote, *The Spirit in Public Theology: Appropriating the Legacy of Abraham Kuyper* (Grand Rapids: Baker Academic, 2005).

As Bacote observes, despite Kuyper's shared convictions with Bavinck on the corporate unity of the human race, Kuyper continued – arguably inconsistently – to evaluate the moral and the purportedly developmental aspects of other ethnicities on the basis of his own Dutch culture. Kuyper assumed the sort of classification scheme that tethered moral and character traits to biology, which was predominant in Europe during the eighteenth to nineteenth centuries.[13] For Kuyper, the unity of the human race cannot elide the enduring inequalities within the species: just as eagles rank higher than owls in the bird species, so are there gradations in the human race.[14] Indeed, Kuyper exemplified what Norma Riccucci and other theorists have described as the oppressive result of a constructed and essentialized notion of race: 'although race is socially constructed and does not stem from natural differences, it produces negative effects in our society.'[15] The social construction of race reifies a perceived gradation of existence that produces unjust structures and prejudices against those who are categorized as 'lower' tiered.

Given, in addition, the use of Kuyper's theology of 'sphere sovereignty' by later South African theologians and pastors as a means of justifying apartheid, a reckoning within neo-Calvinism was and is necessary. Richard Mouw picks up on Bacote's work and emphasizes the need to develop a 'neo'-Kuyperian approach that deploys the better parts of Kuyper against himself.[16] This approach recalls H. Russell Botman's apt remark that Kuyper's influence in South Africa has had a simultaneously 'oppressive' and 'liberative influence'.[17] Theologians who utilize Kuyper to support emancipatory efforts and to develop a positive articulation of

13. See, e.g., Abraham Kuyper, *Lectures on Calvinism* (Grand Rapids: Eerdmans, 1999), pp. 32, 35, 195–6. See also James Bratt, *Abraham Kuyper: Modern Calvinist, Christian Democrat* (Grand Rapids: Eerdmans, 2013), pp. 293–4. Bacote writes, 'These kinds of theories of the inheritance of character and moral stature as connected to racial traits were based entirely on a form of speculation, yet the concept of race as linked to biology came to be regarded as simply the way things are,' 'Erasing Race', p. 126.

14. Kuyper, *Lectures on Calvinism*, p. 196.

15. Norma M. Riccucci, *Critical Race Theory: Exploring Its Application to Public Administration* (Cambridge: Cambridge University Press, 2022), p. 4.

16. Richard Mouw, *Abraham Kuyper: A Short and Personal Introduction* (Grand Rapids: Eerdmans, 2011), pp. 80–5. See also George Harinck, '"Wipe Out Lines of Division (Not Distinctions)": Bennie Keet, Neo-Calvinism and the Struggle Against Apartheid', *Journal of Reformed Theology* 11 (2017): pp. 81–98.

17. H. Russell Botman, 'Is Blood Thicker Than Justice?: The Legacy of Abraham Kuyper for Southern Africa', in Luis Lugo, *Religion, Pluralism, and Public Life: Abraham Kuyper's Legacy for the Twenty-First Century* (Grand Rapids: Eerdmans, 2000), p. 343. Cf. James Eglinton, '*Varia Americana* and Race: Kuyper as Antagonist and Protagonist', *Journal of Reformed Theology* 11 (2017): pp. 65–80.

human diversity thus recognize that they are moving *beyond* Kuyper.[18] As Bacote summarizes: 'we should prune Kuyper's troublesome views on race from his legacy and consider how to make his legacy blossom anew from within as well as considering ways to update and develop this living tradition.'[19]

It is precisely in the attempt to develop this tradition that Herman Bavinck appears within the neo-Kuyperian literature, not least because Bavinck was resisting apartheid and 'racial segregation' as early as the 1910s in response to white South African PhD students at the Free University of Amsterdam.[20] 'Herman Bavinck points Kuyperians in a fruitful direction', writes Richard Mouw, for Bavinck articulates how corporate humanity unfolds itself 'in the rich diversity of humankind spread over many places and times'.[21] This creational unfolding of humanity achieves its aim in redemption and consumation, as the many 'redeemed *peoples*' are 'gathered into the New Jerusalem from many tribes and tongues'.[22] Liou, likewise, points to Bavinck's more nuanced discussion of differences among peoples. Despite 'employing the scientific reasoning of his day and finding support from Darwin for his theological convictions regarding the unity of humanity … Bavinck lists those naturalists and racial theorists who he thinks either under- or overestimate the significance of races.'[23] Liou goes on: 'In other words, however racial lines were drawn and however dully or brightly putative racial boundaries could be articulated, Bavinck considered the unity of humanity to be indissoluble.'[24] George Harinck has also noted that Bavinck (unlike

---

18. This move is parallel to Willie James Jenning's description of the '3B' (third) category of responding to colonial Christianity. He categorizes three ways of response. The first way rejected Christianity altogether, a second way uses Christianity to reconstruct one's own native religion, while a third approach accepted Christianity. This third approach, however, is further divided into two. Three-A referred to those who accepted Christianity and its colonialist expressions, whereas Three-B 'accepted Christianity but did not accept its colonial configuration … The biblical story was [seen to be] the way one entered God's world and life with God that was not a world controlled by white Christianity and certainly not slave-holding society or colonial operations'. Willie James Jennings, 'Black Theology', in *The New Cambridge Companion to Christian Doctrine*, Michael Allen (ed.) (Cambridge: Cambridge University Press, 2022), p. 271.

19. Vincent Bacote, 'Kuyper and Race', in *Calvinism for a Secular Age: A Twenty-First Century Reading of Kuyper's Stone Lectures,* Jessica and Robert Joustra (eds) (Downers Grove: IVP Academic, 2022), p. 158.

20. Harinck, '"Wipe Out Lines of Division (Not Distinctions)"', p. 84.

21. Mouw, *Abraham Kuyper*, p. 84.

22. Mouw, *Abraham Kuyper*, p. 84.

23. Jeff Liou, 'Taking Up #blacklivesmatter: A Neo-Kuyperian Engagement with Critical Race Theory', *Journal of Reformed Theology* 11 (2017): p. 113. Liou is commenting on Bavinck, *RD* 2: p. 526.

24. Liou, 'Taking Up #blacklivesmatter', p. 113.

Kuyper) was 'critical of the notion of defining racial differences'.[25] Finally, Liou points to Bavinck's 'eschatological humanity' as a resource:

> By extension, when Bavinck speaks of the image of God in collectivistic terms, he does so because of the covenant of works. Additionally, if the *vestigia Dei* are distributed over space and time, then the *imago Dei* likewise transgresses space and time. Thus the 'universal' (if the word can be taken to include both unity and diversity) human family throughout history and geography *is* the image of God … The innumerable, diverse multitude of Revelation 7:9 is the 'restoration-plus' of the covenants: a single family that yet includes discernable nations, tribes, peoples, and languages, however those delineations were determined.[26]

Indeed, Bavinck rejected, in a much clearer way than Kuyper, understanding 'race' as an essentialist reality, as if the different people groups differed according to nature or some biological feature. 'Race' is used rather to speak about the localized peoples in their geographical dispersion as the image of God spreads across the globe.

These suggestive yet brief comments on the fruitfulness of Bavinck's thought on race, however, have not resulted in an extended close reading of the relevant texts.[27] The most important recent contribution is James Eglinton's biography of Bavinck, which briefly surveys Bavinck's occasional commentary on matters related to race, especially in relation to his second visit to America in 1908.[28] Drawing from Bavinck's public lectures and *dagboek* entries during his visit, Eglinton notes that Bavinck spoke in 'apocalyptic tones of the unfolding disaster that was racialized hatred in America'.[29] Bavinck predicts that America will be mired in the struggle between Black and white citizens, and was, according to Eglinton, 'struck by the segregated reality of American church attendance'.[30] Eglinton notes that, for Bavinck, 'Unless it also underwent a profound transformation, the American church could not offer a solution to the problem of race.'[31] This sensitivity to the race problem in America further indicates the importance of Bavinck in one's evaluation of neo-Calvinism and its relation to race-talk.

---

25. Harinck, '"Wipe Out Lines of Division (Not Distinctions)"', p. 83.
26. Liou, 'Taking Up #blacklivesmatter', p. 115.
27. As noted in the introduction, Jessica Joustra's 'An Embodied *Imago Dei*' expounds on Bavinck's emphasis on the human body as integral to the image of God in humanity and its potential significance for contemporary conversations on race. While this is an important earlier work pointing to the potential fruitfulness of Bavinck's thought on this issue, the article does not develop this point further.
28. James Eglinton, *Bavinck* pp. 244–9. Eglinton develops some of his claims there in his '"Indignation Would Rise within You": Herman Bavinck on Racial Injustice in Europe and North America' (pre-print): pp. 1–15.
29. Eglinton, *Bavinck*, p. 248.
30. Eglinton, *Bavinck*, p. 248.
31. Eglinton, *Bavinck*, p. 248.

This survey of the literature situates the need to pay further attention to Bavinck's theological writings on corporate humanity, especially as it relates to the emerging 'race-consciousness' of his nineteenth-century European context.[32]

'Jesus Did Not Come from Israel, but from the Aryans': On the Rise of German Nationalism

In two particular texts, *Christelijke wereldbeschouwing* (1904; 1913) and *Philosophy of Revelation* (1908), Bavinck anticipated the rise of German nationalism and its concomitant construction of a gradation of existence, with Aryans centralized as the apex of universal humanity. Bavinck further offered an explanatory genealogical analysis that seeks to account for this ideology emerging at the turn of the twentieth century. He sought to provide such an analysis in a way that anticipates what Sally Haslanger has identified as two key reasons to develop a theory of race and racism: diagnosis and amelioration.[33] For Bavinck, however, diagnosis leads to his view that what is needed is a theological kind of amelioration. If the sources of racism and the uplifting of Aryanism as a new category of humanity by which to demean other peoples are a departure from a particular set of theological doctrines – that of the Creator-creature distinction, the so-called 'classical' attributes of God and the doctrines of revelation and of the image of God (as Bavinck would argue), then the amelioration itself must be of a theological sort.[34] This is not to suggest that doctrinal retrieval is sufficient to generate anti-racist sensibilities, but it is necessary, in Bavinck's perspective. His diagnosis thus leads to a retrieval of

---

32. For an earlier exploration of Bavinck's views of catholicity as it impinges upon diversity and ecclesial pluriformity, see Nathaniel Gray Sutanto, 'Confessional, International, and Cosmopolitan: Herman Bavinck's Neo-Calvinistic and Protestant Vision of the Catholicity of the Church', *Journal of Reformed Theology* 12 (2018): pp. 22–39.

33. Sally Haslanger, *Resisting Reality: Social Construction and Social Critique* (New York: Oxford University Press), pp. 239–40.

34. See Sameer Yadav's essay on theologically motivated amelioration undertaken by Christians, 'whose anti-racist ameliorative interests might thus be aimed at reconstructing or recreating Christian social groups. In that case, theological background beliefs about – and ontological commitments to – e.g., God, divine creation and providence, sin, and salvation, the church, and eschatology … might figure into both the diagnosis and the remedy of racism uncovered by an RRFT [Religious Race Formation Theory] and theological facts might enter into an explanation of both *why* we ought to reconstruct racial and religious identities in conformity with principles of human dignity, equality, etc., as *religiously grounded* norms, and an explanation of what reconfigurations of our current social categories would best serve to exemplify those norms'. Sameer Yadav, 'Religious Racial Formation Theory and Its Metaphysics: A Research Program in the Philosophy of Religion', in *The Lost Sheep in Philosophy of Religion: New Perspectives on Disability, Gender, Race, and Animals*, Blake Hereth and Kevin Timpe (eds) (New York: Routledge, 2020), p. 384. Emphases original.

an alternative theological account that may serve generatively for the sake of amelioration, so long as one retrieves those insights critically. I shall first survey *Christian Worldview*, and then explore Bavinck's elaboration of what he introduces there in the *Philosophy of Revelation*. These texts will not disclose Bavinck's voice to be *the* solution to the racism that he identified (so much of which still persists today). Indeed, while Bavinck's work is contextualized and hence to a certain extent limited to the nineteenth and early twentieth centuries, his challenges to racism are noteworthy and should be drawn upon – albeit not uncritically – by contemporary thinkers in the neo-Calvinist tradition and beyond.

Christian Worldview: Theism and the Origins of Aryanism

Christian Worldview explores the implications of Christianity for the three branches of philosophy: epistemology, metaphysics, and ethics (thinking, being, and acting).[35] Rather than exploring these implications in a deductive, *a priori* fashion, Bavinck uses an inductive approach; he wrestles with the alternatives to Christian faith in his own day, especially given the prominence of German enlightenment philosophies that had become influential in the Netherlands. His organization of the material utilizes the terms *being* (*zijn*) and *becoming* (*worden*) as a framing device. Whereas Christianity posits a firm distinction between being and becoming, an immutable eternal God and a mutable creation formed *ex nihilo*, the various philosophical options that posed an alternative to Christianity (especially in the varieties of German Idealism) sought to merge being and becoming (being-in-becoming), or to form inferences about being from becoming. This context informs his analysis of ethics in the third and longest chapter within the book, and it is in this chapter that he argues that a departure from the Christian principle of the Creator-creature distinction (the chasm between being and becoming) would lead to the unintended consequences of a 'counterfeit nationalism, to a narrow chauvinism, to a fanaticism about race and instinct' (*valsch nationalisme, tot een enghartig chauvinism, tot een dweepen met ras en instinct*).[36] How Bavinck argues for this conclusion, and the significance of its implications, is the burden of this section.

The main figure that prompts Bavinck's analysis is Immanuel Kant, but to understand Kant's role in contributing to the trajectory toward this 'fanaticism', one has to step back and consider Bavinck's placement of Kant within the history of modern philosophy, specifically, the rise of modern science and the so-called

---

35. Herman Bavinck, *Christelijke wereldbeschouwing*, 2nd ed. (Kampen: Kok, 1913); ET: *Christian Worldview*, N. Gray Sutanto, James Eglinton, and Cory Brock (trans. and eds) (Wheaton: Crossway, 2019).

36. Bavinck, *Christian Worldview*, p. 100; *Christelijke wereldbeschouwing*, p. 76.

historical turn and their impact on the status of moral norms.[37] Bavinck begins the chapter by observing the everyday phenomenology of encountering the normative force of ethical requirements: 'as soon as we are awaken to consciousness, we discover that there are laws and norms above us that direct us in order to elevate us above nature.'[38] It is a call to love the 'true, the good, and the beautiful' (*het ware, het goede en het schoone*) that goes beyond the 'strict causality' of the material order.[39] Consciousness awakens us to norms that transcend experience that yet demand our attention. Obligations to render judgments on actions and thoughts, to evaluate ourselves in comparison to others, and to strive toward an ideal confront us on a daily basis. For Bavinck, all of this points to the responsibility one has before God, 'the Father of humanity, who is in heaven', who is the 'moral ideal'.[40]

This anchoring of normativity in the existence of God was presumed, Bavinck continues, until the rise of 'modern science', which began to erode the foundation of 'faith and religion', such that 'the foundation of law, even the moral law, was destabilized'.[41] It was here that Kant began to seek a 'firmer foundation of moral law in the essence of human nature [in its practical reason]', and thus to rescue morality from the skeptical clutches of science.[42] How so? Bavinck sums up Kant's basic epistemology in this way:

> To that end, he first pointed science to her limits. For in order to obtain a place for faith, he first had to deprive knowing of a large part of its terrain. Indeed, in Kant's view, the intellect is bound to empirical reality and cannot rise above it. It knows nothing of unseen and eternal things. It can obtain no certainty about God, the soul, and immortality: if a person had nothing apart from reason, he would know nothing about these things. But yet, he still has a practical reason, a heart, and a conscience, and herein he feels bound to an absolute law, to an ideal norm. This moral bond is grounded in human nature; it is an a priori that cannot

---

37. Cf. Joel D. S. Rasmussen, 'The Transformation of Metaphysics', and Johannes Zachhuber, 'The Historical Turn', in *The Oxford Handbook of Nineteenth-Century Christian Thought*, Joel D. S. Rasmussen, Judith Wolfe, and Johannes Zachhuber (eds) (Oxford: Oxford University Press, 2017), pp. 11–34, 53–71, respectively. In identifying Kant as the progenitor of this particular trajectory, Bavinck's analysis thus parallels (and conceptually anticipates?) J. Kameron Carter's *Race: A Theological Account* (Oxford: Oxford University Press, 2008). Note, however, Carter's caveat: 'the Kantian outlook is only the discursive nurturing of the racial colonialism inaugurated in the mid-to-late fifteenth century. And again it must be said that in the middle of it all was theological discourse, mainly of a Thomist-Aristotelian sort, coupled with the discourse of canon and civil law, which also functioned in relationship to theology', *Race*, p. 6. Cf. Jennings, *Christian Imagination*, chapter 2.
38. Bavinck, *Christian Worldview*, p. 94.
39. Bavinck, *Christian Worldview*, p. 95; *Christelijke wereldbeschouwing*, p. 70.
40. Bavinck, *Christian Worldview*, p. 95.
41. Bavinck, *Christian Worldview*, p. 96.
42. Bavinck, *Christian Worldview*, p. 96.

be derived from experience. Kant works from this given: the absolute validity of obligation is, to him, the basis of morality, theology, and religion. Philosophy, driven out from the domain of science, receives the task of research into the assessment of necessary, generally applicable values.[43]

As others have noted, Bavinck was picking up on Kant's so-called Copernican revolution, or the turn from transcendental realism to transcendental idealism.[44] Bavinck charitably evaluated that 'Kant performed an outstanding service for morality in his day', and displayed an 'intense effort to hold ideal norms, in their superiority, high above human approval and self-interest'.[45] Yet, the question remains, Bavinck argues, whether Kant was able to establish morality on a better footing than the older theism. Ultimately, the failure to root morality in the immanent (human reason) rather than in the transcendent (the Eternal Creator) manifested itself when one observes the rise of a second modern movement: the historical turn. Whereas Kant presumed that human nature was universal and fixed, historicism introduced the notion of evolution to understand not only history but also human nature, and thus 'many began to doubt whether human nature, with its sense of duty, was indeed an objective and immutable given from which one could safely proceed in researching the moral life'.[46] The human being 'had become historical'.[47] And if this were true, then there would be as many moralities as 'humans and peoples', for the human, 'as a moral being, was a product of his environment'.[48]

The historical turn 'fought [Kant] with the weapons he himself had wielded' when Kant untethered moral norms from the knowledge of God.[49] Despite contributing much on the genealogy of humanity and religion, the historical turn led to the demise of the universal moral norm, as an expression of ethical obligation became reducible to historical contingency. From the fact of a particular social expression within time, one cannot deduce a universal moral claim. Furthermore, when there are competing claims of progress and norm, there is nothing to which one can appeal to adjudicate on those competing claims except for one's own culture.

It is precisely here that a sense of chauvinism and racism could arise. Putting the logic tersely: if morality is founded not in God but in humanity, and if humanity is not a universal but is diverse and evolving, then one must decide *which* humanity and *which* point of time will ground all moral evaluation.

On account of the inescapability of moral consciousness and the need for stability, Bavinck is observing that this historical viewpoint is what indeed led to

---

43. Bavinck, *Christian Worldview*, p. 97.
44. See especially Henry Allison, *Kant's Transcendental Idealism*, revised ed. (New Haven: Yale University Press, 2004).
45. Bavinck, *Christian Worldview*, p. 97.
46. Bavinck, *Christian Worldview*, p. 98.
47. Bavinck, *Christian Worldview*, p. 98.
48. Bavinck, *Christian Worldview*, p. 98.
49. Bavinck, *Christian Worldview*, p. 99.

a counterfeit nationalism and a fanaticism about race and instinct. An appeal to a 'generic' or 'universal' humanity is no longer possible or conducive to practice: one drifts now to select a particular human history from which one derives normativity, and by which other nations and peoples might be adjudicated. If one rejects the older theistic claim that God himself is the true, good, and beautiful, then one will have to pick out one particular expression of humanity as the bearer of the same.[50] The most instinctive outcome is to locate that normativity in one's own people. Where does Bavinck see this coming to the fore within his nineteenth-century context? The answer is: in a variety of converging Aryan nationalisms: 'Pan-Germanism, pan-Slavism, and so on, supply proof of this.'[51] Bavinck then cites three influential authors in quick succession as 'eloquent' interpreters of this emerging racism: the French aristocrat, Count Joseph Arthur de Gobineau (1816–82), who developed the idea of an Aryan 'master race'; German art philosopher Julius Langbehn (1851–1907), who wrote *Rembrandt als Erzieher* (*Rembrandt as Educator*); and British-born pan-Germanist propagandist Houston Chamberlain (1855–1927), who was later influential in the National Socialist Movement (Chamberlain in particular will reappear in Bavinck's *Philosophy of Revelation*).[52] While these authors argue from differing angles for the common superiority of Aryanism, what binds them together methodologically, in Bavinck's reading, is the attempt to infer ethics from a particular history or a genealogy: the 'norm was sought in the historical, the ideal identified with reality, the relative exalted to the rank of the absolute'.[53] While these projects look antiquated and groundless today, their influence lies in a utopian projection that lured the popular imagination of many in the late nineteenth century.[54]

Anticipating the contemporary analyses of racism by Jennings and Carter, which trace the sin of white supremacy back to a pseudo-theological supersessionism, Bavinck's next line of reasoning is worth considering in full:

---

50. I began to gesture towards this narrative that Bavinck canvasses in N. Gray Sutanto, 'Christian Worldview: Context, Classical Contours, and Significance', *Reformed Faith and Practice* 5 (2020): pp. 28–39.

51. Bavinck, *Christian Worldview*, p. 100.

52. Bavinck, *Christian Worldview*, pp. 100–1. See esp. Houston Stuart Chamberlain, *Die Grundlagen des neunzehnten Jahrhunderts*, 2 vols (München: Bruckmann, 1903). ET: Houston Stuart Chamberlain, *Foundations of the Nineteenth Century*, 2 vols, John Lees (trans.) (London: John Lane, 1910). See also Michael Biddiss, 'History as Destiny: Gobineau, H. S. Chamberlain, and Spengler', *Transactions of the Royal Historical Society* 7 (1997): pp. 73–100.

53. Bavinck, *Christian Worldview*, p. 101. It is important to note that Bavinck is not arguing that attention to the historical conditions necessarily leads to chauvinism – rather, his argument here is inductive, based on the observation of what was in fact argued during his time.

54. Biddiss, 'History as Destiny', p. 73.

From that [historical] pedestal, even the highest and holiest is grasped at: if Jesus still wants to retain some authority over us, he has to put up with being injected into the Aryan tribe. All significant peoples had their own religious founder: the Persians had their Zarathustra, the Indians their Buddha, the Chinese their Confucius, the Jews their Moses, the Greeks their Homer, the Arabians their Mohammed [sic]; and the most civilized of the Aryans, the Germans, would not have been able to produce such a personality and had, rather, to go to the school of a people like the Jews! How foolish the one who believes Jesus was not a Jew, [that] he was an Aryan, and [that] the Bible, in which every heretic finds his proof text, gives the evidence for the matter. 'The German spirit shall heal the world'. (*Am deutschem Wesen wird dereinst die Welt genesen.*)[55]

Bavinck is observing the pan-Germanist logic that if a particular history is the source of moral norms, then the appeal to Jesus can remain authoritative only if Jesus himself is located within that historical trajectory. The obverse is also the case: if the emerging Aryan and pan-Germanic ideology is to have merit, it needs to appeal to Jesus, but this can only be done if Jesus is reconceived as a representative of Aryanism rather than of Judaism. Michael Biddiss sums it up well: Chamberlain's Aryan-centered narrative of the world needed Jesus to be non-Jewish, and 'Chamberlain even indulged in a highly convoluted argument (about the pronunciation of Aramaic gutterals, and much else) directed against any supposition that the Messiah was, in racial terms, Jewish'.[56] Or, as Bavinck observed in his *Christelijke wetenschap*, every religion depended on identifying a source of revelation, and the new German nationalism refashioned Jesus into 'the purest type of the Aryan or Germanic race. In fact, people take only a few features from the image of Christ in the New Testament that are comfortable to the present-day way of thinking and try to construct an ideal Christ to suit modern taste.'[57]

Bavinck was detecting what Bacote (following Jennings and Carter) has observed regarding the use of the person of Jesus as a justification of these nineteenth-century Aryan ideologies. To use a contemporary term, this use led to a 'baptism' of whiteness as the representation (and substitution) of God's own will: 'One interesting dimension of how this occurs is by cleaving the Jewish ethnic particularity from Jesus and reconceiving him as the ultimate rational and moral autonomous figure. This creation and, if you will, "baptism" of whiteness as the pinnacle of humanity is then woven into the fabric of the modern world.'[58] Bavinck's critique, to the effect that a departure from God's self-revelation leads

---

55. Bavinck, *Christian Worldview*, p. 101; *Christelijke wetenschap*, p. 76. The German quote is from Chamberlain, *Die Grundlagen des neunzehnten Jahrhunderts* (München: Bruckmann, 1903), 1: p. 209.
56. Biddiss, 'History as Destiny', p. 82.
57. Bavinck, *Christianity and Science*, p. 185.
58. Bacote, 'Erasing Race', p. 128.

to a projection of Jesus into one's own history and interests, dovetails well with Carter's pithy summary:

> [A]t the genealogical taproot of modern racial reasoning is the process by which Christ was abstracted from Jesus, and thus from his Jewish body, thereby severing Christianity from its Jewish roots ... In making Christ non-Jewish in this moment, he was made a figure of the Occident. He became white, even if Jesus as a historical figure remained Jewish or racially a figure of the orient.[59]

The upshot of this tendency of thought, for Bavinck, is that the 'so-called historical view turns into the most biased construction of history'. It posits one nation as the arbitrator and pinnacle of history, and sees other and past cultures as primitive, while positing that 'Jesus did not come from Israel but from the Aryans'.[60] By absolutizing a historically relative entity (a nation and a people), it reduces the histories of other peoples, precluding them from being a source of self-correction, untethers oneself from being accountable to God, and disposes one to be a source of oppressive coercion. In Bavinck's reasoning, the immanent is an inadequate substitute as a bearer of moral law: 'Relativism appears, then, to be impartial, as it wants to know of no fixed norms and claims to be concerned with and to speak of only the concrete, the historical. But it makes the relative itself into the absolute and therefore exchanges true freedom for coercion, real faith for superstition.'[61] Remarkably, Bavinck was arguing that relativism and historicism were trojan horses for racism.

Bavinck moves on in the rest of the chapter to defend a retrieval of the older theistic ethics, rooting law not in humanity but in God: '[laws] have absolute and immutable being, but they are not products of history – they merit a transcendent and metaphysical character and because they cannot float in the sky, they have their reality in God's wisdom and will.'[62] By rooting norms back in the Eternal being, no particular people group can subject another by placing itself in the role of the arbitrator and judge; rather, all are judged by the same divine law: evil is not about deviation from a particular culture but about sin. Christ, then, comes not to bring a new law by buttressing a particular nation with the status of normativity, but by bringing the good news of salvation from above.[63]

Philosophy of Revelation: History, Eugenics, and Human Diversity

If *Christian Worldview* observed a pan-Germanist pattern of reasoning according to which racism and nationalism unfold when one substitutes humanity for

---

59. Carter, *Race*, pp. 6–7.
60. Bavinck, *Christian Worldview*, p. 101.
61. Bavinck, *Christian Worldview*, p. 102.
62. Bavinck, *Christian Worldview*, p. 108.
63. Bavinck, *Christian Worldview*, p. 113. Bavinck's move here is similar to Romero and Liou, *Christianity and Critical Race Theory*, pp. 45–6.

God as a source of law, *Philosophy of Revelation* gives a more granular account of that same narrative, albeit with an eschatological tinge. The chapters on history and the future argue that the identification of a particular human society or nation as the bearer of ethical civilization fills an eschatological vacuum given the removal of Christian hope in modern society. If law is not found in the transcendent, but in the immanent, then so is heaven. This occurs not merely when utopian society is located in a particular nationality, depicted as the height of humanity, but also in the emergence of the science of eugenics, which hauntingly foreshadows the horrors of the Holocaust just a few decades after Bavinck's writings. After exploring Bavinck's genealogical analysis of eugenicism and nationalism, I shall lay out his critiques of the same.[64]

The chapter 'Revelation and History' begins by outlining the emergence of the historical consciousness and the desire to determine the main idea, force, or causal chain that propels history forward. While Hegel may have introduced the importance of history for philosophizing, historians rejected his view as overly speculative, reading history in light of one pre-determined idea rather than letting the empirical phenomena of historical investigation speak for themselves. As Bavinck notes, 'It was no longer permissible to construe the facts in accordance with a preconceived idea; but, inversely, from the facts the laws must be learned which controlled them in their environment.'[65] While this reverse process seems more unbiased and objective in method, Bavinck argues that an unproven presupposition remained operative that in truth it was 'just as much dominated by a preconceived idea as the ideological treatment of Hegel'. This presupposition stated that a correct historical analysis will identify 'one and the same causality [that] originates all events and causes them to succeed each other according to the law of progressive development in a straight, upward line'.[66] Through the influence of the success of evolutionary theory in natural science, the notion of evolution is also applied to the nations and the epochs of history. What emerges is a reductionistic monism. The driving force of history is sought in one principle cause, whether in economic and social conditions, psychological factors or biology. Specifically, in the case of 'Gobineau and H. St. Chamberlain', it is sought in the identification of 'race [as] the principle factor in history and asks of ethnology the solution of historical problems'.[67] In hindsight, Bavinck's description of this race-consciousness might be considered a euphemism, as Gobineau and Chamberlain

---

64. Kuyper credited intermarriage as a cause of the development of humanity, though such an argument still betrays the nineteenth- and early twentieth-century move of identifying race and culture with genetic and biological origins. In this regard, Bavinck's suspicion of the enterprise of eugenics is still in contrast to Kuyper. See D. Th. Kuiper, 'Groen and Kuyper on the Racial Issue', in *Kuyper Reconsidered: Aspects of His Life and Work*, Cornelis van der Kooi and Jan de Bruijn (eds) (Amsterdam: VU Uitgeverij, 1999), pp. 69–81 (79–80).
65. Bavinck, *PoR*, p. 95.
66. Bavinck, *PoR*, p. 95.
67. Bavinck, *PoR*, p. 92.

credited the Aryan stock as the dominant and superior race to which all of the greatest achievements of Europe (and hence the world) could be credited – a reading of history that Michael Biddiss aptly called 'racial determinism'.[68]

On the basis of this 'monistic' and evolutionary outlook, various philosophers of history offer differing accounts of the stages of human history, with each stage couched within an 'ascending series of periods' which (conveniently) depict the present age as the most evolved and cultured:

> A distinction is made between the Stone, Bronze, and Iron ages; between hunting, the pastoral life, agriculture, manufacture, and commerce; between an Asiatic-despotic, medieval-feudal, and civil-capitalistic society … between symbolism, typism, conventionalism, individualism, and subjectivism in the history of the German people; between savagery, barbarism, and civilization; between matriarchy, patriarchy, polygamy, and monogamy; between fetishism, polytheism, and monotheism; between theological, metaphysical, and positivistic phases, etc.[69]

Bavinck picks up on these theories of the successive stages of history and focuses on the aspirations of German philosophers to present themselves as the bearers of a kind of eschatological salvation. He observes that these thinkers do not merely reject Christianity because they perceive it to be false, but because it is bad for the development of the future: 'If modern culture is to advance, it must wholly reject the influence of Christianity and break completely with the old worldview.'[70] How so? Bavinck explains that Christianity offers hope in another world, in eternity, heaven, and God, and hence it is purportedly 'indifferent to this life', whereas contemporary hope is wholly 'this-worldly'.[71] Hope in God is replaced with hope in human achievement – the immanent must produce its own eschaton:

> The modern man no longer feels himself a miserable creature, who has fallen from his original destiny … He can conceive nothing more wonderful than this beautiful world, which has evolved itself from the smallest beginnings and has reached its highest point of development in the grand and mighty human … More and more he becomes his own providence … By labor one is divine and becomes continually more godlike. Labor must therefore be the foundation of religion and morality, and also of the entirety of modern society.[72]

---

68. Biddiss, 'History as Destiny', p. 76.
69. Bavinck, *PoR*, p. 101. This racial and historical consciousness is also present at the outset of the rise of the discipline of 'anthropology'; see Matthew Engelke, *How to Think Like an Anthropologist* (Princeton: Princeton University Press, 2018), pp. 58–82.
70. Bavinck, *PoR*, p. 213.
71. Bavinck, *PoR*, p. 213.
72. Bavinck, *PoR*, p. 213.

Bavinck explores the many ways in which modern culture projected an immanent utopia: from education and labor reforms to the rise of socialism, the reconsideration of the sexes and their places, and the generating of new philosophical inquiries about the final end. Though much of this is to be celebrated can be recast in light of revelation, in Bavinck's perspective, not so with the science of eugenics, based as it was on a nationalistic definition of the archetypal *Ubermensch*.

As Bavinck saw it, the rise of evolutionary theory prompts the founding question of eugenics – the question of whether natural selection can be accelerated by way of artificial selection. What, for example, if survival of the fittest was not a by-product of contingency but assisted by conscious deliberation? Thus philosophers, scientists, and psychologists alike joined together to envision the deliverance of humanity from its many miseries and the perfection of the human race. This joint effort was exploring how 'to improve the racial qualities of humankind in an artificial way'.[73] Agreeing that Christianity offers a 'comfortless view' due to its teachings on original corruption, this attempt at improvement presupposes that humanity is an evolving animal, and – further – that humanity should actively partake in furthering that evolutionary process: '[the human] must feel [their] responsibility for the carrying of the process through … and for its advancing through [human effort] to a higher type of being … and to this belongs in the first place the improvement of the human race.'[74] It logically follows that practices such as allowing the weak, sick, and those considered to be mentally underdeveloped to marry freely is a tragedy, and does not lead to the improvement of humanity.

The 'science of "eugenics"' was formally inaugurated by Francis Galton in 1883 at the University of London.[75] Underlying this emerging field, in Bavinck's view, is the assumption that the moral and physical progress of humanity is the responsibility of science, and eugenics correspondingly seeks to determine 'the laws' by which 'propagation and heredity' is governed.[76] As Bavinck describes it,

> [T]he state can at any rate begin to make medical inquiry obligatory before marriage, and forbid marriage in definite serious cases, and so prevent the birth of unfortunate children. Artificial selection shows how genera and species may be modified among plants and animals; if this selection is applied also to the human race, it will promote its well-being and improvement in the highest degree.[77]

Thus eugenics not only seeks the improvement of health and physical powers, but also hopes for the production of a higher culture, as children inherit better traits

---

73. Bavinck, *PoR*, p. 215.
74. Bavinck, *PoR*, p. 216.
75. Bavinck, *PoR*, p. 217. See also Daniel J. Kevles, *In the Name of Eugenics: Genetics and the Use of Human Heredity* (Cambridge: Harvard University Press, 1985).
76. Bavinck, *PoR*, p. 217.
77. Bavinck, *PoR*, p. 217.

from their parents.[78] Luke Powery's recent description of the rise of eugenicism parallels Bavinck's, and indicates that similar movements were arising in the context of the United States:

> Eugenics, this practice of controlled selective breeding of human groups in order to improve the group's genetic makeup, is an example of this social maintenance. It was spearheaded by Francis Galton in Britain and Charles Davenport in the United States. They claimed negative, deviant social behaviors, including criminality, were genetically based and connected these negative social behaviors with particular racialized groups. They applied these ideas about racial difference to immigration, reproduction, and other policies related to races. These 'scientific' ideas claimed some people groups to be unfit or debased; this led to the attempt to discourage breeding between races, especially between those deemed of lower and higher standing.[79]

Bavinck has much to say about this 'science': it is implicitly chauvinistic, eradicates the unity of human nature, and is a great moral evil. Most relevant for my purposes is that he argues that this social ideology is painfully naïve. It misses the point that evil does not reside in one particular human culture or group but in every human heart. Bavinck writes, 'sin and crime increase frightfully, not only in the lowest ranks of population but quite as much in high aristocratic circles … excess, avarice, theft, and murder, jealousy, envy, and hatred – play no less a part in the life of cultured humanity than among the people of a lower culture.'[80] To locate evil in a genetic trait, to identify it with a particular sub-group or a nation, is not only to miss the natural unity of all humanity but also to underestimate the source of misery and to mislocate sin entirely. Bavinck writes: 'Legislation is almost powerless here; internal corruption, moral degeneration, and religious decay cannot be removed by a law of the state; on the contrary, every law has to reckon with the egoism and the passion of man.'[81] Sin is present in every culture.

James Bratt, however, has picked up on this language of 'high' and 'low' cultures in Bavinck's Stone lectures, indicating that such language reflects 'a lingering Victorian, and therefore also imperial, confidence in the self-superiority of European to other civilizations'.[82] Such language indicates that though Bavinck is more perceptive than his contemporaries, and though he would later deploy such language rhetorically against the pan-Germanist logics of his day, the retention of 'high' and 'low' cultures should be jettisoned, for they smuggle in the sort of tiered understanding of humanity that Bavinck himself was so concerned to resist.

---

78. Cf. Engelke, *How to Think Like an Anthropologist*, p. 38.
79. Luke A. Powery, *Becoming Human: The Holy Spirit and the Rhetoric of Race* (Louisville: Westminster John Knox Press, 2022), p. 41.
80. Bavinck, *PoR*, p. 235.
81. Bavinck, *PoR*, p. 235.
82. James D. Bratt, 'The Context of Herman Bavinck's Stone Lectures: Culture and Politics in 1908', *The Bavinck Review* 1 (2010): p. 21.

One can draw out Bavinck's own broader reasoning against his language here. The differences in culture should be enfolded within a properly organic account of humanity that Bavinck himself has recognized, for non-Western societies are no less cultured, as they too are made in the image of God and responding to revelation. The recognition of his prescient criticisms of Euro-centrism must be coupled with the bare admission of his own limitations.

While Bavinck is a few decades away from seeing the future coalescing of the science of eugenics and pan-Germanism in Nazi Germany, he was clear that eugenicism and Aryanism were produced by the same turn to the immanent. Toward the end of his chapter, he turns once again to the emerging nationalism of Germany. The Enlightenment claimed the emancipation and exaltation of universal reason, Bavinck observes, but particular patterns of reasoning within historicism particularized that enlightened reason to the culture of a particular nation:

> The cosmopolitanism of the 'Enlightenment' (*Aufklärung*) was not only exchanged in the nineteenth century for patriotism, but this patriotism was not infrequently developed into an exaggerated, dangerous, and belligerent chauvinism, which exalts its own people at the cost of other nations.[83]

Invoking once again the influence of H. S. Chamberlain, Bavinck notes that a 'race consciousness' particularized that nationalism even further to a specific people group with particular biological and moral traits; in turn, he states, '[t]his race glorification acquires such a serious character and so far exceeds all bounds ... that the virtues of the race are identified with the highest ideal.'[84] Once again, this leads to a kind of pseudo-theological supersessionism. Instead of the subordination of the nation (and nations) under the reign of Jesus and his Israelite history, the history of Jesus is subsumed under a new national identity and ideal. '*Deutschtum*, for example, is placed on a level with Christendom, and Jesus is naturalized into an Aryan in race.'[85] It is clear, Bavinck argues, that the emancipation of science and philosophy from Christian faith has not led to the immanent utopia that 'enlightened' reason once projected, and that 'neither science nor philosophy, neither ethics nor culture, can give that security with regard to the future which we have need of, not only for our thought but also for our whole life and action.'[86] To envision an ethic that might do justice to the whole of humanity now requires an eschatological vision that transcends immanent history.

While Bavinck's genealogical diagnosis is a potent critique in itself, he offers more precise criticisms peppered throughout *Philosophy of Revelation*, in addition to the insistence on the recovery of Christian theistic ethics surveyed above from *Christian Worldview*. I shall briefly pick up on three threads that go together

---

83. Bavinck, *PoR*, p. 236.
84. Bavinck, *PoR*, p. 237.
85. Bavinck, *PoR*, p. 237.
86. Bavinck, *PoR*, p. 238.

within this text: first, that evolutionary historicism produces a simplistic picture of history; second, the unity of the human race; and third, the need to prioritize divine revelation and redemption in order to diagnose and deliver humanity from its miseries.

First, Bavinck offers a pluriform account of humanity and history in contrast to the monistic ideologies of the nineteenth century, discerning insurmountable problems in the latter. The application of the term 'evolution' to the discipline of history, Bavinck argued, was an instance of the Baconian fallacy of *idolum fori* (idol of the marketplace).[87] While Bacon used this term to critique the transposing of common social terms to nature, Bavinck argued in the opposite direction. Those who described history in nontheistic evolutionary ways were unduly transposing a concept that belonged to nature, and to cellular organisms in particular, to the common social history of humanity. But for Bavinck, whatever unity or development can be ascribed to human history is utterly different from that pertaining to cellular organisms, for the former unity is born not simply out of internal growth but also on the basis of freedom and ethics. Bavinck writes: 'Monism overlooks the difference between a biological, a psychical, and an ethical organism, just as it does that between an organism and a mechanism.'[88] It inadvertently reduces the richness of created life into a singular kind of uniformity, as if an explanation that works well in one sphere can be used to explain every other sphere.

Furthermore, the grand-narrative construal of history that neatly divides it into categorized segments runs into another severe problem. Not only does this run against the theological and empirically verifiable unity of humanity, Bavinck observes, these narrative-schemes also wrongly place these predicates in '*succession* to one another' when 'in reality' they had always occurred '*side by side*'.[89] So-called high civilization existed even in antiquity, and vices of all kinds remain in contemporary cultures. Correspondingly, he acknowledges, 'Even if a period is older in history, it is very possible that it may have something which it alone possesses and by which it excels all others.'[90] Indeed, when the desire to explain all of history under 'sharply defined periods' is relinquished, a more thorough investigation reveals that 'high civilization existed even in antiquity; industry and technic, science and art, commerce and society had even then reached a high degree of development.'[91] Human history does not form a neatly linear story of development that culminates in one nation or master-philosophy, but a rich and multifaceted maze of layered phenomena.

---

87. This parallels Gijsbert van den Brink's remark: 'Any attempt to deduce some ideal arrangement of society from evolutionary theory suffers from what has been called … the naturalistic fallacy: one concludes from how things (apparently) *are* to how they *should* be.' Van den Brink, *Reformed Theology and Evolutionary Theory*, p. 232.
88. Bavinck, *PoR*, p. 96.
89. Bavinck, *PoR*, p. 101.
90. Bavinck, *PoR*, p. 101.
91. Bavinck, *PoR*, p. 101.

Second, such grand narratives of history can privilege one nation or people group and overlook the unity of the human race. Undergirding the diversity of nations and peoples is a single humanity disclosed in revelation; when history is read in light of that revelation, what emerges is not a gradation of ethnicities but a diverse humanity. The true historical discipline, conducted in this light, is thus dedicated to the study of *humanity in all of its particularities and locations*. Bavinck argued that sundering historical sciences from their Christian-theistic roots often leads to the denigration of one nation, or the elevation of one phase of history, both of which can lead to supremacist results. The historian requires 'revelation', precisely because in it God has revealed 'a history of the world and a history of humanity, in which all men, all peoples, nay, all creatures, are embraced, and are held together by one leading thought, by one counsel of God'.[92] In short, '[t]he unity of human nature and the human race is the presupposition of all of history, and this has been made known to us only by Christianity'.[93] Preserving differentiation over against a 'false unity', in other words, requires that the

> unity of all creation is not sought in the things themselves but transcendently ... in a divine being, in his wisdom and power, in his will and counsel ... A person alone can be the root of unity in difference, of difference in unity. He alone can combine a multiplicity of ideas into unity, and he alone can realize them by his will *ad extra*.[94]

Affirming Christianity means rejecting monism and embracing human diversity, rather than placing one culture or ethnicity as the universal expression of true humanity, Christianity for Bavinck teaches that 'the unity of humanity does not exclude but rather includes the differentiation of humanity in race, in character, in attainment, in calling, and in many other things.'[95] This 'variety has been destroyed by sin and changed in opposition', Bavinck argues later, and 'the unity of humanity was dissolved into a multiplicity of peoples and nations'; but salvation in Christ and the fellowship of the Spirit restores its unity-in-diversity.[96] It is worth noting that, for Bavinck, the unity of humanity means that race is understood not in terms of an essentialist or biological property that distinguishes one people group from another by virtue of their physical 'stock' (contra Gobineau and Chamberlain), but rather consists in recognizing the particularities of nationalities and cultures, determined as they are by geographic dispersion and local histories.

Bavinck sums up the principle of a Christian practice of historical analysis here as that of treating the peoples as 'side-by-side' rather than as 'one line' or 'in succession'. He will sum this up well in his chapter on the emergence of religion (to be explored further later): 'We must return from the "after-one-another" to the

---

92. Bavinck, *PoR*, p. 113.
93. Bavinck, *PoR*, p. 113.
94. Bavinck, *PoR*, pp. 111–12.
95. Bavinck, *PoR*, p. 114.
96. Bavinck, *PoR*, p. 243.

"by-the-side-of-one-another," from uniformity to multiformity, from the abstract theory of monism to the fullness of life."[97] This reorientation of thought will allow the Christian historian truly to listen to the native, the local, and the foreigner, as it forbids imposing one's own history and narrative upon the other.

Third, then, divine redemption, along with revelation, is necessary to achieve the ideal of true, organic unity. Humanity's unity and differentiation, identity and dignity, are all secured ultimately in Christ – the 'kernel' of history who himself revealed that history has a 'plan, progress and aim' that evacuates the sinful tendency to exalt one's self as the historical ideal.[98] In other words, history's center, aim, progress, and end are not us, but Christ – and this confession simultaneously preserves the unity-and-diversity of, and the meaningful norms within, human history. Bavinck's reasoning there leads us back to the conclusion of *Christian Worldview*: that an 'organic worldview alone answers the diversity and richness of the world'[99] – a worldview that does not only contend that history is governed by an archetypal divine will, but also supposes that the same will itself 'entered into it historically and as such lifts it up to the heights of its particular idea, to a work of God, to the genesis of the kingdom of heaven'.[100]

The kingdom of heaven, then, is not a result of historical progress but a work of God:

> In spite of all striving after unity by means of world conquest, political alliance, and international arbitration, trade unions and economic interests; in spite of the advocacy of an independent, positive, and common world language, world science, world morality, and world culture – unity has not and cannot be realized. For these forces can at the most accomplish an external and temporal unity, but they do not change the heart and do not make the people of one soul and one speech … If there is ever to be a humanity one in heart and one in soul, then it must be born out of return to the one living and true God.[101]

The genealogical diagnosis of the emergence of both eugenicism and nationalism therefore leads Bavinck to a theological amelioration: the heeding of Christian revelation and a retrieval of a transcendent eschatological vision, advanced not by the labor of human hands but brought about by the divine will alone.

Conclusion

This chapter has shown that neo-Kuyperians have recognized the need to ameliorate Kuyper's own problematic views on race by turning to more recent thinkers and

---

97. Bavinck, *PoR*, p. 129.
98. Bavinck, *PoR*, pp. 115–16.
99. Bavinck, *Christelijke wereldbeschouwing*, p. 97.
100. Bavinck, *Christelijke wereldbeschouwing*, p. 95.
101. Bavinck, *PoR*, p. 244.

by retrieving the more level-headed contributions of Bavinck. Bavinck offered a genealogical diagnosis of the origins of racism, and that he analyzed of what might be called a 'top-down' approach to racism. By substituting the transcendent for the immanent in the historical turn, various nineteenth-century movements sought to locate normativity in the historical trajectory of one particular group. Doing so has resulted in identifying the Aryan race or one nation as the measure by which other peoples are to be assessed. Bavinck, indeed, offered several objections to such a move – including that it misinterprets history and wrongly applies notions of evolution and gradation to human civilization, and that it forgets the unity of human nature and the source of norm and salvation. The next chapter shall detail Bavinck's genealogical diagnosis of a 'bottom-up' sort of racism, in which an 'original' or 'primitive' humanity is sought, along with an exploration of Bavinck's own constructive account of human unity and diversity in the states of nature, grace, and glory.

Chapter 7

RACE AND RELIGION

With Bavinck's genealogical diagnosis and critique of the origins of racism in hand, it is now possible to offer a more detailed exposition of Bavinck's positive account of corporate humanity, especially with reference to the diversity of humanity expressed in geographically sustained identities over time. This chapter moves in three steps. First, I revisit Bavinck's comments on the intrinsically religious character of human nature, explored in the first half of this book, focusing particularly on race (which undergirds and precedes national developments) by engaging with his lecture on 'Revelation and Religion' in *Philosophy of Revelation*. Second, I show that, contrary to the Aryan, colonialist, and social-evolutionary impulses of the science of religion in nineteenth-century Holland, Bavinck argued that no one nation has 'special' access to the creational knowledge of God, and that divine revelation precedes and resources the formation of each human civilization. There is thus no linear development or gradation of religious civilizations. Missions, then, should recognize – rather than eradicate – the cultural particularity of each people and be receptive to their potential theological contributions. Finally, I sketch Bavinck's account of human unity and diversity through the three estates that qualify human nature – creation, fall, and redemption. Along the way, I observe the teleological design of human nature, Bavinck's affirmation of the corporate character of sin, and the pluriform character of the church. The conclusion of this chapter summarizes the argument and offers some critical reflections on Bavinck's account of corporate humanity.

Religion and Human Nature

To understand the significance of Bavinck's comments about the religious nature of human beings and their application to the modern notion of race, it is instructive to recall Willie Jennings' description of the colonialist imagination in *The Christian Imagination*. Colonialist expansion, Jennings argues, envisioned

> new lands as systems of potentialities, a mass of undeveloped, underdeveloped, unused, underutilized, misunderstood, not fully understood potentialities. Everything – from peoples and their bodies to plants and animals, from the ground and the sky – was subject to change, subjects for change, subjected to change.[1]

1. Jennings, *Christian Imagination*, p. 43.

Settlers dismissed the local's self-knowledge, and failed to 'imagine a theological appropriation of native knowledge as an act of theological reflection itself'.[2] The colonialist spoke for indigenous peoples, and located them on a graded scale of existence, with the white settler at the pinnacle and brown and Black people at the bottom. They presented 'salvation without the desire for communion'.[3] Indeed, settlers, though Gentiles themselves, located themselves as Israel's replacement and saw it as their vocation to differentiate false and true worship, primitive and pristine religion. As such, the settlers forgot the narrative of redemptive history, which includes their inclusion into Israel's narrative: 'a simple Gentile remembrance that would enable a far more richly imagined possibility of movement toward faith from within the cultural logics and spatial realities of Andean [and other native] life'.[4] Such a remembrance would enable them to turn to the 'other' nations as analogies of their own graced inclusion, with attentive hope that God might teach us something by their inclusion.

While Jennings is commenting on medieval expressions of colonialist sensibilities, these represent the genealogical roots of the modern forms of race-consciousness that Bavinck encountered at the turn of the twentieth century. When Bavinck turns to the subject of religions in the sixth chapter of *Philosophy of Revelation*, he centers his discussion on revelation and its implications for understanding the nature of humanity, its connection to redemptive history and the eroding of the same in the historical and religious studies of his day.

Paralleling his critique of evolutionary historicism and of its claim that one culture represented the height of human development recounted in the previous chapter, Bavinck argues that the phenomenon of religion signifies the fundamental equality of human beings across space and time, as religion arises out of human nature. To grasp the significance of his argument, I first sketch Bavinck's critique of the nineteenth-century search for the 'original' or 'primitive' human prior to the rise of religion, and then move on to Bavinck's depiction of religion as intrinsic to human nature.[5]

First, then, I attend to Bavinck's observations on the search for an 'original' human nature. If his earlier chapter on history shows Bavinck's suspicion of a gradation of cultures that posited 'Aryan' nations as the pinnacle of historical evolution, this sixth chapter shows that Bavinck applies that same suspicion to the distinction between the religionless 'nature-peoples' (*natuurvolken*) and the

2. Jennings, *Christian Imagination*, p. 91.
3. Jennings, *Christian Imagination*, p. 93.
4. Jennings, *Christian Imagination*, p. 98.
5. On the rise of the science of religions in the Netherlands during the nineteenth century, see Arie Molendijk, *The Emergence of the Science of Religion in the Netherlands* (Leiden: Brill, 2005), and his more recent *Protestant Theology and Modernity in the Nineteenth-Century Netherlands* (Oxford: Oxford University Press, 2022), pp. 155–78.

'cultured' people of Western Europe. Indeed, Bavinck's argumentation in *Philosophy of Revelation* is initially predicated as a response to the science of religions – led in the Netherlands by the Leiden professor of the history of religions, Cornelis Petrus Tiele (1830–1902) – which sought to identify the essence of world religions and couched religious studies as an empirical and historical enterprise.[6]

As I will show, his argument is that this distinction is superficial, for there is no gradation between the former and the latter, and culture, religion, and morality can also be found in the so-called nature-peoples, while sin, degradation, and callousness cut across both so-called high and low cultured societies. Although Bavinck's language at times signifies that he remained a man of his time, as noted in the previous chapter, his critiques of the gradation of existence anticipate those offered by scholars in the twenty-first century.

If Aryan superiority was predicated on the search for norms in the historically immanent, the hypothesis of a gradation between the primitive and the cultured human was posited as a result of the search for the 'origin' of religion. Bavinck points to John Lubbock (1834–1913), for instance, who sought to find an original non-religious society in the 'state of savages', or a 'phase of atheism' out of which human beings evolved.[7] Despite the admissions of scientists and historians (Bavinck points to an array of work, citing Cornelis Petrus Tiele, Ludwig Stein, and Oscar Hertwig), to the effect that genealogical histories of the development of humanity and religion are mere hypotheses, these same figures continued to offer accounts of that development with confidence.[8] To support the gradation hypothesis, Bavinck observes that the category of the *natuurvolken* is introduced: 'Study of the animal and the child on the one hand, and on the other study of the so-called nature-peoples (*natuurvolken*) is pressed into service in order to form in some sense an idea of the primitive human still wholly without culture [and, we might add, religion]'.[9] The logic of this research program is that a study of the nature-peoples would unveil, inductively, what the original primitive human would be like.

Bavinck detects the influence of Darwinian evolutionary theory in biology behind these newer studies in history and religion. From the truth of the common descent of humanity, conjectures are offered on the developmental and social

---

6. Bavinck's engagement is with C. P. Tiele, *Inleiding tot de godsdienstwetenschap*, 2 vols, 2nd ed. (Amsterdam: P. N. Van Kampen & Zoon, 1900).

7. John Lubbock, *The Origin of Civilization and the Primitive Condition of Man: Mental and Social Condition of Savages*, 5th ed. (New York: D. Appleton and Co., 1898). Bavinck, *Philosophy of Revelation*, p. 121, was engaging with the German edition: John Lubbock, *Die Entstehung der Zivilisation und der Uruzstand des Menschengechlechtes, erläutert durch das innere und äußere Leben der Wilden*, Deutsch Ausgabe (Jena, 1875).

8. Bavinck, *Philosophy of Revelation*, p. 122. Cf. Tiele, *Inleiding tot de godsdienstwetenschap*, II: p. 183.

9. Bavinck, *Philosophy of Revelation*, p. 122. Cf. Molendijk, 'Ethnology and Religion', in *The Emergence of the Science of Religion in the Netherlands*, pp. 179–222.

conditions of humanity's evolution. The goal, again, is to offer an explanation of – as well as to determine – the precise point at which religion, culture, and art had arisen, as if there were a 'simple', primitive, and 'monistic' point of origin that slowly ascended toward higher expressions of religiosity, culture, and morals.[10] Arie Molendijk posits that this transposition of Darwinian biology to social theory in this way results in 'a theory of culture that claims a unilinear, universal development from a "barbaric" or "savage" to a "civilized" stage of human existence'.[11] Upon encountering 'nature-people' in the present, then, as Matthew Engelke observes, the colonialist concludes that they signify humanity in its more primitive form: 'they were us-as-before. Children, more like, who might become us some day but still had a long way to go.'[12]

This brings us to the second observation: Bavinck disagrees entirely with this search for a gradation of existence. His logic is penetrating and clear: there is no humanity without culture, and the 'other' is not a window into a more 'primitive' humanity positioned at a lower 'grade' of existence. That these communities are deemed 'cultureless' and even 'wild' by some theorists misses the fact that, as would be discovered by non-prejudiced observation, religion and culture permeate them just as much as the so-called cultured societies.[13] As Bavinck wrote:

> The name itself is misleading; nature-people are nowhere to be found, any more than wild or cultureless peoples. The cultured peoples are no less dependent on nature than the so-called nature-peoples …. And wild or cultureless people do not exist either. The ridiculous fancies about men who formerly or even now clamber up into the trees like apes, covered over the whole of their bodies with hair, knowing nothing of fire, without language or religion, reappear, it is true, now and then; but they are antiquated. All men and peoples, though they may be poor in culture yet possess at least its fundamental elements: the erect walk, the average weight of the brain, the hand and the thumb, fire and light, language and religion, family and society.[14]

As he investigates the accounts of missions undertaken in South America, parts of Arabia, Australia, and the Arctic, what emerges is not an encounter, in Bavinck's judgment, with cultureless and atheistic communities but rather with

---

10. Bavinck, *Philosophy of Revelation*, p. 125.
11. Molendijk, *Emergence of the Science of Religion in the Netherlands*, p. 146.
12. Engelke, *How to Think Like an Anthropologist*, p. 66.
13. As it turns out, the language of 'evolution' is compatible with different accounts of the signs or ends of progress and development: 'Evolutionist schemes did not necessarily imply that religion was a superseded stage in human development, but could also be applied within the field of religion to demonstrate, for instance that "primitive" forms of religion … developed through various sorts of polytheism to the highest stage of monotheism.' Molendijk, *The Emergence of the Science of Religion in the Netherlands*, p. 147.
14. Bavinck, *Philosophy of Revelation*, p. 126.

a multiformity of cultures and religions.[15] The empirical evidence points not to a gradation between cultureless and cultured human civilizations, but to a common humanity existing across time and space, manifesting itself in different cultures.[16] In effect, Bavinck identifies in 1908 what anthropologist Johannes Fabian coins in the 1980s as the social evolutionary tendency to deny another people group's 'coevalness' with us – denying that the 'other' co-exists in the same time as one's own 'culture' or 'civilization'.[17]

Equally, Bavinck observes that superstition and all kinds of 'crimes and unnatural sins occur among the [so-called] culture-peoples no less, and sometimes in more aggravated forms, than among the [so-called] nature-peoples'.[18] The doctrine of sin does not mean that the restoration of dignity to the peoples of the past should be identified with the 'idyllic fashion of the age of Rousseau', but that there is a fundamental continuity of culture and brutishness, religiosity and evil, that spans all humanity: 'the notion that all peoples are on the road to progress is as incorrect as that they are continuously declining and degenerating. Neither development nor degeneracy covers the course of history.'[19] The deployment of evolutionary language to describe the history of humanity fails to recognize the pluriformity of human existence across time.

The upshot is that one should consider the history of humanity not as a linear development but as a process of cultural diversification, 'side by side', as it were. This principle is re-invoked here as it was in Bavinck's previous chapter on history. He writes, 'The peoples cannot, therefore, be arranged in succession, one after the other.'[20] Civilization, culture, sin, and evil are not phases that occur one-after-another, but rather always co-exist *side by side*. The key passage where Bavinck makes this point is as follows:

> It is arbitrary to place the nature-peoples at the beginning of the genealogical table of the human race and to represent their condition as the original condition of mankind. The theory of development … is just as one-sided as the theory of degeneracy. History declines to follow in its course a single straight line. Every people and every group of peoples, spread over the globe, has its own life and continues in the midst of the others. We must return from the 'after-one-another' to the 'by-the-side-of-one-another', from uniformity to multiformity, from the abstract theory of monism to the fullness of life.[21]

15. Bavinck, *Philosophy of Revelation*, p. 127. Bavinck points to the work of James Orr, specifically *God's Image in Man and Its Defacement in the Light of Modern Denials* (London: Hodder & Stoughton, 1906), pp. 163ff.

16. 'The facts already adverted to as to the high character of early civilization are adverse to the theory of the slow evolutionary origin and original brutishness of man.' See Orr, *God's Image in Man*, p. 186.

17. Johannes Fabian, *Time and the Other: How Anthropology Makes Its Object* (New York: Columbia University Press, 1983).

18. Bavinck, *Philosophy of Revelation*, p. 127.

19. Bavinck, *Philosophy of Revelation*, p. 128.

20. Bavinck, *Philosophy of Revelation*, p. 128.

21. Bavinck, *Philosophy of Revelation*, pp. 128–9.

Bavinck's alternative, then, is to reject entirely the empirical project of finding a point in time at which religion originates. Not only does such a project go beyond the bounds of our empirical data, it also jeopardizes the fundamental unity of human nature across history. Religion is not something that emerged from primordially 'nonreligious factors', and even if one could find a point at which religion did arise, then to offer an explanation of religion in terms of that nonreligious factor (whether in one's biology, historical circumstances or upbringing) would be to commit the fallacy of *'metabasis eis allo genos'*.[22] The fallacy has to do with 'a change to another genus', that is, of transposing falsely between what is true in one area (biology), as if it were true in another (culture or religion), and hence equivocating. Just because developmental processes are observed in biology, it does not follow that language of 'evolution' can be applied to society, history, or religion.

Bavinck is then arguing that one has to begin with a theory of human nature: if human nature is fundamentally non-religious and brutish, then religion is inexplicable, reducible to something physical (and hence not religious at all).[23] If, however, one begins from the position that human nature is irreducibly religious, as Bavinck does, then religious experience, expression, and formation arise spontaneously across all human beings.

Revelation and Religion

It is precisely this point in Bavinck's reasoning that harkens back to the material covered in the earlier chapters of this book on the religious self. The emergence of religions across the human race is best explained, in Bavinck's judgment, by an appeal to the innate religiosity of human nature. Human beings are 'hardwired' for religion, predisposed to form theistic beliefs and affectively oriented toward moral action and worship of the divine. He writes: 'Openly or secretly, all turn back to an inborn disposition, to a *religio insita*.'[24] Scientists of religion, like Tiele, who disavow an immediate appeal to Christianity or revelation would refer to this inborn disposition by differing names, but the concept remains the same: a 'divine spark', an 'inborn feeling and need of the infinite', and 'an inborn quality of man'. In

---

22. Bavinck, *Philosophy of Revelation*, p. 132.

23. Bavinck cites Troeltsch (*Philosophy of Revelation*, p. 132) to support his point: religion's cause 'is entirely unknown to us … and just as in the case of morals and logic, will always remain unknown to us. An absolute generation [of religion] is denied to us'. Ernst Troeltsch, 'Die Christliche Religion: Mit einschluss der Israelitsch-Jüdischen Religion', in *Die Kultur der Gegenwart* I. VI. (Leipzig: Teubner, 1905), p. 483. German original: 'das ist uns völlig unbekannt und wird wie bei Moral und Logik uns immer unbekannt bleiben. Eine vollige Urzeugung ist uns versagt'.

24. Bavinck, *Philosophy of Revelation*, p. 132.

each case, an appeal to the innate religiosity of human consciousness is made.[25] As Molendijk notes, 'Without using the term, Tiele presupposed a religious a priori'.[26] For Bavinck, then, human nature itself explains the rise of religion.

The question of a religious disposition in human nature, however, brings into view the question of the reality of revelation: does that disposition produce mere phantasms, or does it respond to an irreducibly divine reality? Bavinck notes the seriousness of this question: 'We stand here before essentially the same dilemma as in the case of self-consciousness (*zelfbewustzein*). If this is not a delusion or imagination, the reality of the self is necessarily included in it; hence religion is either a pathology of the human spirit, or it postulates the existence, the revelation, and the knowableness of God.'[27] Does the phenomenon of religion point to the veracity of Calvin's dictum that the knowledge of self (self-consciousness) is inseparable from the knowledge of God? In Bavinck's judgment, if religion points us to the created human disposition to desire the divine, indicating our capacity to respond to creational revelation, and 'what is unknown none desires', then one must answer in the affirmative: 'religion has its foundation in revelation and derives from its origin.'[28]

This grounding of religion in human nature and, further, in humanity's response to a general revelation from God allows Bavinck to describe non-Christian religions in relatively humane ways. Rather than describing these religions in terms of savagery, primitiveness, or as fundamentally less developed than (Western forms of) Christianity, Bavinck argues that 'Certain it is that all religions, in harmony with their own idea, rest upon conscious and spontaneous revelation of God. This is confirmed by the consideration of what humanity seeks in religion.'[29] Sure enough, the religions interpret this revelation 'in harmony with their own idea', but virtually all religions are expressions of the general human reception of divine revelation. This means both that Christianity has much in common with other religions and that other religions ought to be treated with open-minded attentiveness, for they, too, are responding to revelation. If 'revelation is the foundation (*fundament*) of all religion, the presupposition of all its conceptions, emotions, and actions', then it will not suffice to measure religions according to a gradation.[30] Bavinck notes that such gradations 'suffer … from excessive one-sidedness; they ignore other elements, do no justice to the richness and variety of religious life, and all proceed tacitly from the Hegelian notion that the chapters which successively treat of the several religions represent so many

---

25. Bavinck, *Philosophy of Revelation*, p. 132, citing Tiele, *Inleiding tot de godsdienstwetenschap*, II: pp. 108, 202, 204.
26. Molendijk, *The Emergence of the Science of Religion in the Netherlands*, pp. 101–2.
27. Bavinck, *Philosophy of Revelation*, p. 133.
28. Bavinck, *Philosophy of Revelation*, p. 133.
29. Bavinck, *Philosophy of Revelation*, p. 135.
30. Bavinck, *Philosophy of Revelation*, p. 138.

steps in the development of religion'.³¹ If each religion is the result of an affective reception of revelation, however, a developmental gradation of each religion is rendered untenable.

To be sure, Bavinck will argue in the next chapter of his work for the necessity of God's Word (i.e., of special revelation) to appropriately respond to creational revelation.³² But by construing other world religions as a response to creational revelation, he recognizes that the religions stand on the same ground, putting them on an equal footing. Every religion is a response to creational revelation, and religions are all concerned with the idea of 'redemption', and specifically of 'redemption from an evil and the attainment of a supreme good', and each religion locates that redemption or evil in some notion of the divine or in some aspect of creation itself.³³ In the *Dogmatics*, Bavinck argues that in 'general revelation, Christians have a firm foundation on which they can meet all non-Christians', as general revelation provides a 'point of contact'.³⁴ Recently, Joshua Ralston has observed that this led Bavinck to treat other religions – especially Islam – with more nuance than his predecessors (including Calvin, Turretin, and Schleiermacher) in Reformed theology:

> Bavinck shows the most interest in Islam and a seeming awareness, however inchoate, of the internal debates and traditions within Islamic thought and practice …. In addition Bavinck also occasionally references Islam, Muslim piety, and Muhammad … [including] arguments that show a more advanced theological understanding of Islamic thought than any other major Reformed dogmatic theology (an admittedly low bar, but significant nonetheless).³⁵

Bavinck, therefore, demonstrated greater sensitivity in describing the nature of the religious 'other'. Ralston continues to describe Bavinck's critique of the developmental account of religion in the *Dogmatics*:

> [H]e avers that the evolutionary accounts of religion that view religion as a progression from more local and 'primitive' to more advanced depend on an assumption of the 'idea of God' at the beginning of human and religious development. That is to say, Bavinck both critiques scientific studies of religion, but also allows their views to serve as an impetus for him to interrogate Christian

---

31. Bavinck, *Philosophy of Revelation*, p. 138. Cf. G. W. F. Hegel, *Lectures on the Philosophy of Religion: One Volume Edition – The Lectures of 1827*, Peter C. Hodgson (ed.) (Oakland: University of California Press, 1988).

32. As Bavinck would often refrain: 'General revelation leads to special revelation, and special revelation points back to general revelation. The one calls for the other, and without it remains imperfect and unintelligible.' *Philosophy of Revelation*, p. 25.

33. Bavinck, *Philosophy of Revelation*, p. 136.

34. Bavinck, *RD* 1: p. 321.

35. Joshua Ralston, 'Islam as Christian Trope: The Place and Function of Islam in Reformed Dogmatic Theology', *Muslim World* 107 (2017): p. 768.

notions of the divine Logos and general revelation to rethink other religions in a more nuanced way.[36]

Ralston observes that this generous doctrine of general revelation was precisely the resource behind Bavinck's more nuanced treatment of the Prophet Muhammad and of the rise of Islam. Bavinck argued that, owing to the universal human reception of creational revelation, there are always 'elements of truth' present in non-Christian religions, and as such, Muhammad and other religious authorities cannot be reduced into mere enemies of God.[37] Ralston writes,

> Thus, Bavinck would appear to be arguing that Muhammad, and by extension the Qur'an, is not wholly divorced from divine revelation. It is not special revelation, let alone the Word of God in the sense that Muslims understand it to be, but it is a human response to general revelation.[38]

Another doctrine should also be mentioned alongside general revelation to account for Bavinck's nuanced description of Islam noted by Ralston here. That general revelation is accessed, however imperfectly, by human beings is by virtue of the generosity of God in common grace to humanity universally. This non-salvific grace allows sinners access to creational gifts, as Bavinck himself observes: 'In this doctrine of *gratia communis*, the Reformed maintained the particular and absolute character of the Christian religion on the one hand, while on the

---

36. Ralston, 'Islam as Christian Trope', p. 769. It is noteworthy that Jennings describes a similar resource for a more hospitable treatment of local religions (though inconsistently followed by the sixteenth-century Spanish priest, Bartolomé de las Casas): '(1) all peoples operate out of some knowledge of God, even if little or confused; (2) all people are led to worship God by their capacities and cultural ways; (3) the highest way to worship God is through sacrifice; and (4) sacrifice, no matter under what custom, is always offered to the true God as that god is understood by the native peoples' (Jennings, *Christian Imagination*, p. 100). For Jennings, these convictions may help in allowing missiologists to treat 'cultural particularities' seriously, recognizing 'indigenous cultural prescription' for their own theological reasoning. (Jennings, *Christian Imagination*, pp. 147–8) The neo-Calvinist tradition, more broadly considered, would agree with these observations as they dovetail well with an emphasis on the organic emergence of associational structures and their religious directions. See, e.g., Richard Mouw and Sander Griffoen, *Pluralisms and Horizons: An Essay in Christian Public Philosophy* (Grand Rapids: Eerdmans, 1993).

37. Bavinck, *RD* 1: p. 318. In another place, Bavinck would write, 'We can no longer be satisfied with the old formulas and ideas. It is no longer possible to declare that Buddha, Zoroaster, and Muhammad are simply deceivers and instruments of Satan. Psychology and the philosophy of history have brought significant changes in our ideas.' 'Theology and Religious Studies', in John Bolt (ed.), Harry Boonstra and Gerrit Sheeres (trans.), *Essays on Religion, Science, and Society*, p. 55.

38. Ralston, 'Islam as Christian Trope', p. 769. Cf. Matthew Kaemingk, *Christian Hospitality and Muslim Immigration* (Grand Rapids: Eerdmans, 2018).

other they were second to none in appreciating all that God continued to give of beauty and worth to sinful men.'³⁹ The key point is that Bavinck's conviction of the intrinsically religious character of human nature grounds his critique of the gradation of humanity and the development of religion. Again, Bavinck appeals to traditional Christian resources to dispute the emergence of racial and cultural superiority in the modern age. To link this chapter on religion in *Philosophy of Revelation* to his earlier chapter on history, Bavinck argues that it is by retrieving older accounts of God's transcendence and human nature, along with the doctrine of common grace, that one can be guarded from racist ideas.[40]

'Humanity in Its Entirety': Human Diversity in Creation, Fall, Redemption, and Consummation

This section deepens our grasp of Bavinck's account of human nature by sketching his enfolding of cultural diversity into his corporate doctrine of the image of God throughout the *Dogmatics*. This means revisiting Bavinck's account of the telos of the human organism in creation, reckoning with his acceptance of societal sin, and observing the pluriform catholicity of the church in redemption and consummation.

Creation

Bavinck begins his discussion of the unity of the human race in the *Dogmatics* in a way that anticipates his later reflections on the origins of racism. 'The unity of the human race', he writes, 'is a certainty in holy Scripture (Gen. 1:26; 6:3; 10:32; Matt. 19:4; Acts 17:26; Rom. 5:12ff; 1 Cor. 15:f., 45f.) but has almost never been acknowledged by the peoples who lived outside the circle of [special] revelation'.[41] The scriptural texts cited indicate the common creation of humanity and thus the sharing of a common human nature as image-bearers. Bavinck goes on to chronicle the construction of divisions by various philosophies throughout history, from the Greeks who 'looked down on "Barbarians"', through the Indian caste system and the idea of social evolution, to the 'defense of slavery' by many in the

---

39. Herman Bavinck, 'Common Grace' p. 52. The epistemic and theological relationship between common grace, general and special revelation, however, has been explored in depth elsewhere and is not my primary concern here. See Sutanto, *God and Knowledge*.

40. It is precisely these ideas that feed into Johan Bavinck's later missiological reflections that prioritize the twin aims of preserving indigenous cultures while maintaining Christological proclamation, which improved Bavinck's thoughts on missions in important respects. See James Eglinton, 'Planting Tulips in the Rainforest: Herman and Johan Bavinck on Christianity in East and West', *Journal of Biblical and Theological Studies* 6 (2021): pp. 277–92; Daniel Strange, *Their Rock Is Not Like Our Rock: A Theology of Religions* (Grand Rapids: Zondervan, 2015).

41. Bavinck, *RD* 2: p. 523.

eighteenth century.⁴² Such racist constructions betray a forgetfulness concerning the fundamental unity of human nature.

Bavinck acknowledges that the 'existence of various peoples and races within humanity is most certainly an important issue', bringing into view real differences between ideas, customs, and religion.⁴³ The differences between the peoples are not understood in essentialist terms (as if the different peoples and their cultures were pre-determined by some natural or biological reason that distinguished one people group from another). Rather, the differences are the result of geographical and linguistic dispersion. The tower of Babel narrative of Genesis 11 indicates for Bavinck that these differences stem out of a former unity, and God himself is the one who introduces the differences through 'a single act ... by which he intervened in the development of humanity'.⁴⁴ Again, the origins of difference lie in the geographical dispersion of humanity, as the 'more people live in isolation, the more language differences increase. The confusion of languages is the result of confusion in ideas, in mind, and in life.'⁴⁵ In the fourth volume of the *Dogmatics* (to be explored further below), Bavinck would return to the Babel narrative to show that this introduction of human differences cannot be reduced to a mere curse, but must also be construed as a blessing designed to further the mandate to be fruitful and multiply. In this section on human origins, however, Bavinck merely makes the point that the unity of the human race is preserved despite Babel: 'however great the difference between the races may be, upon deeper investigation the unity and kinship of all people nevertheless emerge all the more clearly'.⁴⁶ While Bavinck betrays a nineteenth-century preoccupation with the biological features of the different peoples, he still concludes that the physical differences among the peoples are rather superficial, and, importantly, he insists that the aptitude of humanity for culture and religion remains stable across the cultures:

> [I]n intellectual, religious, moral, social, and political respects, human beings have a wide range of things in common: language, intellect, reason, memory, knowledge of God, conscience, sense of sin, repentance, sacrifice, fasting, prayer, traditions about a golden age, a flood, and so forth. The unity of the human race, as Scripture teaches, is powerfully confirmed by all this. It is finally, not a matter of indifference, as is sometimes claimed, but on the contrary of the utmost importance: it is the presupposition of religion and morality.⁴⁷

If nature precedes grace and grace restores nature, then it is precisely the natural unity of humankind that is presupposed by the Christian teachings on the 'atonement in Christ, the universality of the kingdom of God, the catholicity

---

42. Bavinck, *RD* 2: pp. 523–4.
43. Bavinck, *RD* 2: p. 525.
44. Bavinck, *RD* 2: p. 525.
45. Bavinck, *RD* 2: p. 525.
46. Bavinck, *RD* 2: p. 526.
47. Bavinck, *RD* 2: p. 526.

of the church, and the love of neighbor – these all are grounded in the unity of humankind'.[48] God's renewal, which regenerates sinners and transfers them into the kingdom of God, consists not in a transition from one form of humanity to another, but is a restoration and consummation of original humanity. In other words, the catholicity and pluriformity of the church are not mechanical appendages or forced additions to an otherwise uniform or cacophonous humanity, but rather restore and elevate humanity to its original telos and design. These teachings on creation are key for understanding why it is that the church too will conform to a shape of unity-in-diversity.

It is on the section on human destiny that Bavinck returns to the telos of humanity, harkening back to the observations in previous chapters on the organism of humanity and the covenantal make-up of human beings. If human beings constitute an organic whole, then what is in view is the destiny of a fully developed organism:

> Not as a heap of souls on a tract of land, not as a loose aggregate of individuals, but as having been created out of one blood; as one household and one family, humanity is the image and likeness of God. Belonging to that humanity is also its developments, its history, its ever-expanding dominion over the earth, its progress in science and arts, its subjugation of all creatures. All these things as well constitute the unfolding of the image and likeness of God in keeping with which humanity was created. Just as God did not reveal himself all at once at the creation, but continues and expands that revelation from day to day and from age to age, so also the image of God is not a static entity but extends and unfolds itself in the forms of space and time. It is both a gift (*Gabe*) and a mandate (*Aufgabe*).[49]

Hence, Bavinck speaks about 'humanity in its entirety – as one complete organism', spreading across the whole earth, imaging God as earth's prophet, priest, and king.[50] The path of human development and the consummate end for which it is created reflects the triune God's infinite richness, as human beings disperse throughout space and time. Human sin may distort the harmonious unity-in-diversity for which God has created humanity, 'but by the last Adam, and his re-creating grace they are all the more resplendently restored to their destiny. The state of integrity – either through the fall or apart from the fall – is a preparation of the state of glory in which God will impart his glory to all he creates and be "all in all" [1 Cor. 15:28]'.[51] While Adam failed to confer righteousness and glory to his progeny, Christ, the second Adam, is the head of a new, restored, and eventually consummated humanity.

48. Bavinck, *RD* 2: p. 526.
49. Bavinck, *RD* 2: p. 577. The language of gift and mandate again connects Bavinck conceptually to the *Bildung* tradition of conceiving human formation as a collective task.
50. Bavinck, *RD* 2: p. 577.
51. Bavinck, *RD* 2: p. 588.

Sin – Individual and Social

In Volume 3 of the *Dogmatics*, Bavinck speaks of sin's effects on that original unity. If the image of God refers not merely to individuals but also to corporate humanity, then actual sin takes not only individual but also social forms. As individuals act sinfully, habits of sin are perpetuated; and as each individual's sinful habits develop, others are impacted and corrupted. Bavinck writes: 'Just as a sinful deed, when repeated over and over, fosters a habitual propensity … so sinful mores and habits can also reinforce an innate depravity in a family, among relatives in a family line, or among a people and develop it in a certain direction.'[52] Sin is too complex to be reduced to isolated acts, and Bavinck's corporate account of the image of God produces a more granular picture of sin's perpetuation and effects. Bavinck envisions sin's effects to that of the spread of a disease – from individuals, to the family, to the nations, and from generation to generation. Sin ought not be spoken of merely in the abstract, but has concrete manifestations in each 'line'. The key passage from Bavinck runs as follows:

> that special modification [within a family] of innate depravity often passes from parents to children, from one generation to the next. Human beings are not individuals in an absolute sense … A human being is born from the matrix of a community and from that very moment lives in a certain circle, situation, and period. The immediate and the larger family, society, nation, climate, lifestyle, culture, the spirit of the age, and so on – all of them together impact the individual person and modify his or her innate moral depravity. Sin, therefore, though it is indeed always essentially the same, manifests itself in differing ways and forms in different persons, families, classes, and nations and in different states and times. Also, as a sinner each person has his or her own physiognomy. Sins in the East differ from those in the West, in tropical zones from temperate zones, in rural areas from cities, in civilized states from uncivilized ones, in the twentieth century from earlier centuries. There are family sins, societal sins, and national sins. Statistics show that in certain situations, periods, and circles there is horrifying regularity in the incidence of certain moral offenses such as homicide, suicide, illegitimate births, and so on. In every area of life, we are all subject to the influence of bad habits and sinful examples, of the zeitgeist and public opinion. Aside from what we call original sin, there is also corporate guilt and the corporate action of sin.[53]

Sin is not abstract but takes concrete forms. Each personality is inclined to different sorts of sins, and that, in turn, means that different communities may

---

52. Bavinck, *RD* 3: p. 175.
53. Bavinck, *RD* 3: p. 175. On systemic sin in the Bible, see D. T. Everhart, 'Communal Reconciliation: Corporate Responsibility and Opposition to Systemic Sin', *International Journal of Systematic Theology* (Early View, 2022): pp. 1–23. Cf. Bavinck, *Guidebook*, pp. 90–2.

exemplify differing sinful tendencies. In short: 'As people are interconnected, so also are their sinful inclinations and deeds. Penetrating the infinite riches of all creation, sin also forms a realm that, animated by a single life principle, organizes itself in multiple forms and appearances.'[54] Bavinck cites Schleiermacher's *Christian Faith* §71–2 at this juncture.[55] He has in view Schleiermacher's account of how individuals are corrupted by originated sin, which informs Bavinck's social account of sin's effects. After Bavinck's presentation of this organic account of the imputation of Adam's sin, he was keen to maintain the balance between communal guilt – which acknowledges the reality of inherited sin as a law and reality – and the individual guilt that accrues from actual sin. Here, Bavinck appeals to Schleiermacher, agreeing that humanity is caught up in one another's guilt:

> It is … completely true that we can never with complete accuracy indicate the boundaries that separate personal guilt from communal guilt. What Schleiermacher says of original sin is something very different from what Scripture and the church say concerning it, but by itself is completely true of sin in general that it is the collective deed and collective guilt of the human race as a whole. In other words, the sinful state and sinful deeds of each individual are, on the one hand, conditioned by those of the previous generation, and, on the other, they in turn condition the sinful state and acts of later descendants. Sin is "in each the work of all and in all the work of each".[56]

Bavinck thus accepts an account of collective sin, which prompts an analysis of concrete manifestations of systemic sins in families, nations, and cultures across time. The pluriform diversity of the peoples, meant to signify analogically the infinite riches of God's being, becomes a cacophony of sinful patterns in conflicting directions. This corporate manifestation of sin bestows sin with a cosmic sense. Sin is mysterious and ever-present, leading philosophers like Schelling – Bavinck notes – to conclude that 'the irrational, the darkness, the chaotic' is that which is 'fundamental to everything'.[57] As each locus in space and time bears a distinct sinful pattern, so does suffering take on particularities: 'A stream of spiritual and physical misery in individual persons, families, generations, and nations, in state, church, society, science, and art has its origin in sin.'[58] These observations correspond to Bavinck's description of the work of redemption, which must also be recognized concretely, as God sanctifies sinners in ways that correspond to their distinct personalities and sinfulness.

---

54. Bavinck, *RD* 3: pp. 175–6.
55. Friedrich Schleiermacher, *CF*, §71–2. See also Derek R. Nelson, *What's Wrong with Sin: Sin in Individual and Social Perspective from Schleiermacher to Theologies of Liberation* (London: T&T Clark, 2009).
56. Bavinck, *RD* 3: p. 116, quoting Schleiermacher, *CF*, §71.1.
57. Bavinck, *RD* 3: p. 177.
58. Bavinck, *RD* 3: p. 179. See also similar comments in Johan Bavinck, *Between the Beginning and the End: A Radical Kingdom Vision* (Grand Rapids: Eerdmans, 2014), p. 60.

Redemption and Consummation

Regenerated humanity is restored natural humanity. Regeneration recreates new individuals, unites them to a new federal head in Christ, and thus forms a new humanity, the church. The church, too, is an organic unity, developing across space and time. Bavinck expounds on these themes on the corporate and historical account of the church from his earlier to his more mature works.[59]

The church anticipates the eschatological manifestation of the kingdom of God, where God's rule will be made manifest in the union of the new heavens and the new earth. This eschatological vision is the consummation of creation's original trajectory. Originally, 'the notion of a Kingdom of God that fosters the development of both individual and community, that is both the content and goal of world history, encompassing the whole earth and all nations' was the destiny of humanity, as it obeys God throughout the earth.[60] Now, after the fall, the church witnesses to this Kingdom. While the church is not synonymous with God's kingdom, it signals the eventual consummation of that kingdom – a future wherein God's rule is fully realized and Christ returns. Bavinck writes: 'Apart from sin, the Kingdom of God would have existed among humanity from the very beginning and would have developed completely normally. Through sin, the Kingdom of God was disrupted, the various goods contained in the Kingdom were torn asunder', and so 'the Kingdom of God is a Kingdom that does not yet exist fully but is coming into fuller existence'.[61] It is the 'unity, the inclusion, the totality of all moral goods, of earthly and heavenly, spiritual and physical, eternal and temporal goods', of which the church is one constituent part.[62] This unity and diversity motif of the Kingdom signals its organic character: 'the unity of an organism becomes the more harmonious, the more rich, and the more glorious to the degree that the multitude of parts increases'.[63] The eschatological Kingdom is the unity-and-diversity of humanity in its consummate, sinless form.

The fullness of the Kingdom is witnessed to in the church's geographic and temporal locations now, and finally manifested in glorified humanity:

> Viewing nothing human as foreign but as spiritual in nature, the Kingdom of God is universal, bound to no place or time, embracing the whole earth and everything human, independent of nation and country, of nationality and race, of language and culture. In Christ Jesus what is legitimate is only what has been created anew, with no exceptions. This is why the gospel of the Kingdom must

---

59. I draw from his 'Kingdom of God, the Highest Good' (1881), his 'Catholicity of Christianity and the Church' (1888), his *Dogmatics*, then, finally from his *Guidebook on the Christian Religion* (1913).
60. Herman Bavinck, 'The Kingdom of God, the Highest Good' (Nelson Kloosterman, trans.); *The Bavinck Review* 2 (2011): p. 136. Hereafter, *KGHG*.
61. Bavinck, *KGHG*, p. 146.
62. Bavinck, *KGHG*, p. 141.
63. Bavinck, *KGHG*, p. 144.

be brought to all nations, to all creatures, not only to people but to the entire creation (Mark 16:15). The Kingdom of God extends as far as Christianity itself.[64]

That first clause on the Kingdom of God 'viewing nothing as foreign' foreshadows Bavinck's emphasis in his 1888 address on catholicity. If the kingdom of God is only against sin, and not nature as such, then the entrance of Christianity into a particular culture or nation means that the particularities of that culture or nation can be preserved. Each culture can be leavened by the transformative powers of the Spirit, and can signal a final day in which cultural and national pluriformity will characterize the kingdom.[65] Pre-empting Jennings' emphases, Bavinck depicts the influence of Christian faith as culture-preserving, as the Kingdom takes up the 'cultural particularities' of each nation.[66]

Indeed, Bavinck's 1888 address included extensive discussions on the *leavening* power of Christianity as part of its catholicity. Christianity, precisely because it is not tethered to a particular nation, culture, or perennial *Sitz im Leben*, has the capacity to embrace and leaven any culture with which it comes into contact, thereby maintaining multiformity. In Bavinck's words, Christianity 'can enter into all situations, can connect with all forms of natural life, is suitable to every time, and beneficial for all things, and is relevant in all circumstances. It is free and independent because it is in conflict only with sin and in the blood of the Cross there is purification for every sin.'[67] In this last claim, Bavinck is echoing his oft-quoted axiom that Protestantism 'traded the quantitative antithesis of the natural and the supernatural for the qualitative, ethical antithesis of sin and grace.'[68] Christianity is only against sin, not culture as such.

If this is the case, then the catholicity of the church is best expressed not *in spite* of diversity but precisely *in* diversity. Catholicity consists not in mechanical uniformity but in a 'richness', a 'many-sidedness', and in 'pluriformity'.[69] Continuing with the idea that Christianity is a world religion and thus for every time and place, Bavinck argues for the inherent desirability of confessional and international diversity in the church on distinctly Reformed grounds in this way:

---

64. Bavinck, *KGHG*, p. 148.
65. Bavinck writes: 'the history of the nations and of their states finds its principal idea and explanation to be the Kingdom of Heaven'. *KGHG*, p. 163.
66. Jennings, *Christian Imagination*, p. 147.
67. Bavinck, 'Catholicity of Christianity', p. 249. Bavinck's understanding of common grace and the universal character of the Christian vocation also ground these claims. See especially his 'Calvin and Common Grace', in *Calvin and the Reformation: Four Studies*, William Park Armstrong (ed.) (New York: Fleming Revell Co., 1909), pp. 99–130. '[Calvin's] ethics is diametrically opposed to all asceticism, it is catholic and universal in scope,' in 'Calvin and Common Grace', p. 128.
68. Bavinck, *RD* 4: p. 410. Cf. James Eglinton, *Trinity and Organism: Toward a New Reading of Herman Bavinck's Organic Motif* (London: T&T Clark, 2012), pp. 40–1, 96.
69. Bavinck, 'Catholicity of Christianity', p. 250.

That church is most catholic that most clearly expresses in its confession and applies in its practice this international and cosmopolitan character of the Christian religion. The Reformed had an eye for it when in various countries and churches they confessed the truth in an indigenous, free, and independent manner and at the Synod of Dort invited delegates from all over Reformed Christianity.[70]

Reformed theology wishes for no uniformity, and the diverse confessions of the Reformed tradition witness to its catholic commitments. This means that Christian theologians should not expect that the Christian expression of one culture should be replicated or repeated by another: American Christianity is not Dutch Christianity, or German Christianity, for example. As Harinck aptly comments, Bavinck was committed to a kind of 'cultural relativism'.[71] While Bavinck may not use the same terms as Jennings, who envisions a sort of pluriformity of the church that recognizes 'Christianities and various visions of orthodoxy', Bavinck certainly recognizes the inevitability and goodness of various cultures expressing Christian faith according to their own language and ideas.[72]

The diversity of cultures and nations thus does not pose a threat but rather represents an asset to the kingdom of God, and will find its culmination in consummation: 'Tribes, peoples, and nations will make their own particular contribution to the enrichment of life in the new Jerusalem …. The great diversity that exist in all sorts of ways is not destroyed in eternity but is cleansed from all that is sinful and made serviceable to fellowship with God and each other.'[73] In a way that directly contradicts the monolingual vision of the eschaton in the *Leiden Synopsis*,[74] Bavinck argues that multi-lingualism was the teleological intention of the divine command to be 'fruitful and multiply' and was thus consummated in the final state. Revisiting the tower of Babel narrative in the fourth volume of the *Dogmatics*, Bavinck argues that diversity was the goal before the fall, was initiated

---

70. Bavinck, *RD* 4: p. 323.
71. George Harinck, 'Calvinism Isn't the Only Truth: Herman Bavinck's Impressions of the USA', in *The Sesquicentennial of Dutch Immigration: 150 Years of Ethnic Heritage; Proceedings of the 11th Biennial Conference of the Association for the Advancement of Dutch American Studies*, Larry J. Wagenaar and Robert P. Swierenga (eds) (Holland: The Joint Archives of Holland, Hope College, 1998), pp. 151–60, 154.
72. Jennings, *Christian Imagination*, p. 114. For more on Bavinck on cultural pluralism and catholicity, see Brock and Sutanto, *Neo-Calvinism*, chapter 3.
73. Bavinck, *RD* 4: p. 72.
74. The Leiden Synopsis states: 'It is not as clear as to which language the blessed will use, although it is certain that the variety of languages – which is a consequence of sin – will cease there, according to the apostle (1 Cor. 13:18 [*sic*]). Hence some also draw the not improbable conclusion that the use of the Hebrew language will remain, because it is not a consequence of sin, and because Christ when he spoke to Paul from heaven even though the latter was originally Greek, used the Hebrew language, as the apostle explicitly observes in Acts 26:14.' *Leiden Synopsis*, 3: p. 609.

again by God in Babel, and was finally re-affirmed in Pentecost and consummated in eternity:

> In unity God loves the diversity. Among all creatures there was diversity even when as yet there was no sin. As a result of sin that diversity has been perverted and corrupted, but diversity as such is good and important also for the church. Difference in sex and age, in character and disposition, in mind and heart, in gifts and goods, in time and place is to the advantage also of the truth that is in Christ. He takes all these differences into his service and adorns the church with them. Indeed, though the division of humanity into peoples and languages was occasioned by sin, it has something good in it, which is brought into the church and thus preserved for eternity. From many races and languages and peoples and nations Christ gathers his church on earth.[75]

These patterns of reasoning on the unity and diversity of consummated humanity inform Bavinck's comments in his *Guidebook on Christian Religion*. There, Bavinck crystallizes all of these ideas succinctly, especially in its chapters on the church and the consummation of the world. On the church, Bavinck argues that God gifts his Spirit so that the 'fellowship that unites believers together' emerges, and states: 'He [God] does not hand [these blessings] out to a few isolated individuals but to a large number of people, who from the beginning forms a historical continuity, an organic whole'.[76] If there was a 'close connection between ethnic unity (*volkseenheid*) and the religious community' in the old covenantal administration of Israel, Pentecost 'freed [the church] from every national bond and organized them into their own community, independent from nation (*volk*) and country (*land*) in the midst of the world'.[77] This does not mean that cultural particularities are now rendered unimportant, but that the gospel is 'suitable and necessary for all people, in all times, in all circumstances, and in all situations'.[78] Catholicity means that there is not merely 'one denomination', but instead there is 'the Christian congregation in which all churches together, in different degrees of purity, come to

---

75. Bavinck, *RD* 4: p. 318. See also James Eglinton, 'From Babel to Pentecost via Paris and Amsterdam: Multilingualism in Neo-Calvinist and Revolutionary Thought', in *Neo-Calvinism and the French Revolution*, George Harinck and James Eglinton (eds) (London: Bloomsbury T&T Clark, 2014), pp. 31–60. Liou similarly observes: 'Scripture repeatedly uses the phrase "wealth of nations" and related ideas … The usages refer to material *and* cultural wealth of distinct cultures and nations beyond Israel. In Scripture, their diverse cultural productions are made pleasing to God,' in 'Critical Race Theory', pp. 246–7. Cf. Richard Bauckham, *Theology of the Book of Revelation* (Cambridge: Cambridge University Press, 1993), pp. 132–5.
76. Bavinck, *Guidebook*, p. 161.
77. Bavinck, *Guidebook*, pp. 161–2.
78. Bavinck, *Guidebook*, p. 166.

revelation'.⁷⁹ This pluriformity of the church witnesses to the final manifestation of the kingdom of God, as Bavinck observes:

> In this consummated kingdom, diversity will be preserved in unity. There will be little and great (Rev. 22:12), first and last (Matt. 20:16); the distinctions between ethnicities (*geslacht*) and nations will remain; Israel and the nations (*volken*) will not be dissolved into one another, but each will hold their own place and task (Matt. 19:28; 25:32; Acts 3:19-21; Rom. 11:26); the nations (*volken*) that are saved will walk in the light of the new Jerusalem, and the kings of the earth will bring their glory and honor into it (Rev. 21:24; 22:2). Although all share in the same salvation, the same eternal life, and the same fellowship with God, yet there will be all sorts of differences among them in rank and position, in gift and calling, in glory and radiance.⁸⁰

This diversity does not eclipse true unity, and Bavinck maintains that the true end of humanity in its entirety is the vision of God: 'for all will see God's face and be like him (Matt. 5:8; John 3:2; Rev. 22:4); all will know as they are known (1 Cor. 13:12); and all will be prophets, priests, and kings'.⁸¹ This eschatological vision is not merely indicative of what is to come, but ought to inform the church's calling in the present moment.

Conclusion and Critical Considerations

Chapter 6 surveyed Bavinck's genealogical diagnosis of the origins of racism and denoted the significance of departing from classical theistic moorings as paving a way for racism. By seeking ethical norms no longer in the divine ideas but rather in the historically immanent, pan-Germanist philosophers and theologians located normativity in the Aryan race throughout history and in the German nation particularly. This is what I have in view when I referred to 'top-down' racism. On the other hand, a 'bottom-up' trajectory emerged in the positing of 'nature-peoples' as indicative of an original and primitive humanity out of which more civilized peoples evolved. If top-down racism identified one nation or people as the source of norms, bottom-up racism identified another nation as underdeveloped and primitive. Instead of recognizing the pluriformity of cultures as an inherent good, where each nation is depicted as responding to the general revelation of God, these nineteenth-century ideological movements that Bavinck critiqued depicted the peoples in terms of a gradation of existence – from less to more developed, from atheism to theism, from less cultured to more, and from the immoral (or amoral) to the moral and spiritually conscious.

---

79. Bavinck, *Guidebook*, p. 166.
80. Bavinck, *Guidebook*, p. 193.
81. Bavinck, *Guidebook*, p. 194.

I have suggested that Bavinck's rather prophetic critiques of the 'race-consciousness' of his day and his positive construal of corporate humanity are generative, and should be considered as a resource for critical reflection on the origins of Euro-centric racism and on human diversity. Of course, not all of Bavinck's particular comments should be carried over in contemporary discourse, despite how prescient he was at the turn of the twentieth century. Contemporary writers ought to develop his claims rather than merely repristinate them, and I offer two critical suggestions here.

First, while Bavinck recognizes that all peoples have their own culture, and what exists is not a historical or ethnic gradation between the primitive and the developed, there is in his work still, on some occasions, talk of 'higher' and 'lower' cultured societies.[82] While I have shown that such language was utilized precisely against the linear views of civilization that Bavinck found, and was thus deployed for the sake of argument against his interlocutors, contemporary discourse on matters of race and anthropology would do well in critically considering whether such usage leads to precisely the sort of gradationism that Bavinck himself was criticizing. It is thus unsurprising, as James Eglinton has noted, that despite Bavinck's account of corporate humanity, improvement over his contemporaries over the issue of race, and recognition of the distinction between ethnicity and culture, he inconsistently retained problematic comments related to cultural hierarchy and colonial policy.[83] Terms like 'culture' and 'civilization' are recognized now as being linked with decidedly colonialist origins, and while they do continue to have some limited usefulness (if only due to their ubiquity), one should guard against the smuggling in of new gradations by which to adjudicate upon the relationship between one community and another through the use of these terms. What emerges in the discipline of anthropology is the manifestation of plurality and difference. Thus, for example, the so-called hunter-gatherer community is not to be adjudicated on the basis of 'Western civilization' or the like but each ought to be described (and evaluated) on its own terms.[84]

This is not to succumb to pure relativism but rather to issue a call for a chastened use of critical reason, refusing to confuse one's localized intuitions with some higher universal, which is precisely Bavinck's point. This fortifies the arguments I offered earlier regarding Bavinck and affect theory – namely, that our intuitions are themselves culturally and temporally situated, and there is no access to a naked, universalized reason. Here, the diversity of the human cultures and intuitions manifests God's call for diversity within the corporate image of God. This chastening thus wards away not merely the more insidious kinds of racism that sees the other races as essentially lower and ripe for domination, but also the more benevolent forms that identify one's self or people as the savior-figure over

---

82. Bavinck, *Philosophy of Revelation*, p. 235.
83. Eglinton, 'Planting Tulips in Rainforests'.
84. Cf. Engelke, *How to Think Like an Anthropologist*; Eglinton, 'Planting Tulips in Rainforests'; Yadav, 'Religious Racial Formation Theory and Its Metaphysics'.

against the other, helping them along the way to see just what they are missing and moving them from a 'lower' life to a 'higher' one.

Second, while the appeal of Bavinck (and Herdt) to God's revelation is indeed a way to chasten projects of *Bildung* and is a potential guardrail against imperialism, that revelation still requires interpretation and is thus mediated by a community of scholars, who are localized themselves. One would thus do well not to suggest that one particular class, group, or, say, Dutch Reformed theologians, has unique or immediate access to that Word, and hence that they are the ones through whom one might exclusively hear revelation. Hence, while the setting aside of appeals to the transcendent leads to identifying one particular history as the source of normativity, the appeal to a transcendent revelation might itself risk conflating our *reception* of revelation with revelation itself (or, as a matter of colonialist history, one might conflate one's own localized culture with the Universal Good, or with the most developed phase of salvation history).[85] If divine revelation is to be an operative norming norm, the interpretive process requires not merely listening to one tradition, but is itself a catholic and ecumenical process that takes into account the global context of revelation's reception.[86] Developing a Christian worldview is more like constructing a map, and one needs investigators from every corner of the globe to form a reliable map, which itself is not to be confused with the reality which the map is approximating. Bavinck himself recognizes this, when he argues that Reformed theology is not co-extensive with Christianity, despite connoting that it is precisely through Reformed theology that the capaciousness of Christian faith might be best recognized.[87] In Bavinck's oft-cited words, after reflecting on the ways in which American Christianity differs from the Dutch: 'Calvinism', after all, 'is not the only truth!'[88]

However, these critical considerations from the vantage point of the contemporary outlook should not detract from the value of the genuine yet contextualized insights that Bavinck offers, remarkable as they are given that they come from 1904 to 1908. These reflections on humanity as a unity-in-diversity lead us to the topics of the final chapters: the telos of humanity as mediated by a federal head, and the implications of that representational principle for what Bavinck considers to be a 'Reformed' account of the beatific vision.

85. Klaas Schilder, a second generation neo-Calvinist, critiqued Kuyper's account of history and pluriformity along precisely these lines. Schilder strongly rejects identifying the course of human history with God's salvation history. See *The Klaas Schilder Reader*, George Harinck, Richard Mouw, and Marinus De Jong (eds) (Bellingham: Lexham Press, 2022), pp. 90–7, 281–8.

86. Andrew Ong, 'World Christianity', in *T&T Clark Handbook of Neo-Calvinism*, Nathaniel Gray Sutanto and Cory C. Brock (eds) (London: Bloomsbury T&T Clark, 2024), pp. 426–38.

87. Cf. Herman Bavinck, *What Is Christianity?*, Greg Parker (trans.) (Peabody: Hendricksen, 2022).

88. Herman Bavinck, 'My Journey to America: Appendix One', in Eglinton, *Bavinck*, p. 314.

Chapter 8

CONSUMMATION ANYWAY

I turn now to the corporate end of humanity in its organic unity in diversity: fellowship with God. Indeed, this logically follows from the observations already in place on the irreducibly religious nature of human beings as image-bearers. If humans are image-bearers, their natures inform them spiritually and physically, and also orient them toward forming religious cultures and ultimately toward fellowship with God as their ultimate end. As Bavinck writes, 'religion, the moral law, and man's final destiny are essentially the same ... a kingdom of God, a holy humanity, in which God is all in all'.[1] Humans are thus oriented from the very beginning for an everlasting fellowship with the God that they image. As religious creatures, consummation consists in a glorified existence where God and humanity are united in communion.

This chapter will consider how Bavinck envisions the means by which humans might obtain that consummate existence, and unfold Bavinck's logic of what has been called consummation anyway in a constructive fashion. Bavinck proposes a version of consummation anyway that, I suggest, evades some potential objections against the logic. In doing so, I show that Bavinck's view hinges on a deployment of the covenant idea (already explored in Chapter 5 on organic humanity) to ground the creator-creature relation in time. The rest of this chapter, then, moves in four steps. First, I establish the logic of consummation anyway by putting Bavinck's view in dialogue with what has come to be known as the incarnation anyway thesis. Second, I sketch a Bavinckian and Reformed account of the consummation anyway model that addresses certain challenges put forth by an incarnation anyway thesis. Third, then, I consider three potential objections against Bavinck's account of consummation anyway, the first two of which are inspired by a recent argument offered by James T. Turner, and a third which questions whether such a model compromises the Christo-centricism which Bavinck advances elsewhere.[2]

---

1. Bavinck, *RD* 2: pp. 577–8.
2. James T. Turner, 'Perfect Obedience, Perfect Love, and the (So-Called) Problem of Heavenly Freedom', in *Love, Divine and Human: Contemporary Essays in Systematic and Philosophical Theology*, Oliver Crisp, James M. Arcadi, and Jordan Wessseling (eds) (Bloomsbury: T&T Clark, 2019), pp. 239–57.

Incarnation or Consummation Anyway?

To illumine Bavinck's view, it is instructive to put him in dialogue with some recent work on the question of whether the incarnation would obtain in worlds without a fall. Arguments for the incarnation anyway thesis typically involve at least these two claims: (1) a state of eschatological glory that goes beyond nature for God's people was the intended goal of creation; and (2) Christ's incarnation, as the locus of the Son's mediation, is a necessary or essential means by which such eschatological consummation is achieved.[3] Hence, it is claimed, irrespective of humanity's fall into sin, the second person of the Trinity would have graciously become incarnate anyway in order that nature's telos could be fulfilled.

In a recent work, Marc Cortez continues this lively discussion by critically considering four separate objections or alternatives to incarnation anyway.[4] The first involves an argument from the Bible to the effect that the incarnation seems to be most linked to redemption, rather than creation and consummation. The second is what he calls 'Consummation Anyway', which argues that consummation without the fall could have been achieved apart from the incarnation. The third is the 'no consummation' view, according to which creation does not after all presuppose a teleological end of consummate greater glory. The fourth objection is the 'sin anyway' thesis, a kind of *felix culpa* argument according to which both consummation and incarnation presuppose the ordination of sin as a means by which God brings about greater good. After outlining the reasons given for these objections and alternatives, Cortez responds to each of them, concluding that none of these objections are conclusive in rejecting incarnation anyway.

Cortez offers a few reasons for adopting the incarnation anyway thesis as a fitting implication of his reading of 1 Cor. 15. In this generative Pauline passage, the contrast between the created body and the heavenly body is a contrast between the state of innocence (or protology) and the state of glory (eschatology). Moreover, there is a clear logical link between the two, as established in 1 Cor. 44b: *if* there is a natural, *then* there is a spiritual, namely, *if* there is a creational order, *then* there is an eschatological consummation that moves natural, created bodies, into heavenly, glorious bodies. Paul indicates that the one who bears the heavenly body is Christ, the life-giving Spirit (1 Cor. 15:45b). It follows that Jesus is the one through whom humanity would receive a heavenly, glorified existence.[5] Drawing also from the

---

3. Other than Marc Cortez's work, see also on the question of incarnation anyway: Marilyn McCord Adams, *Christ and Horrors: The Coherence of Christology* (Cambridge: University Press, 2006); Edwin Ch. van Driel, *Incarnation Anyway: Arguments for Supralapsarian Christology* (Oxford: University Press, 2008); Oliver Crisp, 'Incarnation without the Fall', *Journal of Reformed Theology* 10 no. 3 (2016): pp. 215–33; *Analyzing Doctrine: Toward a Systematic Theology* (Baylor University Press, 2019).

4. Marc Cortez, *Resourcing Theological Anthropology: A Constructive Account of Humanity in the Light of Christ* (Grand Rapids: Zondervan, 2017).

5. For an elaboration of this exegetical claim, see N. Gray Sutanto, 'Consummation Anyway: A Reformed Proposal', *Journal of Analytic Theology* 9 (2021): pp. 223–37.

recent work of Marilyn McCord Adams, Edwin Ch. van Driel, and Oliver Crisp,[6] he argues for incarnation anyway in three ways. First, the incarnation is the means by which all of creation is united to a single head; second, Christ is 'essential' to eschatological consummation; and third, Christological union is the fitting means by which God ordains to be united with humanity. In each of these lines of reasoning, Christ is fitting or essential for the bringing about of consummation.[7]

It is at this point that Cortez brings up consummation anyway as an alternative to his own position. The central claim of consummation anyway is that God could bring about consummation – the telos of created humanity – apart from the incarnation of Christ. Cortez acknowledges that one benefit of this model is that it 'would thus be able to affirm many of the key aspects of the above arguments without granting that the incarnation would have happened even if creation had never fallen'.[8] Here, however, Cortez raises two objections: first, that such a proposal is overtly speculative, and second, that such a proposal claims that humanity is capable of transitioning from creation to consummation apart from intervening grace. In truth, these two objections coalesce, in that they are implications that follow if one does not suppose that the incarnation of Christ is necessary to achieve the greater good of consummation. That is, if the incarnate Jesus is not fundamentally necessary for humanity to achieve their eschatological end, then there must be some other way to achieve that goal independently of Jesus. But we do not know of any other way – all we have is that Christ indeed was the way. So, the CA model must 'pry into counterfactual realities about what might be', Cortez argues, rather than making theological judgments about what *is* the case, or what was actually revealed.[9] The second objection is also an implication of denying that the incarnation is necessary for consummation. Cortez's reasoning here is as follows: grace is necessary for humanity to achieve its eschatological end. On pain of speculation, that grace is encapsulated in the incarnation of Christ. Hence, it follows that the incarnation is necessary to achieve humanity's eschatological end. If one denies the incarnation, then one must also deny that grace is necessary for humanity to achieve their eschatological end.

Bavinck and the Logic of Consummation Anyway

In order to respond to these two objections on speculation and the necessity of incarnation as that which constitutes God's grace, one would have to attend to Bavinck's deployment of the covenant idea. I suggest that considering how God could bring about the eschatological end of humanity by his free benevolence, but without the incarnation, would also respond to the argument from speculation.

6. Marilyn McCord Adams, *Christ and Horrors*; Edwin Ch. van Driel, *Incarnation Anyway*; Oliver Crisp, 'Incarnation without the Fall.'
7. Cortez, *Resourcing Theological Anthropology*, pp. 86–90.
8. Cortez, *Resourcing Theological Anthropology*, p. 93.
9. Cortez, *Resourcing Theological Anthropology*, p. 93.

God's condescending goodness, indeed, is necessary in order for natural humanity to achieve its consummate (and supernatural) end. And here Bavinck draws from the federal Reformed tradition by deploying covenant theology. Indeed, according to the Reformed tradition, Jesus Christ brings those in union with him into their consummate telos not because the incarnation – or the fall – per se is necessary to bring about that consummation, but because God has decided to work with humanity covenantally and by way of a promise. God promises a reward that is disproportionate to the obedience humanity can offer. As Bavinck summarizes:

> [Human beings] expect salvation and eternal life from him. All this is possible solely because God in his condescending goodness gives rights to the creature. Every creaturely right is a given benefit, a gift of grace, undeserved and nonobligatory. All reward from the side of God originates in grace; no merit, either of condignity or congruity is possible. True religion, accordingly, cannot be anything other than a covenant: it has its origin in the condescending goodness and grace.[10]

The 'right' that a creature has to the reward of that covenant, were the creature to offer that obedience, is thus a graced right: 'In that sense the "covenant of works" is not a "covenant of nature" … There is no natural connection here between work and reward.'[11] For Bavinck, then a covenant is gracious, not in the qualified postlapsarian sense that involves the forbearance of sin, but in the sense that it cannot be obligated or coerced out of God, but comes from his *free benevolence*. Grace, in the sense of God's free benevolence, then, is necessary for humanity to achieve their consummate end.

The Westminster Standards might be brought into view to show that Bavinck's view is reflective of a broader Reformed orthodox argument, which continues to distinguish between a covenant of works with Adam, and a covenant of grace that became necessary in Christ because of the fall. On the former, it says this:

> II. The first covenant made with man was a covenant of works, wherein life was promised to Adam, and in him to his posterity, upon condition of perfect and personal obedience.[12]

Here, the reward of eternal life promised in return for Adam's obedience to the covenant of works is due solely to God's voluntary condescension, not to a natural right by virtue of Adam's (even unfallen) merit (WCF 7:1). Furthermore, the logic

---

10. Herman Bavinck, *RD* 2: p. 570; Cf. Mattson, *Restored to Our Destiny*.
11. Bavinck, *RD* 2: p. 571.
12. WCF 7:2.

and trajectory of creation being oriented toward consummation are embedded within the second article of the Confession here. 'Life' was promised to Adam and his posterity, upon condition of perfect and personal obedience. The language of life here harkens one back to the first article of the same Chapter of the Confession, which refers to the gift of God as one's blessedness and reward.[13] The twentieth question in the Westminster Larger Catechism (WLC) thus associates this first covenant with Adam as a covenant of *life:*

> Q. 20. What was the providence of God toward man in the estate in which he was created? A. The providence of God toward man in the estate in which he was created, was the placing him in paradise, appointing him to dress it, giving him liberty to eat of the fruit of the earth; putting the creatures under his dominion, and ordaining marriage for his help; affording him communion with Himself; instituting the Sabbath; entering into a *covenant of life* [emphasis added] with him, upon condition of personal, perfect, and perpetual obedience, of which the tree of life was a pledge; and forbidding to eat of the tree of knowledge of good and evil, upon the pain of death.[14]

The rewards that come by way of a covenant are rather distinct from natural rewards. No amount of finite obedience can bring about the reward of eternal, blessed fellowship with God. In theological language, the rewards tied to a covenant are owed to the covenant-keeper *ex pacto*.[15] Francis Turretin correspondingly argues that the value of the obedience offered can have no intrinsic purchase upon 'the infinite reward of life', and as such the giving of the reward depends on the character of the covenant-maker: 'the fidelity of him making it'.[16] In sum, Turretin argues that this covenantal pact was 'gratuitous, as depending upon a pact or

---

13. So, Petrus van Mastricht, on the eternal life promised to Adam in the covenant of nature, writes: 'an eternal life, insofar as God was his God, insofar as he rejoiced in the love, benevolence, communion, enjoyment, and glorification of God, in which eternal life consists', in *Theoretical-Practical Theology*, vol. 3, *The Works of God and the Fall of Man*, Joel Beeke (ed.), Todd M. Rester (trans.) (Grand Rapids: Reformation Heritage Books, 2022), p. 393.

14. See also the exposition in Chad Van Dixhoorn, *Confessing the Faith: A Reader's Guide to the Westminster Confession of Faith* (Edinburgh: Banner of Truth, 2014), pp. 97–8.

15. On the development of merit *ex pacto* in the Reformed tradition, see Harrison Perkins, '*Meritum Ex Pacto* in the Reformed Tradition: Covenantal Merit in Theological Polemics', *Mid-America Journal of Theology* 31 (2020): 57–87.

16. Francis Turretin, *Institutes of Elenctic Theology*, 3 vols, James T. Dennison Jr. (ed.), George Musgrave Giger (trans.) (PLACE: Presbyterian & Reformed Publishing, 1997), 1: p. 578. Cf. Van Mastricht, *Theoretical-Practical Theology*, 3: p. 395.

gratuitous promise (by which God was bound not to man, but to himself and to his own goodness, fidelity, and truth).'[17] As Bavinck would put it:

> the first human beings, being created in God's image, rested in it and *saw in this covenant* a revelation of *a way to a higher blessedness*. The covenant of works, accordingly, does justice to both the sovereignty of God – which implies the dependency of creatures and the nonmeritoriousness of all their works – and to the grace and generosity of God, who nevertheless wants to give the creature a higher than earthly blessedness.[18]

Bavinck, in consonance with the broader Reformed orthodox on this issue, thus offers resources that respond to Cortez's argument regarding the necessity of grace.

This language of life, however, also includes not merely the beatific vision – though that is indeed the central reward for the Christian, having God as their blessedness – but also the attaining of glorious human natures. The ninth chapter of the Westminster Confession makes this clear. In contrast to the will of man in the state of innocence, 'the will of man is made perfectly and immutably free to do good alone in the state of glory only'.[19] This language distinguishes between the creational goodness that Adam enjoyed, and the immutable goodness that glory bestows. They show that denying that the incarnation is necessary (or essential) to achieve the eschatological end does not entail that grace (or, gratuitous free benevolence) is unnecessary to achieve that supernatural end. God has offered a way to achieve that end by the grace of establishing a covenant through the federal headship of Adam. Embedded within the creation of the first humans in paradise is thus the telos of a higher life: consummation anyway is the logic of the Reformed tradition. Grace is indeed necessary, but that grace is first manifested in the covenant that made possible Adam's entrance into a higher life, conditioned on his obedience. That is, consummation is the original telos that was possible through *Adam's* federal headship.

How, then, does Christ fit within this picture? Rather than arguing that the incarnation of the second person of the Trinity per se is what is necessary for humanity to obtain their eschatological end, Bavinck is arguing that Christ obeyed in Adam's place, and thus, to borrow Brian Mattson's pithy phrase, Christ has

---

17. Turrentin, *Institutes of Elenctic Theology*, 3: p. 395.

18. Bavinck, *RD* 2: p. 572. Emphasis mine. Turretin observes the same point: 'However, the received opinion among the orthodox is that the promise given to Adam was not only of a happy life to be continued in paradise, but of a heavenly and eternal life (to which he was to be carried after the course of perfect obedience and perseverance had been run and which God had prescribed to him as a trial of his faith) ... The question is not whether the promise was given to him of happiness and life perpetually to endure, if he had persisted in integrity ... Rather the question is whether that happiness and life were to be passed in heaven or only upon the earth and in paradise. The latter they affirm; we, the former.' *Institutes of Elenctic Theology*, p. 583.

19. WCF 9:5.

restored us to our destiny.[20] That is, Christ restored us to the blessed destiny to which *Adam* would have taken us, had he remained upright:

> For the Reformed, who walked in the footsteps of Augustine ... Adam did not possess the highest kind of life. The highest kind of life is the material freedom consisting of not being able to err, sin, or die. It consists in being elevated absolutely above all fear and dread, above all possibility of falling. The highest life is immediately bestowed by grace through Christ upon believers. They can no longer sin (1 John 3:9) and they can no longer die (John 3:16) since by faith they immediately receive eternal, inamissable life. Theirs is the perseverance of the saints; they can no longer be lost. Hence, Christ does not [merely] restore his own to the state of Adam before the fall. *He acquired and bestows much more, namely, that which Adam would have received had he not fallen. He positions us not at the beginning but at the end of the journey Adam had to complete.* He accomplished not only the passive but also the active obedience required; he not only delivers us from guilt and punishment, but out of grace immediately grants us the right to eternal life.[21]

Christ, then, offered an obedience with two aspects, as Bavinck observed here. The passive obedience of Christ is that aspect of Christ's obedience that suffers the conditions of a fallen world and the penal consequences of Adam's disobedience in the fall, having its climax in his death on the cross. Christ's active obedience, however, is that aspect of Christ's obedience that Adam, too, had to offer in the state of innocence to the covenant of works.

The upshot of this exposition of these rather traditional moves in Bavinck's covenant theology is that denying that the incarnation per se is necessary for achieving the eschatological end does not entail the denial of the necessity of grace for achieving that end. That end could have been achieved, by God's intended covenantal design, by way of the obedience of the original federal head, namely, Adam.

This leads us directly to a response to Cortez's objection regarding speculation. Finding a way to achieve consummation apart from the incarnation involves no illegitimate speculation beyond the bounds of divine revelation. That Adam's federal obedience to the covenant of works is the way by which humanity was originally meant to enter into consummate glory is embedded within the very texts that Cortez himself exegetes: in 1 Cor. 15, in the Adam-Christ parallel in Rom. 5, and in the Genesis narrative itself.[22] The if-then structure of 1 Cor. 15:44b specifically, I suggest, is better read from the model of consummation anyway: the text 'if there is a natural body, then there is a spiritual body' involves a logical link

---

20. Mattson, *Restored to Our Destiny*.
21. Bavinck, *RD* 2: p. 573. Emphasis mine.
22. For an exposition and defense of the covenant of works, see John V. Fesko, *The Covenant of Works: The Origins, Development, and Reception of the Doctrine* (Oxford: Oxford University Press, 2020).

between creation and glory, not between creation and incarnation. Furthermore, as Bavinck recognizes, Scripture positions the incarnation mission of Christ within the context of redemption: 'Scripture ... always and exclusively connects the incarnation of Christ with sin and regards it as the most magnificent proof of God's compassion.'[23] Bavinck appeals to 1 Tim. 1:15, which records that Christ came specifically for sin: to posit another primary reason for the incarnation, or to suggest that God is incapable of bringing humanity to consummate existence without the incarnation are arguably the positions that require undue speculation.[24]

If Adam had obeyed with his natural body, he would have moved himself and his progeny to the spiritual state, with God bestowing upon them their eschatological heavenly bodies, perhaps in the same way that believers who are still alive at the time of Christ's second coming will receive a transformed body 'in the twinkling of an eye'.[25] Indeed, not only, as Cortez notes, can consummation anyway accommodate his fine reading of 1 Cor. 15, this argument also shows that consummation anyway has a venerable precedent within the Reformed tradition.

Objections

It is instructive to anticipate at least three objections to the argument above, and thus also to consider how invoking the covenant of works might aid in responding to these objections. Doing so affords us with the opportunity to clarify the argument sketched above in constructive ways while remaining within the lines of Bavinck's argument, and also further to show that the view of consummation anyway is less speculative than one might first think.

The first potential objection is the impossibility thesis recently raised and clarified by James T. Turner in his essay 'Perfect Obedience, Perfect Love, and the (So-Called) Problem of Heavenly Freedom'. While the impossibility thesis is initially raised as an objection to the idea that one can ground the impeccability of consummate human beings in heaven on their freely lived earthly lives, the thesis might also have implications for advocates of CA. The objection has to do with the impossibility of those redeemed to change themselves in such a way as to bring about their consummate bodies. By parity of reasoning, then, it is impossible for those in the state of innocence to bring themselves into the heavenly, consummate existence. Turner uses the terms inaugurated new nature (INN) to refer to the redeemed before the second coming of Christ, and consummated new nature (CNN) to refer to the consummate life. Just as it is physically impossible for those with an impaired vision to restore clarity to their eyes, so is it metaphysically

---

23. Bavinck, *RD* 3: p. 279.
24. See Justus Hunter, *If Adam Had Not Sinned: The Reasons for the Incarnation from Anselm to Scotus* (Washington DC: Catholic University of America Press, 2020), pp. 183–4. As we shall see, this does not rule out other congruent goods that the incarnation would bring about.
25. 1 Cor. 15:52.

impossible for those with redeemed natures to bring about consummate natures for themselves. In Turner's words:

> Now, when I suggest that plausibly it is metaphysically impossible for a human with INN to change her character such that she becomes a human with CNN, I mean it in the same way that one might plausibly suggest that it is *physically or nomologically* impossible that a human with CVN [Correctable Vision Nature] change her vision, by internal effort, such that she becomes a human with PVN [Perfected Vision Nature]. (Note here that the idea is *not* that a human could not change from having CVN to having PVN; rather, it is that a human cannot do this through visual training or exercise.)[26]

Humankind in the state of innocence and sinners with an INN are in possession of bodies that fall short of consummation. Hence, in the same way that those with INN would not be able to bring about the CNN for themselves, so too, is it impossible for those with innocent natures (like Adam) to bring about the CNN for themselves. Only the miraculous power of God can bring about the transition from INN to CNN, for that transition is obtained by way of resurrection. And since resurrection presupposes human death, and human death presupposes the fall, so too does consummation presuppose the redeeming work of Christ on which the resurrection of the redeemed is based. In this story, then, consummation anyway is impossible, for at least two reasons: (1) Adam could not bring about the change from innocent natures to consummate natures, and (2) the resurrection promised by Christ's redeeming work is that which is necessary to bring about the transition into glory.

What might proponents of consummation anyway say to this objection? It is here that the covenant idea once again comes to aid us. Proponents of consummation anyway here would heartily agree that Adam could not, 'by internal effort', bring about the consummate nature for himself. Indeed, one would argue that the transition from innocence/regeneration to consummation is not one of gradual ascent but of a real qualitative transition from two non-overlapping *sources*: from nature or the Spirit. Again, the consummate (and resurrected) body is spiritual precisely because it comes from the power of the Spirit. Only God can bring about this transition.

The covenant of works protects the divine origins of this transition. It is not Adam's obedience that naturally brings about the consummate body. No amount of obedience from Adam can bring it out. The consummate body is granted to Adam by God's free benevolence in setting up the covenant of works. It arises from the promise and power of God, and it tethers this disproportionately glorious reward to Adam's finite obedience.

---

26. James T. Turner, 'Perfect Obedience', p. 241.

The response to the idea that the resurrection is necessary to bring about the consummate natures, too, can be responded to in brief. Just as believers who are still alive during Christ's second coming would instantly receive their transformed, consummate bodies (so 1 Cor. 15:52), so too would Adam, had he obeyed, receive a transformed, consummate body. What is required to bring about the consummate body is thus not resurrection per se, but a miraculous working of God's initiative – either by way of resurrection or by way of instant transformation.[27]

This brings me to the second, perhaps more serious, potential objection, that is, the objection from vagueness. Suppose we grant that the consummate body is granted to Adam if Adam obeys. The vagueness objection concerns the perceived difficulty of identifying the particular sort of obedience Adam had to offer in order to secure the reward of the covenant of works. The stipulation of the covenant seems to be exceedingly vague; it is also unclear how many acts of obedience Adam must offer in order to secure the reward. To make matters worse, it seems that offering an answer to this objection involves no small amount of speculation.

An initial response to this worry is by clarifying that the obedience that Adam was to offer to God is not to be conceived quantitatively, as a collection of a numerical sum of obedient acts. Rather, just as the 'one act' of righteousness in Romans 5:12-18 refers not to a singular act by Christ, but rather to the whole of his life and work as a completed act of obedience, so too must Adam offer an obedience that is 'complete' before God.

Sceptics of consummation anyway might contrast the difficulty of specifying how Adam might complete this obedience to the clarity of the biblical witness concerning the completion of Christ's obedience. It was precisely at the point of death on the cross that Christ declared that his obedience was finished.[28] Embedded within this account of Christ's obedience is perhaps another indicator to the effect that Christ's work of redemption is a necessary pre-requisite to bring about glorious bodies for the redeemed: Christ had to offer himself as a sacrifice, become the first fruits of those who would be resurrected, in order that we too might partake of the consummate life. Hence, instead of speculating about some other means of consummation, why not simply follow the biblical plotline that seems to imply that it is Christ's completed obedience – to the point of death – that brings about consummate estates? This is not so much an endorsement of incarnation anyway but a rejection of consummation anyway as the original telos of Adam.

While a full response to this objection would take us beyond the scope of this chapter (requiring a full biblical-theology of the covenant and the work of Christ as the second Adam), I think a preliminary response can be canvassed in the following way.

---

27. As Hunter recognizes, this means that the union between God and consummate humanity without the fall would be a union of wills, as human beings are perfectly ethically conformed with God's goodness. *If Adam Had Not Sinned*, p. 203.

28. Cf. Jn. 19:30 and Phil. 2:6-11.

Granting the biblical witness that suggests that Christ comes as the second Adam, fulfilling that which Adam had failed to complete, we can infer that Christ's life tells us exactly what would have been required for Adam to offer complete obedience in the absence of the fall. Christ was led by the Spirit to be tempted in the wilderness, for example, in order to recapitulate the temptation of the serpent against Adam in the garden. Christ was also sent to crush the serpent,[29] and this is precisely what his death on the cross accomplished – all things were subjected to him in his exaltation. His death succeeded in this because he had 'disarmed' the rulers and authorities by 'cancelling the record of debt that stood against us'.[30] I take this to mean that Christ had to obey and die in our place in order to disarm the serpent's accusations against the guilt of the redeemed. But this is just one part of the serpent's 'works', the part which presupposes the post-lapsarian order – and the 'Son of God' came precisely in order to 'destroy the works of the devil',[31] namely, in the context of 1 John 3, to destroy the works of the devil in defiling God's creation with sin, and in tempting God's people to sin.

It is worth mentioning at this point that Adam, too, is called the 'Son of God.' Luke 3–4 indicate precisely that Jesus is God's beloved son, in connection (or by contrast) to Adam, the 'son of God'.[32] Here is the key observation: if Jesus, the faithful Son of God, came to fulfil what Adam should have fulfilled, and Jesus' mission was to destroy the works of the devil, so, too, would Adam have completed his own obedience by destroying the serpent, but without requiring his own death (which presupposes guilt and sin). In other words, what we can infer from the biblical witness is that the obedience that Adam had to offer in order to receive the consummate state is not entirely vague after all, and we can gain some progress toward specifying what that completion must entail. Adam would have completed his obedience if he had destroyed the serpent, banishing him from God's holy garden, by resisting the serpent's temptations and by obeying God's word against it. In traditional Reformed terminology, Adam had to offer active obedience but not passive obedience, whereas Christ had to offer both.

While this response does involve drawing some informed inferences from the biblical witness, as well as the task of disentangling what part of obedience presupposes the fall (passive obedience) and what part is present regardless (active obedience), I do not believe that it is reducible to unhealthy speculation. At worst, what is involved here is a speculation of a theologically fruitful kind, and at best I do believe that it is a hypothesis that goes along the grain of the biblical text, in consonance with Bavinck and the older Reformed tradition sketched above. If this story is plausible (and I submit that it is), then we have a response, too, to the objection from vagueness.

Finally, then, we turn to a third potential objection, which challenges the internal coherency of Bavinck's own thought on this matter. While it may be clear

---

29. Gen. 3:15.
30. Col. 2:14-15.
31. 1 Jn. 3:8; cf. Ps. 91:11-13.
32. Lk. 3:38.

that Bavinck follows the logic of consummation anyway, surely, such a model cannot affirm that the Son's mediation is 'central' for human redemption. For the incarnation to be 'central', it must be considered not as a mere response to the fall, but as the focal point of God's plan. However, Bavinck, in other places, does say that the Son is the final cause and the central point of God's plan.

Consider these two important statements from Bavinck on the relation between Jesus Christ and last things. On the one hand, Bavinck maintains that the Son is the telos of creation, and the mediator of union between God and his creatures: 'The Son is not only the mediator of reconciliation (*mediator reconciliationis*) on account of sin, but even apart from sin he is the mediator of union (*mediator unionis*) between God and his creation. He is not only the exemplary cause (*causa exemplaris*) but also the final cause (*causa finalis*) of creation.'[33] On the other hand, Bavinck insists that the incarnation is prompted by the fall of humanity to sin; again: 'Scripture ... always and exclusively connects the incarnation of Christ with sin and regards it as the most magnificent proof of God's compassion.'[34] It appears that there is an inconsistency here, for it is not immediately obvious how it is that Bavinck can maintain the mediation of the Son as the final cause of all of creation, when the Son's incarnation was exclusively occasioned by the entrance of sin.

If the Son is the mediator between God and humanity in the state of creation (and not merely for the sake of reconciliation), as Bavinck claims, this would seem to imply that Bavinck, on the pain of inconsistency, would have to affirm the thesis that the incarnation would obtain anyway, even in a world without sin. It would seem difficult otherwise to hold together the claim that the Son is the mediator between God and humanity in general and yet posit that the reason for the incarnation is 'exclusively' humanity's redemption from sin. To use the language of the contemporary debate, a stress on the former claim would seem to lead Bavinck to an incarnation anyway thesis, according to which the incarnation would obtain even in possible worlds without a fall, whereas the latter would place Bavinck in a contrary position.

To respond properly to this third objection and to illumine Bavinck's own account, I draw from Justus Hunter's recent analysis of medieval debates on the reasons for the incarnation.[35] As one shall see, that Bavinck argues here that the incarnation is 'exclusively' tied to sin should be understood in terms of the 'primacy' question for the incarnation. The primary reason for the incarnation is sin, but Bavinck would not deny that the incarnation has brought about other goods, and that other congruent reasons might be put forward for the incarnation, including that Christ is the crown of all creation and revelation, as well as the focal point of humanity's fellowship with God, or that Christ is the final cause of all of creation in the logical ordering of God's decrees.

As Hunter shows, thirteenth-century debates on incarnation anyway rested on distinguishing between the primary reason for the incarnation and other

---

33. Bavinck, *RD* 4: p. 685.
34. Bavinck, *RD* 3: p. 279.
35. Hunter, *If Adam Had Not Sinned*.

congruent reasons. A proper response to the hypothetical question of whether the incarnation would obtain without a fall depends on a prior answer to the primacy question. If the incarnation's primary reason is redemption from sin, then all other congruent reasons are annexed to the primary reason. In other words, to identify the primary reason for the incarnation is not to exclude other reasons, but it does order them logically in a particular way.

Suppose, then, that the incarnation was motivated primarily by humanity's redemption from sin. It does not follow that the incarnation could not bring about other congruent goods, or that God could not have other congruent reasons for the incarnation. God might send the incarnate Son so that humanity might have a revelation of divine goodness, and so that humanity might enjoy not merely an intellectual but also a sensible fellowship with God, but primarily so that humanity might be redeemed from sin. This, in fact, was the argument of Bonaventure (and Thomas) for answering the hypothetical with the negation, while affirming the possibility that the incarnation could bring about other goods.[36] Furthermore, Bonaventure and Thomas argue that answering with the negation to the hypothetical is less speculative and more reliant on divine revelation, for Scripture indicates that Christ came in order to save sinners (1 Tim. 1:15).[37] Hunter's conclusion, then, is that while those who affirmed incarnation anyway might argue that they uphold the centrality of the incarnation of Christ in an absolute sense, as the incarnation would obtain in possible worlds without a fall, those who reject incarnation anyway can still uphold Christ's primacy, despite saying that it is occasioned by sin: 'Christ enjoys primacy in a significant sense in Thomas, as in Bonaventure.'[38]

This is consistent with Bavinck's position, though he speaks about the primacy of the incarnation in terms of the logical ordering of the decree. While the covenant of grace involves the sending of the incarnate Son to redeem sinners, it 'does not hang in the air but rests on an eternal, unchanging foundation. It is firmly grounded in the counsel and covenant of the triune God and is the application and execution of it that infallibly follows.'[39] This appeal to the eternal counsel (the *pactum salutis*) as the backdrop for the sending of the incarnate Son in the third volume of the *Dogmatics* refers back to the discussion on the divine counsel in the second volume: 'the one simple and eternal decree of God unfolds itself before our eyes in time in a vast multiplicity of things and events.'[40] In Bavinck's perspective, history is the manifestation and unfolding of the divine decree in time, and the

---

36. Hunter, *If Adam Had Not Sinned*, p. 184.
37. Hunter, *If Adam Had Not Sinned*, p. 183.
38. Hunter, *If Adam Had Not Sinned*, p. 231. Cf. Bavinck, *RD* 3: p. 278.
39. Bavinck, *RD* 3: p. 215.
40. Bavinck, *RD* 2: p. 374. For recent defenses of the *pactum salutis* from the concerns of Karl Barth that shows its consonance with the singular divine will, see Duby, *Jesus and the God of Classical Theism*, pp. 112–30; Scott Swain, 'Covenant of Redemption', in *Christian Dogmatics: Reformed Theology for the Church Catholic*, Michael Allen and Scott Swain (eds) (Grand Rapids: Baker Academic, 2016), pp. 107–25.

logical order of the eternal decree might differ from the order of execution within time. Analogically, just as an artist might specify the sort of house she desires first in the order of her plan, but in the order of action she might actually gather the requisite tools first before beginning the construction of the house, so the logical order of God's decrees might differ from the order of execution within time.

If human history is the unfolding of the divine decree, then one can logically hold together the claims that the Son was fore-ordained as the final cause of all creation and is the only mediator between God and humanity *and* that Christ came primarily in order to save sinners in the order of execution.[41] In eternity past, God predestined the incarnation as the manifestation of his own glory and the central way in which humans would commune with God, but in the order of execution and history this incarnation is occasioned and predicated on the fall. So, Bavinck argues that 'even before the fall Adam was already a type of Christ (1 Cor. 15:47ff), yet in Scripture the incarnation is always based on the fall of the human race'.[42] To unpack it in another way, the incarnation was the focal point of God's decrees, and was thus ordered within the decrees prior to the fall, in a supralapsarian sense. God created the world with the incarnate Son in view as the mediator of all creation. Thus, the creation of the first human as a representative of all humanity logically anticipates the coming of the superlative representative in Christ. Adam was created first in the order of execution in order to point to Christ, because Christ was logically prior to Adam in the order of the decrees.

This concatenation of logical and historical orders dovetails with Bavinck's insistence on the need for coupling supra- and infra-lapsarian positions together:

> Accordingly, neither the supralapsarian nor the infralapsarian view of predestination is capable of incorporating within its perspective the fulness and riches of the truth of Scripture and of satisfying our theological thinking. The truth inherent in supralapsarianism is that all the decrees together form a unity; that there is an ultimate goal to which all things are subordinated and serviceable; that the entrance of sin into the world was not something that took God by surprise, but in a sense willed and determined by him; that from the very beginning the creation was designed to make re-creation possible; *that even before the fall, in the creation of Adam, things were structured with a view to Christ*. But the truth inherent in infralapsarianism is that the decrees, though they form a unity, are nevertheless differentiated with a view to their objects; that in these decrees one can discern not only a teleological but also a causal order; that the purpose of the creation and fall is not exhausted by their being means to a final end; and that sin was above all and primarily a catastrophic disturbance of creation, one which of and by itself could never have been willed by God.[43]

---

41. One should also keep in mind that the Son was already mediator apart from and before the incarnation: see Bavinck, *RD* 3: p. 214.

42. Bavinck, *RD* 2: p. 391.

43. Bavinck, *RD* 2: p. 391. Emphasis mine.

If supralapsarianism highlights the unity of the divine purpose and the way in which all things point to Christ, infralapsarianism emphasizes that the fall was no happy incident, reducible to a mere 'means' to an end. That redemption by incarnation follows the fall in the order of execution, then, does not mean that the incarnation was a mere reaction, or that it was never centrally part of the plan of God as the focal point of God's revelation and goodness – God, as Bavinck indicated, has always planned for Christ to be the mediator of all humanity:

> while the incarnation is certainly different from all other revelation, it is also akin to it: it is its climax, crown, and completion. All revelation tends toward and groups itself around the incarnation as the highest, richest, and most perfect act of self-revelation ... In the act of creation, God already had the Christ in mind. In that sense the creation itself already served as preparation for the incarnation. The world was so created that when it fell, it could again be restored; humanity was organized under a single head in such a way that, sinned, it could again be gathered together under another head. Adam was so appointed as head that Christ could immediately take his place; and the covenant of works was so set up that, broken, it could be restored in the covenant of grace. People were therefore wrong in thinking that the incarnation of the Son of God would also have taken place without sin.[44]

The incarnation is, as Bavinck indicates here, the very reason for Adam's creation, and Christ's coming brought about the congruent goods of manifesting the climax of God's condescension in divine revelation, uniting humanity under a single head, and so on. However, the primary reason for the incarnation remains the redemption of humanity from sin. God planned all things so that this story of redemption, centered on Christ's incarnate mission, would be actualized. In sum, by considering the presence and ordering of the decree of God as described in the *pactum salutis*, one can hold together both that the Son is the final cause of God's creation, reflecting the telos of God's decree, and that the Son became incarnate as occasioned by sin, in the order of execution.

Conclusion

This chapter has illumined Bavinck's position on corporate humanity's consummate end by putting his covenant theology in constructive dialogue with the thesis of incarnation anyway. Bavinck follows the logic of consummation anyway. More specifically, consummation anyway agrees that eschatological consummation was the original telos of humanity's creation, but disagrees that the incarnation itself was the essential or necessary means by which humanity would obtain that eschatological end. Hence, there is another hypothetical possibility that

---

44. Bavinck, *RD* 3: p. 278.

humanity could obtain that eschatological end apart from Christ, namely, by way of the obedience of Adam, humanity's original federal head, to the stipulations of the covenant of works. This covenantal theology, found within Bavinck (and the broader Reformed tradition), evades the two charges against consummation anyway by Marc Cortez, namely that consummation anyway would seem to entail that grace is unnecessary for humanity to achieve their eschatological end, and that it involves undue speculation. The consummation anyway model argues that the covenant idea grounds the gracious character of humanity's achievement of that supernatural end through Adam's obedience to the covenantal stipulations and shows that no excessive speculation is necessary to show that another way apart from the incarnation was possible to achieve eschatological consummation. I have also responded to three potential objections, further showing how the covenant idea can be fruitfully deployed in this debate. Finally, I showed that Bavinck's appeal to the order of the decrees can hold together two claims that initially seem to be contradictory: that the incarnation of the Son is the telos or aim of God's plan for creation (per the supralapsarian logic), while the incarnation in particular is occasioned by sin (per the infralapsarian logic).

With Bavinck's position on the role of the covenant in place for understanding humanity's end, then, one now turns to Bavinck's much-debated view on the beatific vision. As we shall see, covenantal theology continues its pivotal role there as well. In the next chapter, we shall see that Bavinck continues this line of reasoning concerning the mission of the Son as the central point of the divine decree. This incarnational emphasis was precisely the consequence of developing, in Bavinck's view, a 'Protestant principle' for considering the sort of fellowship humans might have with God.

Chapter 9

BEATIFIC VISION

Christ is the final cause of all creation, and the focal point of God's decreed purposes. Christ is the one *from* whom are all things, and he is the one *to* whom all things are pointed (Col. 1:15-17). The second person of the Trinity was always the mediator between God and humanity in creation and redemption, and revelation has its focus in him. God, condescending throughout history to dwell with his people, prefigures this climactic revealing and redemptive act in the incarnation.

This Christological emphasis on revelation and redemption is significant, as we shall see, for grasping Bavinck's conception of the beatific vision – and it is a Christological emphasis that is not diminished but rather emphasized by Bavinck's articulation of the covenant of works. If the organism of the human race is tied together by way of a federal head, then the beatific vision too will be covenantally shaped. Christians will enter into a consummate fellowship with the incarnate and ascended Christ.

To articulate Bavinck's covenantal account of the beatific vision is to enter into controversy. Critics have argued not only that Bavinck fails to engage with wide swaths of the Christian tradition on the beatific vision, but also that Bavinck lacks a positive account at all, perhaps because he was too preoccupied with a 'naturalized' picture of the eschaton.[1] While Cory Brock has demonstrated that Bavinck does indeed affirm the beatific vision, a substantive and positive sketch of the vision itself according to Bavinck was left underdetermined. Thus it is the burden of this chapter to demonstrate that Bavinck does offer a positive account of the beatific vision, and that this positive account is conditioned by his Christology and his description of the nature-grace relation. Much like my analysis of Bavinck's use of the organic motif, the exposition involves piecing together statements that Bavinck makes in various places (and though other interpreters have appealed

---

1. Hans Boersma, *Seeing God: The Beatific Vision in the Christian Tradition* (Grand Rapids: Eerdmans, 2018), pp. 34-8; Cory Brock, 'Revisiting Bavinck and the Beatific Vision', *Journal of Biblical and Theological Studies* 6 (2021): pp. 367-82. See also Michael Allen, *Grounded in Heaven: Recentering Christian Hope and Life on God* (Grand Rapids: Eerdmans, 2018), pp. 6, 61-3 (see also his recent clarification and expansion in Michael Allen, 'On Bavinck, the Beatific Vision, and Theological Practice', *Reformed Faith and Practice* 7 (2022): pp. 57-62), and Eglinton, *Bavinck*, pp. 195-6.

to the particular relevant sections in Volumes 1, 2, and 4 of the *Dogmatics*, a key section on the person of Christ in Volume 3 has been left untouched). Indeed, what emerges is an implication of what Bavinck calls the 'Protestant principle', with the *visio* being characterized as covenantal, ethical, and mystical in character.

Bavinck's Covenantal Account of the Beatific Vision

A close reading of the salient portions of Bavinck's lengthy chapter on the person of Christ will disclose three closely related aspects of his understanding of the beatific vision: it is ethical, covenantal (personal), yet mystical.[2] I discuss them under three sections below: the first on Bavinck's critiques of Eastern Orthodox, Catholic, and Lutheran views from which the ethical dimensions of his view of the vision first emerge; the second on his appeal to John Owen and the 'Protestant principle', which has to do with the covenantal (or personal) dimension; the third on how Bavinck defines the 'mystical' character of the vision.

An Ethical, Not Physical, Problem

The first two aspects of the vision – the ethical and covenantal – regularly appear together in Bavinck's text, first emerging in the historical section of a chapter in *Reformed Dogmatics* 3 on the person of Christ that follows a survey of the biblical material. The biblical material, Bavinck argues, was too rich to be 'absorbed into the Christian consciousness', and that means that certain Christological conflicts inevitably took place in the early church and beyond.[3] While the formulation of Chalcedon formed 'clear-cut boundaries … within which the Church's doctrine of Christ would be further developed', further debates continued about the reasons for the incarnation and the particular relation between Christ's divine and human natures.[4]

It is here that Bavinck brings up a significant difference (in his view) between East and West. A basic question that emerges: what is the *problem* that the incarnation addresses? In Bavinck's reading, the Eastern Orthodox position argues that the reason for the incarnation was *metaphysical*, rather than ethical; according to this view, human nature in itself was considered unfit to be one with God. In his words: 'In the theology of the East, the basic idea remained that God himself had to become a human so that human beings might become partakers in the divine nature, immortality, eternal life, divinization (*theosis*).'[5] Though later Bavinck would himself use the word 'mystical' to refer to our communion with God in Christ, here, Bavinck would critique the Eastern Orthodox view as a form of mystic*ism*, as the incarnation was posited to address a 'physical' problem:

2. Bavinck, *RD* 3: pp. 223–319.
3. Bavinck, *RD* 3: p. 253.
4. Bavinck, *RD* 3: p. 255.
5. Bavinck, *RD* 3: p. 255.

The consequences of sin are much more physical than ethical in nature; consequently, a current of mysticism always flows alongside rationalism in the Greek church. The result of this mysticism had to be that, though the human nature of Christ was recognized as well, the major emphases fell on his deity, on the penetration of the divine into the human nature, on the union of the two, on Christ's essential being more than on his historical appearance, on his incarnation rather than on his satisfaction. Hence, with respect to the person of Christ, what mattered most was his divine essence, which was communicated in human form and thus received and enjoyed by human beings. No particular need was felt, therefore, for a sharp distinction between the two natures.[6]

Whether Bavinck was right in his reading of the Eastern church is controversial. What is of interest here is how Bavinck's own positive account begins to emerge in his polemic against the Eastern Orthodox position. For Bavinck, the problem the incarnation sought to address is primarily *ethical*. Thus the renewal of our human nature is needed so that we can once again display righteousness and hence have our relationship with God restored. For the Eastern church, in Bavinck's reading, however, the problem is wrongly supposed to be human nature itself, which needs to be deified in some way in order to be united with God. And the mystic*ism* that Bavinck finds so problematic in this view is that the incarnation *itself*, rather than the incarnation that led to *satisfaction*, is found to be salvific. Through the deification of Christ's human nature ('the penetration of the divine into the human nature'), human beings are also deified. This is mysticism – for Bavinck – in the sense that nature itself (rather than sin) is considered problematic and must be gifted with something above nature in order to become fitting for God.[7]

The Western church, on the other hand, 'made a sharp distinction between the divine and the human nature of Christ', precisely because the 'emphasis was more on the ethical than on the physical; on Christ's satisfaction, his suffering and death, than on his incarnation'.[8] Yet though the Eastern church was never influenced by this position of the West, the West later took on 'the mysticism of the East', and as 'result the idea of a deification of the human also penetrated the Latin church and Latin theology'.[9] The doctrinal outcomes of this influence were the very things that Bavinck critiques about the beatific vision – especially as it is expressed in Roman Catholicism – in the second volume of his *Dogmatics*. He worries that such a mystical account compromises the Creator-creature distinction, and presents a dualistic construal of the relationship between nature and super-nature. In his words: 'Mystical contemplation, the doctrine of the superadded gifts, the theory of transubstantiation, all rest on the idea that the finite is incapable of participating

---

6. Bavinck, *RD* 3: p. 255.
7. For similar comments, see Kevin Vanhoozer, *Biblical Authority after Babel: Retrieving the Solas in the Spirit of Mere Protestant Christianity* (Grand Rapids: Brazos, 2016), pp. 44–50.
8. Bavinck, *RD* 3: pp. 255–6.
9. Bavinck, *RD* 3: p. 256.

in the infinite.'[10] Here, Bavinck argues that there is an analogy between the Roman Catholic view of the incarnation and their view of the believer's ultimate union with God: 'If mystics participated in it by contemplation and were in a sense divinized, then this had to be true in much greater measure of the human being Christ, in whom the fullness of God dwelt bodily.'[11] Bavinck would later revisit this analogy between Christ's two natures and the believer's union with God, but derive a different depiction of what mystical union entails. The point here is that for the East, from the start, and for the West, in due course, the beatific vision was considered to be a metaphysical union, and the incarnation was considered necessary precisely because human nature was metaphysically incapable of partaking in the divine.

Bavinck goes on to emphasize the influence of John of Damascus in this debate. He links John of Damascus with later Roman Catholic theology, especially regarding their shared argument that the human nature of Christ participates in the divine energies or gifts. This, in turn, leads to the view that Christ enjoys the beatific vision even in his estate of humiliation:

> Entirely in accordance with John of Damascus, scholastic and Roman theology therefore taught that, though each nature in Christ remains itself and the communication of the divine attributes to the human nature must not be conceived realistically, yet the divine nature completely permeates and sets aglow the human nature, as heat does iron, and makes it participatory in the divine glory, wisdom, and power .... From this premise it was then inferred that Christ as a human being on earth already possessed the blessed knowledge, the beatific vision of God ... walking not by faith but by sight.[12]

It is crucial to note the analogy: If Christ shows us what it means to behold God, and his beholding of God consists in the participation of the human nature in the divine energies, then human beings too, will participate in the divine energies. Bavinck then argues that this same basic idea exists in Lutheran theology.[13] In response to Boersma's critique that Bavinck never considers the Eastern position, then, it is evident not only that Bavinck engages with John of Damascus and the Eastern tradition, but also that his critiques of Lutheran and Roman Catholic views on the beatific vision are extensions of his critiques of the Eastern tradition.

Though Lutheran and Roman accounts of the risen Christ certainly differ, especially on matters such as the doctrine of ubiquity, Bavinck insists that there is 'kinship' between them. 'Materially, Roman and Lutheran theology agree in the sense that both elevate the human nature above the boundaries set for it and

---

10. Bavinck, *RD* 3: p. 256.
11. Bavinck, *RD* 3: p. 256.
12. Bavinck, *RD* 3: p. 256.
13. For a recent Christological account that engages with Lutheran and Eastern Orthodox ideas on Christology, see Ian McFarland, *The Word Made Flesh: A Theology of the Incarnation* (Louisville: Westminster John Knox, 2019).

dissolve into mere appearance both the human development of Jesus and the state of his humiliation.'[14] By elevating the human nature of Christ through participation in the divine properties or gifts, Lutherans risk dissolving the firm distinction between divine and human natures as well as the real transition between the 'state of humiliation and exaltation', for, that participation in the supernatural gifts obtains even in Christ's humiliation.[15] This perceived blurring of the human and divine natures of Christ informs Bavinck's rather scathing critique in the section on the communication of properties, to the effect that both 'Lutheran and Catholic Christology, consequently, contain within them a docetic element. The purely human development [of Christ] does not come into its own in them.'[16] Notice again the parallel between Christology and the beatific vision in Bavinck's mind. If Lutheran and Roman views of Christology compromise the genuine human nature of Christ, then so too would their doctrine of the beatific vision compromise the human nature of each of us.

In contrast, Bavinck asserts, Reformed Christology has 'fundamentally overcome the Greek-Roman and Lutheran commingling of the divine and the human', thus securing 'space for a purely human development of Christ, for a successive communication of gifts, and for a real distinction between humiliation and exaltation', even while it avoided Nestorianism.[17] Bavinck's answer appears in a crucial passage:

> Reformed theology stressed that it was the *person* of the Son who became flesh – not the *substance* but the *subsistence* of the Son assumed our nature. The unity of the two natures, despite the sharp distinction between them, is unalterably anchored in the person. As it does in the doctrine of the Trinity, of humanity in the image of God, and of the covenants, so here in the doctrine of Christ as well, the Reformed idea of conscious personal life as the fullest and highest life comes dramatically to the fore.[18]

Bavinck's reasoning in this passage is as follows. For the Greek, Roman, and Lutheran views of Christology, a focus was placed on the divine nature that assumes human flesh precisely because communion with God was conceived *substantially* rather than *personally*. The 'problem' Christology was addressing was physical or metaphysical, rather than personal and ethical. For the Reformed, however, the focus was on the unity of the divine person in the incarnation, precisely because Christ came to restore the *personal* relationship we have with God. The goal of restoration was personal communion rather than physical fusion. And this personal communion is communicated to creatures by way of covenant.

---

14. Bavinck, *RD* 3: p. 257.
15. Bavinck, *RD* 3: p. 258.
16. Bavinck, *RD* 3: p. 309.
17. Bavinck, *RD* 3: pp. 258–9.
18. Bavinck, *RD* 3: p. 259. Emphasis original.

As we have seen in Chapter 5, this is precisely the sort of bond that believers enjoy with Christ. The unity that believers have with Jesus is one of ethical, personal fellowship, and this ethical bond is what Bavinck considers to be the core of the covenantal relation: 'The covenant of works and the covenant of grace are the forms by which the organism of humanity is maintained also in a religious and an ethical [*ethischen*] sense.'[19] Christ is our federal representative, the organic ethical center of the organism of humanity. The incarnation and mission of the Son consist in the restoration of this fellowship with God through him.

John Owen and the 'Principle' of Protestantism

A crucial detail is a source that Bavinck cites at the end of that paragraph on the 'Reformed idea of conscious personal life': John Owen. Owen expresses a view that represents the sort of personal communion with Christ that Bavinck believes to be more in line with a 'principle' of Protestantism. Specifically, Bavinck cites Owen's 'Declaration of the Glorious Mystery of the Person of Christ, God and Man'.[20] While Bavinck does not provide a particular page reference or quotation, the signal toward Owen is astute, for Owen, too, sought to 'reform' the beatific vision. As Suzanne McDonald has shown, Owen sought to reform the understanding of the beatific vision in accordance with Reformed instincts by keeping it in line with the modesty of the scriptural witness and by providing a Christocentric lens. McDonald puts it well: 'The beatific vision ... for Owen [means specifically] to behold the glory of God in the face of Jesus Christ.'[21] There is thus a continuity between the sight that believers have of Christ in the last day and the faith they exercise in the present order – both are focused on Christ. Our faith in Christ now will become our sight of Christ in the eschaton. The specific focus of the beatific vision is on the 'hypostatic union', once again: 'The beatific vision is the beholding of the glory of God, and to behold the glory of God is to behold it in the person of Christ, fully divine and fully human.'[22] The vision is not of God apart from Christ, but of God *incarnate*.

Owen's personal reformation of the beatific vision in terms of the vision of Jesus Christ has several benefits over what Suzanne McDonald considers the Thomist

---

19. Bavinck, *RD* 3: p. 106.
20. John Owen, 'Declaration of the Glorious Mystery of the Person of Christ, God and Man', in *The Works of John Owen*, vol. I, William H. Goold (ed.) (reprint. Edinburgh: T&T Clark, 1882).
21. Suzanne McDonald, 'Beholding the Glory of God in the Face of Jesus Christ: John Owen and the "Reforming" of the Beatific Vision', in *The Ashgate Research Companion to John Owen's Theology*, Kelly M. Kapic and Mark Jones (eds) (Farnham: Ashgate, 2012), p. 146.
22. McDonald, 'Beholding the Glory of God', p. 146.

or Roman Catholic account.²³ By focusing on the person of the Son, the human nature of Christ is not to be considered a hindrance to the beatific vision, but a constituent of it. His humanity is not per se the reason for worshipping Christ; rather his divine person is, but his humanity remains united to his person and is thus a vehicle of fellowship with the divine person. As McDonald observes: 'For Owen, we must ensure not only that Christ remains at the centre of our *thinking about* the beatific vision. He is absolutely insistent that we must recognize that it is *the person of Christ, in his ascended, glorified humanity*, who is at the heart of the beatific vision itself.'²⁴ Furthermore, a focus on the person of Christ as the object of the vision can include the sight of the glorified creature's physical resurrected body. While 'the vision of God is principally intellectual, precisely because it entails understanding the fullness of the person of Christ, it is not exclusively so. To Owen, to deny a place to our glorified bodily senses is scripturally and theologically wrong-headed.'²⁵ By refocusing the vision on the fellowship believers have with the incarnate Christ, Owen was able to account for the importance of the resurrected body for beholding God in Christ.

While Bavinck may not have given as much detail to the beatific vision as Owen, he was clearly aware of the broader Reformed (perhaps, specifically Owenian) reshaping of the beatific vision and appealed to it in this crucial juncture. This in turn puts to rest Boersma's claim that Bavinck never drew from the broader Puritan and Reformed accounts to give a positive sketch of the beatific vision. The reference to Owen should also be kept in mind when one revisits the passage on the centrality of the Son, explored in the last chapter: 'The Son is not only the mediator of reconciliation (*mediator reconciliationis*) on account of sin, but even apart from sin he is the mediator of union (*mediator unionis*) between God and his creation. He is not only the exemplary cause (*causa exemplaris*) but also the final cause (*causa finalis*) of creation.'²⁶ In fact, Bavinck's overall description of the beatific vision is consistent with Boersma's summary of Owen's account: '(1) Christ in his human nature will always be the immediate head of the glorified creation; (2) Christ will forever be the means and way of communication between God and the saints; (3) Christ in his human nature will be the eternal object of divine glory, praise, and worship – contemplation will lead to praise.'²⁷ Both Owen

---

23. Boersma makes the same observation regarding the difference between Owen and Aquinas: 'In many respects Owen's approach is simply traditional, probably taken directly from Thomas Aquinas. The one major difference is that Owen uses this theological framework to speak of the saints' beatific vision of Christ (the glory of his incarnation and redemption) – rather than the essence of God', *Seeing God*, p. 325.
24. McDonald, 'Beholding the Glory of God', p.153. Emphases original.
25. McDonald, 'Beholding the Glory of God', p. 157.
26. Bavinck, *RD* 4: p. 685.
27. Boersma, *Seeing God*, p. 326. I suggest that Bavinck's use of Owen here indicates that his account improves on Kuyper's, which, as Boersma notes, leaves Christology behind in the eschaton as believers are considered to directly behold the essence of God (see Boersma, *Seeing God*, pp. 340, 343).

and Bavinck center the beatific vision on the fellowship believers have with the incarnate Christ.

This central place that Christ occupies in Bavinck's account of the final communion with God is further signaled a few pages following the appeal to Owen, where he argues that Christology is the 'central point of the whole system of dogmatics', such that 'all other dogmas either prepare for it or are inferred from it'.[28] Crucially for our purposes, Bavinck specifies that Christology is 'the heart of dogmatics', in which the '*religious-ethical life* of Christianity' is found.[29] What Bavinck means by this Christocentric claim can be inferred from the earlier sections. In and through Christ our religious and ethical fellowship with God is restored, and this is precisely because Christ is, uniquely, God incarnate.[30] Christ is God in a metaphysical sense (in his divine nature and person), but Christians, who are merely metaphysically human, are one with God only ever in that religious and ethical sense.

These observations illumine what Bavinck means when he appeals to what he calls 'the principle of Protestantism'.[31] To worship Jesus on account of his humanity alone, for Bavinck, whether in the Harnackian sense where he is only venerated as such by the Christian consciousness or in the Catholic sense of the deification of Jesus's human nature is to run against this principle. Bavinck writes, 'naming Jesus "God" and venerating him as God, if he is in fact only a human, is a pantheistic mixing of the Creator with the creature, a return to pagan idolatry and Roman Catholic creature deification, both of them things that are diametrically opposed to the principle of Protestantism'.[32] While Bavinck does not define the so-called principle explicitly on this immediate passage, he does indicate the antithesis of the principle: any account or doctrine that may lead to the ontological blurring of the creator-creature distinction.

There are further clues in Bavinck's corpus on what he means by this principle, and they are usually found in those passages where he is contrasting Reformed and Roman Catholic accounts of the relation between (human) nature and grace. In Bavinck's mind, whereas a Reformed account recognizes the intrinsic goodness of created human nature and its fittingness for communion with the divine, Roman Catholic accounts consider nature to be, by itself, unfit for the supernatural and is thus intrinsically in need of super-added grace. That super-added grace elevates nature and makes it able to reach the supernatural end. Hence, 'Rome replaced the antithetical relation of sin and grace with the contrast between natural and supernatural religion.'[33] Whereas the Reformed recognizes that an antithetical

---

28. Bavinck, *RD* 3: p. 274. The question of Bavinck and Christology as the central dogma proves to be quite complex. See Pass, *The Heart of Dogmatics*.
29. Bavinck, *RD* 3: p. 274. Emphasis mine.
30. Bavinck, *RD* 3: p. 285.
31. Bavinck, *RD* 3: p. 285.
32. Bavinck, *RD* 3: p. 285.
33. Bavinck, 'Common Grace', p. 45.

relation exists between humanity's sin and divine favor, Roman Catholicism locates the antithesis in human nature *as such* over against the supernatural.

The problem with humanity, in Bavinck's view, is not that it lacks the supernatural gifts to reach a supernatural existence, but that it refuses God and turns against God in sin: sin and the failure to obtain divine favor are an *ethical* and not an ontological problem. As Bavinck writes, this is what sets Protestantism apart from Roman Catholicism:

> Precisely because Protestants combat sin more seriously than Rome does, they are also able to appreciate the proper worth of the natural order. In Protestantism the mechanical relation of nature and grace gives way to an ethical relation. The Christian faith is not a quantitative reality that spreads itself in a transcendent fashion over the natural but a religious and ethical power that enters the natural in an immanent fashion and eliminates only that which is unholy.[34]

Grace, therefore, is not against nature as such but only against sin, which is the ethical misdirection of persons against God and neighbor. There are many implications from this passage that cannot be teased out here but has been treated elsewhere – that the image of God and original righteousness are concreated with human nature before the fall, that sin is not an ontological reality but an ethical violation of the covenant of works, and that grace, therefore, restores all that is natural and does not hang above natural life – but what is most relevant for our present purposes here is that, in Bavinck's mind, to define communion with God as an ontological elevation of human nature (in deification) is to violate this Protestant principle, for the positing of the need for deification presupposes that sin is an ontological problem that arises from an intrinsically unfit human nature.[35] Rather, if sin is an ethical issue, indeed, a violation of a *covenant* between God and humanity, then communion with God ought to be defined covenantally as well, the restoration of the ethical relation between God and humanity: 'Thus the Reformation based her position not on the *religio supernaturalis* but on the covenant of grace, *foedus gratiae*.'[36] This ethical relation between nature and grace is so important to Bavinck that he would evaluate other wings of the Protestant

---

34. Bavinck, 'The Catholicity of Christianity and the Church', p. 236. See also parallel comments in Bavinck, *RD* 2, pp. 545–7, and *RD* 4, p. 410.

35. On the implications of the nature-grace relation in neo-Calvinism, see Jennifer Patterson, 'Neo-Calvinism and Roman Catholicism', in *T&T Clark Handbook of Neo-Calvinism*, Nathaniel Gray Sutanto and Cory Brock (eds) (London: Bloomsbury T&T Clark, 2024), 337–50, Mattson, *Restored to Our Destiny*, and Brock and Sutanto, *Neo-Calvinism*, chapters 3, 6, 7, and 8. Bavinck's judgments on this issue are shared broadly by others in the Reformed tradition; see, for instance, Francis Turretin's comments in *Institutes of Elenctic Theology* I, p. 471. See also Harrison Perkins, *Righteous by Design: Covenantal Merit and Adam's Original Integrity* (Fearn: Christian Focus, 2024).

36. Bavinck, 'Common Grace', p. 50.

reformation to be inconsistent with Protestant principles insofar as they revert back to a qualitative antithesis between nature and grace.[37]

Thus, for Bavinck, the principle of Protestantism, when applied to the beatific vision, refers to that life in union with God which consists in the religious-ethical fellowship we have with God in Christ, rather than a metaphysical union between God and humanity, which would require the ontological elevation of human nature. Focusing on our ethical communion with Christ as our covenant lord preserves the principle, for the restoration that grace brings about is described here ethically rather than ontologically. The problem to be addressed by Christ, again, is not metaphysical but rather ethical.

It is unsurprising that critics might be disappointed in the briefer treatment Bavinck offers in the fourth volume on the beatific vision if they fail to attend to these broader Christological and covenantal concerns in volume three of the *Dogmatics*. Boersma argues that Bavinck's treatment of the beatific vision in the fourth volume is rather malformed, in that Bavinck spends too much space criticizing past accounts of the vision, and left only 'perfunctory' and 'passing' remarks by way of positive description of the vision.[38] Indeed, the brief section where Bavinck explicitly mentions the contemplation (*visio*) and enjoyment of God as the 'essence of our future blessedness' is, for Boersma, a perfunctory historical description of medieval views on the matter that merely notes Bavinck's preference for Bonaventure's position over Aquinas and Scotus.[39]

Moreover, Boersma makes the judgment that Bavinck did not develop his own account of the beatific vision because his eschatology was 'too this-worldly to do so'.[40] Observing the sections on the renewal of creation in the fourth volume, Boersma rightly observes that Bavinck was concerned to maintain the metaphysical continuity between this world and the next, and that even Sabbath rest in the last day does not preclude cultural and natural activity.[41] However, this pre-occupation with continuity functionally sidelines the role of the beatific vision in Bavinck's actual treatment of the eschaton, despite formal affirmations of the latter as the central benefit of eternal life. Bavinck, then, functions as Boersma's foil in *Seeing God*'s attempt to retrieve a properly catholic and Christological account of the beatific vision.

When one revisits the salient sections on the beatific vision in the fourth volume of Bavinck's *Dogmatics*, however, one sees important markers that point back to those Christological emphases that we have explored above from the third volume. It is worth noticing, first, the Christological glosses with which Bavinck highlights the spiritual blessings of the eschaton: 'Still the spiritual blessings are

---

37. See, e.g., Bavinck's critiques of Luther and Zwingli, in 'Catholicity of Christianity', pp. 237–8.
38. Boersma, *Seeing God*, p. 34.
39. Bavinck, *RD* 4: p. 722.
40. Boersma, *Seeing God*, p. 38.
41. 'Bavinck waxes eloquent about the combination of action and contemplation in the eschaton'. Boersma, *Seeing God*, p. 39.

the most important and innumerable … eternal life (Matt. 19:16-17, 29; etc.); the vision of, and conformity to *God and Christ* … and fellowship with, and the service and praise of, *God and Christ*'.[42] Second, Bavinck defines fellowship with God as *religious*, and that he juxtaposes his religious view of communion with what he takes to be the Roman Catholic perspective:

> It does not consist in the contemplation of God (*visio Dei*) in a Catholic sense, a contemplation to which human nature can only be elevated by a superadded gift. On the other hand, neither is it a slow and gradual development of the Christian life as led by believers already on earth …. In that [consummated] life, *religion – fellowship with God – is primary and central*'.[43]

And after arguing that this communion with God is amplified by the fellowship believers have with the triumphant church, Bavinck refocuses attention on the biblical descriptions of Christ's final lordship and his role in the *covenant* of grace, writing: 'All the saints together will then fully comprehend the breadth and length and height and depth of the love of *Christ* (Eph. 3:18-19). They will together be filled with all the fullness of God, *inasmuch as Christ, himself filled with the fullness of God*, will in turn fill the believing community with *himself* and make it his fulness'.[44] The previous administrations of the covenant of grace, such as the one through the representation of Abraham, Moses, or David, anticipate Christ's representational headship over the earth, when he becomes the object of worship in the eschaton: 'In this dispensation all things in heaven and earth will be gathered up under Christ (Eph. 1:10). And one day at the end every knee will bow before Christ and [every] tongue will confess him as Lord (Phil. 2:10-11).'[45] It is precisely through the human being bowing down to the Christ that 'God

---

42. Bavinck, *RD* 4: p. 722. Emphases mine.

43. Bavinck, *RD* 4: p. 722. Emphasis mine. Bavinck often uses the terms 'vision of God', 'communion' with God, and 'dwelling' with God (and Christ) interchangeably, in order to indicate that the vision is not a metaphysical union with God but rather consists in an ethical fellowship with the incarnate Christ, who is the mediator between glorified humanity and the triune God. For example, Bavinck writes, 'to know God in the face of Christ – by faith here on earth, by sight in the hereafter – not only *results* in blessedness but *is* as such blessedness and eternal life', *RD* 1, p. 53, emphasis original. On some occasions, however, Bavinck wants to emphasize that the vision of God and communion go together because humanity's eschatological knowledge of God is both intellectual and ethical (contemplative and volitional): see, for example, *RD* 4, p. 722, and 'Kennis en leven', in *Kennis en leven: Opstellen en artikelen uit vroegere jaren*, C. B. Bavinck (ed.) (Kampen: Kok, 1922), p. 222: 'a beholding of God and a fellowship with God … go far beyond the usual opposition between knowing and doing, of theory and practice; it embraces head and heart together and employs both mind and will'. I am thankful to Israel Guerrero for pointing me to this latter source.

44. Bavinck, *RD* 4: p. 723. Emphasis mine.

45. Bavinck, *RD* 4: p. 723.

will be all in all (1 Cor. 15:28)'.⁴⁶ If one reads these admittedly briefer statements on the beatific vision in volume four in isolation, one might indeed receive the impression that Bavinck was uninterested in the doctrine. However, read within the overall shape of Bavinck's Christology, the material in Volume 4 signals back to Bavinck's analysis of Christology provided in Volume 3 and presupposes it. Communion with God consists in the communion of renewed humanity with the risen and ascended Christ, and that communion is religious in character.

Therefore Bavinck does, indeed, contra Boersma, offer a positive account of the final beatific vision. He does not just formally affirm that the communion that saints have with God on the last day is of the highest importance; he also specifies that this union consists in a religious, ethical, and personal fellowship with God in Jesus Christ, one that is consistent with Puritan reformations of the beatific vision and a Reformed emphasis on the covenantal, personal relation. In this way, Bavinck argues that his account of the communion bond that saints have with Christ is a distinctly Reformed account, rather than an Eastern Orthodox, Roman, or Lutheran one.

On the 'Mystical'

This final sub-section addresses this potential issue: Bavinck still did not give as much detail on the nature of the beatific vision within the *Dogmatics* as Owen did, which prompts one to ask why that is the case. Addressing this issue requires us to revisit the analogy that Bavinck establishes between the hypostatic union of the incarnation and the saint's final union with God, and to attend to his definition of what is properly 'mystical'.

On one level, the observations above on the Protestant principle already address the potential issue on why Bavinck did not give as much detail on the beatific vision in the fourth volume: he had already done so in the third volume, and he refuses to provide metaphysical explications of the nature of that final communion. But there is a deeper way to address this question, and that lies in his perceived analogy between the incarnation and the believer's communion with God, and in his definition of the term 'mystical'.

Bavinck draws on the Chalcedonian formula to defend his priority on scriptural fidelity and epistemic modesty in the presence of mystery: '[the Chalcedonian definition] has the advantage that it does not neglect any of the scriptural data, maintains the name of Christ as the only mediator between God and humankind, and in addition still offers the plainest and clearest understanding of the mystery of the incarnation.'⁴⁷ These characteristics of Chalcedon – criteria for what makes a particular doctrinal construction sound, as it were – inform Bavinck's account of the final communion with God: 'When this communion with God is truly – not as a fiction but as true reality – understood, its kinship with and analogy to the incarnation leap out at us.'⁴⁸ Bavinck's reasoning here is subtle and careful.

46. Bavinck, *RD* 4: p. 724.
47. Bavinck, *RD* 3: p. 304.
48. Bavinck, *RD* 3: p. 304.

Chalcedon, in his mind, affirmed the Scriptural data by outlining the formula of the hypostatic union, namely, that the divine second person of the Trinity is united to an impersonal human nature. Chalcedon did not explain *how* the divine person might indwell the human, but merely affirmed *that* this was so. Similarly, a Reformed account of the beatific vision should uphold the Scriptural data and outline that, in Christ, we are *united* with God without going in excess by explicating *how* that union works that goes beyond Scriptural data: 'it [the incarnation] is integrally connected with the essence of religion.'[49] When Bavinck uses the term 'mystical' union, then, the sense of mystical for Bavinck consists merely in denoting a mystery that cannot be explained. To say it another way: *Just as Chalcedon defined Christology in ways that outline both what must be affirmed and the boundaries of orthodoxy, without explicating the central mystery confessed, so should a Protestant conception of the beatific vision do the same.*[50]

As Bavinck writes, 'communion with God' is mystical in the sense that it goes beyond our understanding:

> Religion is communion with God. Without it humans cannot be truly and completely human. The image of God is not a superadded gift but belongs to human nature. That communion with God is a mystical union. It far exceeds our understanding. It is a most intimate union with God by the Holy Spirit, a union of persons, an unbreakable and eternal covenant between God and ourselves, which cannot be at all adequately described by the word 'ethical' and is therefore called 'mystical'. It is so close that it transforms humans in the divine image and makes them participants of the divine nature (2 Cor. 3:18; Gal.: 2:20; 2 Pet. 1:4).[51]

Though Bavinck rejects *mysticism* (as shown in the earlier sections above, defined as an ontological deification of human nature for communion with God), he insists that the term 'mystical' is still appropriate to describe the final union humans will have with God, insofar as it is purified of its physical connotations (on pain of denying the 'principle of protestantism').[52] He can, with the passages cited above from Paul and Peter, continue to speak of a partaking of the divine nature, so long as we remain modest about what that partaking precisely entails. The union is mystical in the sense that it is, like the incarnation itself, something to be believed, outlined, but not apprehended as such, since 'it far exceeds our understanding'.

This point on epistemic modesty confirms Cory Brock's observation that Bavinck's reticence to speak in great detail on the nature of the beatific vision is

---

49. Bavinck, *RD* 3: p. 304.

50. This epistemological point, coupled with Bavinck's 'principle of Protestantism', explains why Bavinck does not follow many in the medieval Reformed scholastic tradition (including the Leiden Synopsis) in specifying or explicating how the intellect also beholds the divine essence. On this issue, see Zachary Seals, 'The Beatific Vision in the *Synopsis Purioris*: Its Medieval Context', *Reformed Theological Review* 82 (2023): pp. 1–24.

51. Bavinck, *RD* 3: p. 304.

52. Bavinck, *RD* 3: p. 305.

due to the brevity of Scripture itself on the matter. As Bavinck writes: 'modesty is certainly in keeping with Scripture. The Bible indeed teaches that the blessed in heaven behold God, but does not go into any detail, and elsewhere expressly calls God invisible.'[53] Scriptural brevity entails epistemic modesty with regard to any particular doctrine. Hence, Brock argues that perhaps the main spirit that fuelled Bavinck's many objections to past discussions on the vision was that they were too metaphysically speculative, going beyond the bounds of our epistemic jurisdiction given the paucity of revealed material on the doctrine. 'For Bavinck, the theologian must take one's understanding of salvation as far as Scripture, but disallow the imagination to over-determine that for which there is no definitive answer.'[54] Brock also ably shows that Bavinck continued to affirm the centrality of the beatific vision as humanity's telos in many places outside of the *Dogmatics*, while resisting undue speculation about the metaphysical workings of the vision. From an early text like 'The Kingdom of God, the Highest Good', to his more mature *The Wonderful Works of God*, Brock notes that Bavinck always stressed beholding and communing with God as the Christian's ultimate hope. As Brock writes: 'In the WWG [*Wonderful Works of God*], in fact, he spends very little time explaining the secondary benefits of life in the kingdom, only describing the bounty of material life in one paragraph.'[55] When one zooms out and surveys Bavinck's overall *oeuvre*, then, the central hope of the beatific vision is not eclipsed by Bavinck's emphasis on the metaphysical continuity between this world and the next, thus challenging Boersma's claim that Bavinck's eschatology was unduly naturalized or too 'this-worldly'.

To return to our point on the principle of mystery upheld in the Chalcedonian formula, the parallel between the personal union of the divine and human natures in Christ and the believer's communion with God should not lead one to overlook real differences between the two. After disclosing the analogies between the incarnation and the believer's communion with God, Bavinck goes on to describe the discontinuities. Attending to these discontinuities further illumines Bavinck's positive account. The incarnation consists in the union of a divine person with an impersonal human nature, whereas the union we have with God in Christ is covenantal, made between two personal parties: 'A covenant is not something that can be improvised; it has to be made with a people in the person of its king or representative. Similarly, God, to make his communion with humankind a reality, united himself with it in Christ as its head.'[56] Christ, therefore, is united to God in a unique way, for he is the representative of humanity and is himself none other than the Second person of the Trinity. We are united to God, not in that hypostatic way, but covenantally and ethically through Christ's federal representation. As Bavinck

---

53. Bavinck, *RD* 2: pp. 189–90.
54. Brock, 'Revisiting Bavinck and the Beatific Vision', p. 378.
55. Brock, 'Revisiting Bavinck and the Beatific Vision', p. 376. Hence, Bavinck on Adam's end: 'his nature was kindred with the divine, and his destiny was the vision of God'. *Guidebook*, p. 85.
56. Bavinck, *RD* 3: p. 305.

elaborates, while the believer and God enjoy a 'religious relation', a 'covenant', consisting in God communing with a people through a 'representative [Christ]', the incarnation is not a 'union of persons; it is a personal and substantial union; it is not a moral union like a marriage, not a matter of agreement in disposition and will, no communion of love alone. It is, however, a natural union ... as Athanasius and Cyril called it.'[57] The enjoyment of God in the beatific vision is thus a personal and religious union, more akin to a marriage or a communion of love. God is united to humanity not physically but covenantally. Human beings behold God in Christ as their husband. Once again, covenant plays an operative role in Bavinck's eschatology – this time in his participation in the 'reformation' of the beatific vision, and the term mystical denotes a unique yet *personal* and *covenantal* union that is in view between God and the faithful.

In sum, by affirming that the beatific vision is mystical, personal, ethical, and religious in this *covenantal* sense, Bavinck's account has several strengths without sacrificing epistemic modesty. Bavinck's view affirms the mystery of the beatific vision, is shaped Christo-centrically, is in line with the covenantal emphases of the Reformed tradition, integrates the resurrected body and physical sight as essential to the beholding of God, and does not compromise the Creator-creature distinction.

Conclusion

This chapter offers an argument that puts to rest claims to the effect that Bavinck was uninterested in engaging with the traditioned debates on the beatific vision, or that he refrained from giving a positive account of the doctrine. Furthermore, the muted discussion of the vision in Volume 4 of the *Dogmatics* is explainable in part due to the sustained engagement with it in Volume 3 of the same. With Bavinck's view in hand, Protestants have yet another resource from which to reflect on the beatific vision, for Bavinck utilizes covenant theology in order to articulate a positive account of that final communion with God. Furthermore, Bavinck's appeal to the 'Protestant principle' to ground his claim that a construal of the vision should be disciplined by Christology and the brevity of the Scriptural witness calls for more research, as other Protestants, unlike Bavinck, continued to argue for a spiritual vision of God that nonetheless did not deify the creature.[58]

All in all, this chapter has investigated Bavinck's doctrine of the beatific vision: that it is mystical, covenantal, personal, religious, and christologically focused. The

---

57. Bavinck, *RD* 3: p. 305. Bavinck goes on to clarify, on the same page, that this 'is not to say that that union was necessary and automatically resulted from one of the two or from both natures; rather, it is so called because it is not moral in nature, but a union of natures in the person of the Son, not a natural but a personal union'.

58. Along with Kuyper, cf. Turretin, *Institutes of Elenctic Theology*, 3, pp. 610–1; *Leiden Synopsis*, 3, pp. 589–601.

fellowship we have with one another as Christ's bride in a renewed and glorified creation should not eclipse this real destiny that all of redeemed humanity will enjoy with Christ. As such, this chapter contributes to the book by exploring, again, the ultimate telos of humanity as a whole. As all fell in Adam, all can be risen by, in, and for Christ.

CONCLUSION

This book has provided a sustained close reading of Herman Bavinck's contributions to theological anthropology and positions him in conversation with current and historical dialogues on embodiment, revelation, affect, phenomenology, the cognitive science of religion, ethics, race, covenant, and the beatific vision. The emphasis throughout has been on the holistic character of Bavinck's vision of humanity, suggesting ways in which his theological anthropology cuts across several potential binaries in contemporary discourse, between affect and reason, body and soul, animality and religiosity, unity and diversity, and between a this-worldly or other-worldly eschatology.

Let us take stock of the arguments of the whole work.

Chapter 2 offers a chronological analysis of Bavinck's account of the body–soul relation, and observes his increased focus on the unconscious and personality as important features of the self. While not identifying the precise point of contact between the body and the soul, Bavinck argues that the two are closely enmeshed yet remain distinct. In seeking to articulate that close relation, Bavinck argues that there is a parallel between the body and soul that centers on the unconscious life and personality. Just as the soul has an 'ego', an 'I' that animates the ways in which it exercises its faculties that are irreducible and often mysterious to the self, so is the body animated by unconscious stirrings that move its actions and direction. In other words, beneath the body and soul is a central unity, an unconscious self, a personality that determines the direction of the human being as a psychosomatic whole. Tracing through Bavinck's works chronologically, from his *Beginselen der psychologie* (Foundations of Psychology) to *Overwinning der ziel* (Triumph of the Soul), I show that he remains consistent in his thought on this matter, despite differing emphases in certain writings. This chapter also shows how Bavinck sought to negotiate classical orthodox convictions on the metaphysics of the soul while also doing justice to newer psychological and physiological studies that sought to give a fuller account of the human person.

The third and fourth chapters constructively relate Bavinck's theological anthropology to current discussions on affect theory, Heideggerian phenomenology, and the cognitive science of religion. Chapter 3 attends to Bavinck's construal of the human self as an essentially *religious* self, as the self is always exposed to God's general revelation and lives *coram deo*. As such, I show that Bavinck's characterization of human psychology and the religious psyche interweaves the insights of these fields by suggesting that all human cognition arises from an affective, embodied existence. The fourth chapter applies Bavinck's phenomenological insights into current debates in the cognitive science of religion regarding how to interpret the cognitive or noetic consequences of sin, and especially regarding whether one is born 'believer' or 'idolater'. In so doing, I advance an alternative model that emphasizes the *psychical effects* of sin – a model of sin's effects on the human self that is more phenomenological than epistemological.

The fifth chapter follows the insight of the holistic, situated, and social view of the self and examines humanity considered as an organic whole. It then shows the implications of this organic anthropology for Bavinck's account of original sin and the concomitant doctrines of actual sin and renewal. I show that although Bavinck accepts covenantal federalism – the thesis according to which Adam represents his progeny by virtue of a divine constitution – Bavinck was able to evade the charge that federalism involves believing in a legal fiction by incorporating certain moves within realism. That is, Adam represents humanity fittingly due to the organic character of the human race. If an organism consists in displaying a pattern of a unity-in-diversity, then Adam's federal headship represents the organism's unity. His representational character thus fits in with humanity's organic ontology. This reference to the corporate whole of humanity as that which comprises the image of God, based on the Trinitarian character of creational ontology, is a distinct contribution of Bavinck, especially from the vantage point of Reformed orthodoxy. Actual sin then takes the form of egocentricity, and the corresponding grace of renewal turns the self toward others, re-creating bonds of love. Egocentricity ruptures the relational ties that bind humanity's organism, and renewal restores those bonds that in turn form a new humanity in the kingdom of God. I then show how Bavinck's work here can be fruitfully put in dialogue with certain emphases in Jonathan Edwards studies and Jennifer Herdt's recent work on the *Bildung* tradition.

One of the differences between Bavinck's account of corporate humanity with the *Bildung* tradition is the latter's vulnerability to be allied with a form of German nationalism. Herdt directs attention to Karl Barth's critique of the tradition, according to which it is called to adopt a posture of attentive listening to the Word of God. Alertness to the divine Word disrupts our sinful attempts to render God's will immanent, and to identify that will with a particular nation's historical trajectory. The sixth and seventh chapters, then, take their cue from this critique to argue that Bavinck, like Barth, offered resources to resist identifying the divine will with a particular nation or culture. I argue here that Bavinck offered a genealogical diagnosis of the origins of racism in the nineteenth century and identified two, mutually coordinated trajectories: a 'top-down' form of racism identifying one particular race's history (Aryanism) as the norm by which all other cultures ought to be normed; and a 'bottom-up' trajectory pointing back to an 'original' or 'primitive' human being, out of which Western civilization, religion, and culture evolved. Provocatively, Bavinck argues that it is precisely by rejecting transcendent norms and locating morality in the immanent that one is led to the tragedies and sins of racism, as showcased by particular movements of German philosophy near the turn of the twentieth century. I locate Bavinck's argument within the broader reception of neo-Calvinism on race and thus hope to show that, though most of the attention has been given to Kuyper and his complicated legacy for understanding the intersection of theology and race, Bavinck offers more stable and potentially fruitful grounds for understanding racial diversity, especially as one pays attention to his appreciation of the pliability and catholicity of the Christian faith, resulting in its multiform character. Chapter 7 continues this exploration by tracing the connection between the religious self and race, and it sketches a theological account of human diversity in the three states of creation, sin, and grace. Together, these chapters also put Bavinck in conversation with contemporary and neo-Kuyperian theologians on the intersection of theology and race.

With humanity's corporate renewal from sin and the telos of glory in view, Chapter 8 considers human destiny and the question of whether the incarnation is necessary for union with God absent the fall. Bavinck's position is what I have called the 'Consummation Anyway' view, according to which the incarnation was a post-fall remedy for sin, and hence would not be necessary for humanity to achieve its consummate end prior to the fall. Centering on covenant theology, Bavinck offered a unified voice with other texts in the high orthodox period of the Reformed tradition that obedience to the covenant of works would be the means by which human beings would achieve consummation absent the fall. In this regard, I show how Bavinck's position provides an alternative to the recent Christological anthropological construction of Marc Cortez and his arguments for the necessity of the incarnation for union with the divine, and I respond to three further objections: (1) that the 'Consummation Anyway' position compromises the claim that grace is necessary for salvation, (2) whether finite human obedience can attain an eternal weight of glory, as signified by consummation, and (3) that Bavinck's 'Consummation Anyway' is inconsistent with the Christo-centric statements he made elsewhere.

The final chapter focuses on Bavinck's view of just what this consummation entails and presents Bavinck's covenantal and Christo-centric account of the beatific vision. I thus challenge the criticism that Bavinck's eschatological outlook was too pre-occupied with 'this-wordliness' and that he lacked interest in providing a positive account of the beatific vision. Bavinck had theological reasons to resist unduly speculative investigations of the vision, and he was motivated by what he perceives to be the logic of Protestantism to depict the vision not metaphysically (as a deification of the human nature or in the vision of the divine essence), but personally and ethically, as an everlasting covenantal fellowship one will have with the risen Christ.

There remains constructive questions and avenues to be explored on Bavinck's anthropology, especially in relation to topics like gender and sexuality, nonhuman animals, eco-theology, and humanity's relation to technology. On gender and sexuality, one can, for instance, explore Bavinck's maturation on the question of the role of women in society, from his 1908 work on *The Christian Family* to his 1918 treatise on *The Woman in Contemporary Society*. On the question of nonhuman animals and eco-theology, one can explore Bavinck's comments on the representational and embodied connection of humanity with its physical habitat and environment, and the ethical consequences of the so-called 'cultural mandate', which dovetails well with current observations on the vocational aspect of what it means to be made in the image of God. On humanity's relation to technology, one can explore the implications of Bavinck's account of the unconscious and personality as intrinsic features of the soul, especially in relation to conversations about artificial intelligence and consciousness.

This book, however, has provided a panoramic overview of Bavinck's anthropology and is a constructive exploration of its relation to current and historical dialogues on human embodiment, revelation, cognition, diversity, covenant, and consummation. I hope that this work charts the way forward for others to take up the work of constructive engagement with Bavinck and the broader neo-Calvinist tradition on other important issues. Equipped with a greater understanding of Bavinck and this tradition within context, Anglophone scholarship on Bavinck is now freed from merely engaging in interpretive debates and throat-clearing. The time for further constructive theological work is at hand, and one can now work to engage in such theological exploration, not merely *on* Herman Bavinck, but by working from, along, and beyond Bavinck's line. This book is one such step in that direction.

BIBLIOGRAPHY

Primary Sources

Bavinck, Herman. *Beginselen der psychologie*. Kampen: Bos, 1897.
Bavinck, Herman. *Bijbelsche en religieuze psychologie*. Kampen: Kok, 1920.
Bavinck, Herman. 'Calvin and Common Grace'. In *Calvin and the Reformation: Four Studies*, 99–130. Edited by William Park Armstrong. New York: Fleming Revell Co., 1909.
Bavinck, Herman. 'Catholicity of Christianity and the Church'. Translated by John Bolt. *Calvin Theological Journal* 27 (1992): 220–51.
Bavinck, Herman. *Christelijke wereldbeschouwing*. 2nd Edition. Kampen: Kok, 1913.
Bavinck, Herman. *Christelijke wereldbeschouwing*. 3rd Edition. Kampen: Kok, 1929.
Bavinck, Herman. *Christian Worldview*. Edited and translated by Nathaniel Gray Sutanto, James Eglinton, and Cory Brock. Wheaton: Crossway, 2019.
Bavinck, Herman. 'Common Grace'. Translated by Raymond C. Van Leeuwen. *Calvin Theological Journal* 24 (1989): 38–65.
Bavinck, Herman. *De vrouw in de hedendaagsche maatschappij*. Kampen: Kok, 1918.
Bavinck, Herman. 'Foundations of Psychology'. Translated by Jack Vander Born, Norman Kloosterman, and John Bolt. *The Bavinck Review* 9 (2018): 1–270.
Bavinck, Herman. *Gereformeerde dogmatiek*. 4 Volumes. 3rd Editon. Kampen: Kok, 1918.
Bavinck, Herman. *Guidebook for the Christian Religion*. Edited and translated by Gregory Parker Jr. and Cameron Clausing. Peabody: Hendrickson Academic, 2022.
Bavinck, Herman. 'Head and Heart'. Translated by Gregory Parker Jr. In *Modern Reformation*. 2021: https://modernreformation.org/resource-library/articles/head-and-heart/ (accessed November 10, 2021).
Bavinck, Herman. *Het christelijke huisgezin*. 2nd Edition. Kampen: Kok, 1912.
Bavinck, Herman. 'Hoofd en Hart'. *Christophilus: Jaarboekje Nederlandsch Jongelings-Verbond* (1892): 71–5.
Bavinck, Herman. 'Kennis en leven'. In *Kennis en leven: Opstellen en artikelen uit vroegere jaren*. Edited by C. B. Bavinck. Kampen: Kok, 1922.
Bavinck, Herman. 'My Journey to America: Appendix One'. In *Bavinck: A Critical Biography*, 301–14. Edited by James Eglinton. Grand Rapids: Baker Academic, 2021.
Bavinck, Herman. *Over het onbewuste: Wetenschappelijke samenkomst op 7 juli 1915*. Amsterdam: Kirchner, 1915.
Bavinck, Herman. *Philosophy of Revelation: A New Edition*. Edited by Cory Brock and Nathaniel Gray Sutanto. Peabody: Hendrickson, 2018.
Bavinck, Herman. *Reformed Dogmatics*. 4 Volumes. Edited by John Bolt. Translated by John Vriend. Grand Rapids: Baker Academic, 2004.
Bavinck, Herman. *Reformed Ethics*. 2 Volumes. Edited and translated by John Bolt. Grand Rapids: Baker Academic, 2022.
Bavinck, Herman. *The Christian Family*. Translated by Norman Kloosterman. Grand Rapids: Christian's Library Press, 2012.

Bavinck, Herman. 'The Kingdom of God and the Highest Good'. Translated by Norman Kloosterman. *The Bavinck Review* 2 (2011): 133–70.
Bavinck, Herman. 'Theology and Religious Studies'. In *Essays on Religion, Science, and Society*, 49–60. Edited by John Bolt. Translated by Harry Boonstra and Gerrit Sheeres. Grand Rapids: Baker Academic, 2008.
Bavinck, Herman. 'The Primacy of the Intellect or the Will'. In *Essays on Religion, Science, and Society*, 199–204. Edited by John Bolt. Translated by Harry Boonstra and Gerrit Sheeres. Grand Rapids: Baker Academic, 2008.
Bavinck, Herman. 'The Unconscious'. In *Essays on Religion, Science, and Society*, 199–204. Edited by John Bolt. Translated by Harry Boonstra and Gerrit Sheeres. Grand Rapids: Baker Academic, 2008.
Bavinck, Herman. *What Is Christianity?*. Translated by Greg Parker. Peabody: Hendricksen, 2022.
Bavinck, Herman. *Wijsbegeerte der openbaring*. Kampen: Kok, 1908.
Bavinck, Herman. *Wonderful Works of God*. Translated by Henry Zylstra. Glenside: Westminster Seminary Press, 2019.

Secondary Sources

Adams, Marilyn McCord. *Christ and Horrors: The Coherence of Christology*. Cambridge: University Press, 2006.
Allen, Michael. *Grounded in Heaven: Recentering Christian Hope and Life on God*. Grand Rapids: Eerdmans, 2018.
Allen, Michael. 'Future Prospects for Reformed Theology'. In *Oxford Handbook to Reformed Theology*, 623–30. Edited by Michael Allen and Scott Swain. Oxford: Oxford University Press, 2021.
Allen, Michael. 'On Bavinck, the Beatific Vision, and Theological Practice'. *Reformed Faith and Practice* 7 (2022): 57–62.
Allen, Michael. 'Review of Herman Bavinck, *Reformed Ethics*, vol. 1: *Created, Fallen, and Redeemed Humanity*'. *Reformed Faith and Practice* 4, no. 2 (2019): 69–72.
Allison, Henry. *Kant's Transcendental Idealism*. Revised Edition. New Haven: Yale University Press, 2004.
Ayres, Lewis. *Nicaea and Its Legacy: An Approach to Fourth Century Trinitarian Theology*. Oxford: Oxford University Press, 2004.
Ayers, Lewis. 'Seven Theses on Dogmatics and Patristics in Catholic Theology'. *Modern Theology* 38 (2022): 36–62.
Bacote, Vincent. 'Erasing Race: Racial Identity and Theological Anthropology'. In *Black Scholars in White Space: New Vistas in African American Studies from the Christian Academy*, 123–38. Edited by Anthony Bradley. Eugene: Pickwick, 2015.
Bacote, Vincent. 'Kuyper and Race'. In *Calvinism for a Secular Age: A Twenty-First Century Reading of Kuyper's Stone Lectures*, 146–62. Edited by Jessica and Robert Joustra. Downers Grove: IVP Academic, 2022.
Bacote, Vincent. *Reckoning with Race and Performing the Good News: In Search of a Better Evangelical Theology*. Leiden: Brill, 2021.
Bacote, Vincent. *The Spirit in Public Theology: Appropriating the Legacy of Abraham Kuyper*. Grand Rapids: Baker Academic, 2005.

Barret, Justin. 'Foreword'. In *God and the Brain: The Rationality of Belief*. Edited by Clark, Kelly James. Grand Rapids: Eerdmans, 2019.

Barret, Justin. *Why Would Anyone Believe in God?*. Walnut Creek: Altamitra Press, 2004.

Bauckham, Richard. *Theology of the Book of Revelation*. Cambridge: Cambridge University Press, 1993.

Bavinck, J. H. *Between the Beginning and the End: A Radical Kingdom Vision*. Grand Rapids: Eerdmans, 2014.

Biddiss, Michael. 'History as Destiny: Gobineau, H. S. Chamberlain, and Spengler'. *Transactions of the Royal Historical Society* 7 (1997): 73–100.

Boersma, Hans. *Seeing God: The Beatific Vision in the Christian Tradition*. Grand Rapids: Eerdmans, 2018.

Boesak, Allan. *Black and Reformed: Apartheid, Liberation, and the Calvinist Tradition*. Eugene: Wipf & Stock, 1984.

Bonaventure. *Breviloquium*. Edited and translated by Dominic Monti, O.F.M. New York: The Franscan Institute, 2005.

Botman, H. Russell. 'Is Blood Thicker Than Justice? The Legacy of Abraham Kuyper for Southern Africa.' In *Religion, Pluralism, and Public Life: Abraham Kuyper's Legacy for the Twenty-First Century*, 342–59. Edited by Luis Lugo. Grand Rapids: Eerdmans, 2000.

Bowleg, Lisa. 'Intersectionality: An Underutilized but Essential Theoretical Framework for Social Psychology'. In *The Palgrave Handbook of Critical Social Psychology*, 507–29. Edited by Brendan Gough. London: Palgrave Macmillan, 2017.

Bratt, James. *Abraham Kuyper: Modern Calvinist, Christian Democrat*. Grand Rapids: Eerdmans, 2013.

Bratt, James. 'The Context of Herman Bavinck's Stone Lectures: Culture and Politics in 1908'. *The Bavinck Review* 1 (2010): 4–24.

Brock, Cory. *Orthodox yet Modern: Herman Bavinck's Use of Schleiermacher*. Bellingham: Lexham Press, 2020.

Brock, Cory. 'Revisiting Bavinck and the Beatific Vision'. *Journal of Biblical and Theological Studies* 6 (2021): 367–82.

Brock, Cory and N. Gray Sutanto. *Neo-Calvinism: A Theological Introduction*. Bellingham: Lexham Press, 2023.

Caldwell-Harris, Catherine, Caitlin Fox Murphy, and Tessa Velasquez. 'Religious Belief Systems of Persons with High Functioning Autism'. *Proceedings of the Cognitive Science Society* 33 (2011): 2262–6. Austin: Cognitive Science Society.

Calvin, John. *Institutes of the Christian Religion*. Edited by John T. McNeill. Translated by Ford Lewis Battles. Library of Christian Classics. London: SCM, 1961.

Carter, J. Kameron. *Race: A Theological Account*. Oxford: Oxford University Press, 2008.

Chamberlain, Houston Stuart. *Die Grundlagen des neunzehnten Jahrhunderts*. 2 Volumes. München: Bruckmann, 1903.

Chamberlain, Houston Stuart. *Foundations of the Nineteenth Century*. 2 Volumes. Translated by John Lane. London: John Lane, 1910.

Clark, Kelly James. *God and the Brain: The Rationality of Belief*. Grand Rapids: Eerdmans, 2019.

Clark, Kelly James and Justin Barret. 'Reidian Religious Epistemology and the Cognitive Science of Religion'. *Journal of the American Academy of Religion* 79 (2011): 639–75.

Cochran, Elizabeth Agnew. *Receptive Human Virtures: A New Reading of Jonathan Edward's Ethics*. University Park: Pennsylvania State University Press, 2011.

Cochran, Elizabeth Agnew. 'The Moral Significance of Religious Affections: A Reformed Perspective on Emotions and Moral Formation'. *Studies in Christian Ethics* 28 (2015): 150–62.
Cortez, Marc. *Resourcing Theological Anthropology: A Constructive Account of Humanity in the Light of Christ*. Grand Rapids: Zondervan, 2017.
Crenshaw, Kimberlé. 'Demarginalizing the Intersection of Race and Sex: A Black Feminist Critique of Antidiscrimination Doctrine, Feminist Theory and Antiracist Politics.' *University of Chicago Legal Forum* 8 (1989): 139–67.
Crisp, Oliver. *Analyzing Doctrine: Toward a Systematic Theology*. Waco: Baylor University Press, 2019.
Crisp, Oliver. 'Incarnation without the Fall'. *Journal of Reformed Theology* 10, no. 3 (2016): 215–33.
Crisp, Oliver. 'Moral Character, Reformed Theology, and Jonathan Edwards'. *Studies in Christian Ethics* 30 (2017): 262–77.
De Cruz, Helen and Johan De Smedt. *A Natural History of Natural Theology: The Cognitive Science of Theology and Philosophy of Religion*. Massachusetts: MIT Press, 2015.
De Cruz, Helen and Johan De Smedt. 'Reformed and Evolutionary Epistemology and the Noetic Effects of Sin'. *International Journal for the Philosophy of Religion* 74 (2012): 49–66.
Dennett, Daniel. *Breaking the Spell: Religion as a Natural Phenomenon*. New York: Penguin Books, 2006.
Diller, Kevin. *Theology's Epistemological Dilemma: How Karl Barth and Alvin Plantinga Offer a Unified Response*. Downers Grove: IVP Academic, 2015.
Dreyfus, Hubert. 'Overcoming the Myth of the Mental: How Philosophers Can Benefit from the Phenomenology of Everyday Expertise'. In *Skillful Coping: Essays on the Phenomenology of Everyday Perception and Action*, 104–24. Edited by Mark Wrathall. Oxford: Oxford University Press, 2014.
Du Bois, William E. B. 'Talented Tenth: Memorial Address'. *Boule Journal* 15 (1948): 3–13.
Duby, Steven. *God in Himself: Scripture, Metaphysics, and the Task of Christian Theology*. Downers Grove: IVP Academic, 2020.
Duby, Steven. *Jesus and the God of Classical Theism*. Grand Rapids: Baker Academic, 2022.
Eglinton, James. *Bavinck: A Critical Biography*. Grand Rapids: Baker Academic, 2020.
Eglinton, James. '"Indignation Would Rise within You": Herman Bavinck on Racial Injustice in Europe and North America' (pre-print): 1–15.
Eglinton, James. 'Planting Tulips in the Rainforest: Herman and Johan Bavinck on Christianity in East and West'. *Journal of Biblical and Theological Studies* 6 (2021): 277–92.
Eglinton, James. *Trinity and Organism: Toward a New Reading of Herman Bavinck's Organic Motif*. London: T&T Clark, 2012.
Eglinton, James. '*Varia Americana* and Race: Kuyper as Antagonist and Protagonist'. *Journal of Reformed Theology* 11 (2017): 65–80.
Engelke, Matthew. *How to Think Like an Anthropologist*. Princeton: Princeton University Press, 2018.
Everhart, D. T. 'Communal Reconciliation: Corporate Responsibility and Opposition to Systemic Sin'. *International Journal of Systematic Theology* 25 (2023): 134–56.
Fabian, Johannes. *Time and the Other: How Anthropology Makes Its Object*. New York: Columbia University Press, 1983.
Feser, Edward. *Scholastic Metaphysics: A Contemporary Introduction*. Piscataway: Editiones Scholasticae, 2014.
Fesko, John V. *The Covenant of Works: The Origins, Development, and Reception of the Doctrine*. Oxford: Oxford University Press, 2020.

Gould, Paul and James Dew. *Philosophy: A Christian Introduction*. Grand Rapids: Baker Academic, 2019.

Green, Adam. 'Cognitive Science and the Natural Knowledge of God'. *The Monist* 96 (2013): 399–416.

Green, Adam. 'The Maturational Naturalness of Original Sin'. *TheoLogica* 6 (2022): 20–43.

Harinck, George. 'Calvinism Isn't the Only Truth: Herman Bavinck's Impressions of the USA'. In *The Sesquicentennial of Dutch Immigration: 150 Years of Ethnic Heritage; Proceedings of the 11th Biennial Conference of the Association for the Advancement of Dutch American Studies*, 151–60. Edited by Larry J. Wagenaar and Robert P. Swierenga. Holland: The Joint Archives of Holland, Hope College, 1998.

Harinck, George. '"Wipe Out Lines of Division (Not Distinctions)": Bennie Keet, Neo-Calvinism and the Struggle Against Apartheid'. *Journal of Reformed Theology* 11 (2017): 81–98.

Harris, Harriet A. 'Should We Say That Personhood Is Relational?'. *Scottish Journal of Theology* 51 (1998): 214–34.

Haslanger, Sally. 'Racism, Ideology, and Social Movements'. *Res Philosophica* 94 (2017): 1–22.

Haslanger, Sally. *Resisting Reality: Social Construction and Social Critique*. New York: Oxford University Press.

Hegel, Georg W. F. *Lectures on the Philosophy of Religion: One Volume Edition – The Lectures of 1827*. Edited by. Peter C. Hodgson. Oakland: University of California Press, 1988.

Heidegger, Martin. *Being and Time*. Translated by John Macquarrie, and Edward Robinson. Oxford: Blackwell, 1962.

Helm, Paul, *Human Nature from Calvin to Edwards*. Grand Rapids: Reformation Heritage Books, 2018.

Herdt, Jennifer. *Forming Humanity: Redeeming the German* Bildung *Tradition*. Chicago: University of Chicago Press, 2019.

Hunter, Justus. *If Adam Had Not Sinned: The Reason for the Incarnation from Anselm to Scotus*. Washington DC: Catholic University of America Press, 2020.

Ince, Irwyn. *Beautiful Community: Unity, Diversity, and the Church at Its Best*. Downers Grove: InterVarsity Press, 2020.

Inkpin, Andrew. *Disclosing the World: On the Phenomenology of Language*. Cambridge: MIT Press, 2016.

Jaarsma, Cornelius. *The Educational Philosophy of Herman Bavinck: A Textbook in Education*. Grand Rapids: Eerdmans, 1935.

Jennings, Willie James. 'Black Theology'. In *The New Cambridge Companion to Christian Doctrine*, 267–81. Edited by Michael Allen. Cambridge: Cambridge University Press, 2022.

Jennings, Willie James. *The Christian Imagination: Theology and the Origins of Race*. New Haven: Yale University Press, 2010.

Jochemsen, Henk and Gerrit Glas. *Verantwoord medisch handelen: Proeve van een christelijke medische ethiek*. Amsterdam: Buijten and Schipperheijn, 1997.

Johnson, Dru. *Biblical Philosophy: A Hebraic Approach to the Old and New Testaments*. Cambridge: Cambridge University Press, 2021.

Johnson, Mark. *The Body in the Mind: The Bodily Basis of Meaning, Imagination, and Reason*. Chicago: University of Chicago Press, 1987.

Jones, Paul Dafydd. *Patience – A Theological Exploration: Part One, from Creation to Christ*. London: Bloomsbury T&T Clark, 2022.

Jong, Jonathan, Christopher Kavanaugh, and Aku Visala. 'Born Idolators: The Limits of the Philosophical Implications of the Cognitive Science of Religion'. *Neue Zeitschrift für Systematische Theologie und Religionsphilosophie* 57 (2015): 244–66.

Joustra, Jessica. 'An Embodied Imago Dei: How Herman Bavinck's Understanding of the Image of God Can Help Inform Conversations on Race'. *Journal of Reformed Theology* 11 (2017): 9–23.

Kaemingk, Matthew. *Christian Hospitality and Muslim Immigration*. Grand Rapids: Eerdmans, 2018.

Kevles, Daniel J. *In the Name of Eugenics: Genetics and the Use of Human Heredity*. Cambridge: Harvard University Press, 1985.

Kilby, Karen. *God, Evil, and the Limits of Theology*. London: Bloomsbury, 2020.

Kuiper, D. Th. 'Groen and Kuyper on the Racial Issue'. In *Kuyper Reconsidered: Aspects of His Life and Work*, 69–81. Edited by Cornelis van der Kooi and Jan de Bruijn. Amsterdam: VU Uitgeverij, 1999.

Kuyper, Abraham. 'Common Grace'. In *Abraham Kuyper: A Centennial Reader*, 165–201. Edited by James Bratt. Grand Rapids: Eerdmans, 1998.

Kuyper, Abraham. *Lectures on Calvinism*. Grand Rapids: Eerdmans, 1999.

Kuyper, Abraham. *The Problem of Poverty*. Translated by James Skillen. Sioux Center: Dordt College Press, 2011.

Lapine, Matthew. *The Logic of the Body: Retrieving Theological Psychology*. Lexham: Bellingham, 2020.

Launonen, Lari and Ryan T. Mullins. 'Why Open Theism Is Natural and Classical Theism Is Not'. *Religions* 12, no. 956 (2021): 1–16.

Leidenhag, Joanna. 'The Challenge of Autism for Relational Approaches to Theological Anthropology'. *International Journal of Systematic Theology* 23 (2021): 109–34.

Levering, Matthew. *Engaging the Doctrine of Creation: Cosmos, Creatures, and the Wise and Good Creator*. Grand Rapids: Baker Academic, 2017.

Lewinsky, Monica and Max Joseph. *15 Minutes of Shame*. A+E Networks: Six West Media, 2021.

Liou, Jeff, and Robert Chao Romero. *Christianity and Critical Race Theory: A Faithful and Constructive Conversation*. Grand Rapids: Bakerr Academic, 2023.

Liou, Jeff. 'Critical Race Theory, Campus Culture, and the Reformed Tradition'. In *Reformed Public Theology: A Global Vision for Life in the World*, 237–49. Edited by Matthew Kaemingk. Grand Rapids: Baker Academic, 2021.

Liou, Jeff. 'Taking Up #blacklivesmatter: A Neo-Kuyperian Engagement with Critical Race Theory'. *Journal of Reformed Theology* 11 (2017): 99–120.

Lubbock, John. *Die Entstehung der Zivilisation und der Uruzstand des Menschengechlechtes, erläutert durch das innere und äußere Leben der Wilden*. Deutsch Ausgabe. Jena, 1875.

Lubbock, John. *The Origin of Civilization and the Primitive Condition of Man: Mental and Social Condition of Savages*. 5th Edition. New York: D. Appleton and Co., 1898.

MacDonald, Scott. 'Augustine'. In *The Oxford Handbook of the Epistemology of Theology*. 354–68. Edited by William Abraham and Frederick Aquino. Oxford: Oxford University Press, 2017.

MacIntyre, Alistair. *After Virtue: A Study of Moral Theory*. 3rd Edition. Notre Dame: University of Notre Dame Press, 2007.

Mattson, Brian, *Restored to Our Destiny: Eschatology and the Image of God in Herman Bavinck's Reformed Dogmatics*. Leiden: Brill, 2012.

McCall, Thomas. *Against God and Nature: The Doctrine of Sin*. Wheaton: Crossway, 2019.

McCall, Thomas. 'What's Not to Love? Rethinking Appeals to Tradition in Contemporary Debates in Trinitarian Theology'. *International Journal of Systematic Theology* (Online First: 2022): 1–21.
McDonald, Suzanne. 'Beholding the Glory of God in the Face of Jesus Christ: John Owen and the "Reforming" of the Beatific Vision'. In *The Ashgate Research Companion to John Owen's Theology*, 141–58. Edited by Kelly M. Kapic and Mark Jones. Farnham: Ashgate, 2012.
McFarland, Ian. *From Nothing: A Theology of Creation*. Louisville: Westminster John Knox, 2014.
McFarland, Ian. 'God, the Father Almighty: A Theological Excursus'. *International Journal of Systematic Theology* 18 (2016): 259–73.
McFarland, Ian. *The Word Made Flesh: A Theology of the Incarnation*. Louisville: Westminster John Knox, 2019.
McNabb, Tyler Dalton. *Religious Epistemology*. Cambridge: Cambridge University Press, 2019.
McNabb, Tyler and Michael DeVito. 'Cognitive Science of Religion and Classical Theism: A Synthesis', *Religions* 13 (2022): 1–7.
McFayden, Alistair. *Bound to Sin: Abuse, Holocaust, and the Christian Doctrine of Sin*. Cambridge: Cambridge University Press, 2000.
McKirland, Christa. *God's Provision, Humanity's Need: The Gift of Our Dependence*. Grand Rapids: Baker Academic, 2022.
Molendijk, Arie. *Protestant Theology and Modernity in the Nineteenth-Century Netherlands*. Oxford: Oxford University Press, 2022.
Molendijk, Arie. *The Emergence of the Science of Religion in the Netherlands*. Leiden: Brill, 2005.
Mouw, Richard and Sander Griffoen. *Pluralisms and Horizons: An Essay in Christian Public Philosophy*. Grand Rapids: Eerdmans, 1993.
Mouw, Richard. *Abraham Kuyper: A Short and Personal Introduction*. Grand Rapids: Eerdmans, 2011.
Nelson, Derek R. *What's Wrong with Sin: Sin in Individual and Social Perspective from Schleiermacher to Theologies of Liberation*. London: T&T Clark, 2009.
Orr, James. *God's Image in Man and Its Defacement in the Light of Modern Denials*. London: Hodder & Stoughton, 1906.
Oviedo, Lluis. 'Explanatory Limits in the Cognitive Science of Religion: Theoretical Matrix and Evidence Levels'. In *New Developments in the Cognitive Science of Religion: The Rationality of Religious Belief*, 15–35. Edited by Hans Van Eyghen, Rik Peels, and Gijsbert van den Brink. Cham: Springer, 2018.
Owen, John. 'Declaration of the Glorious Mystery of the Person of Christ, God and Man'. In *The Works of John Owen*. Volume I. Edited by William H. Goold. Edinburgh: T&T Clark, 1682.
Pass, Bruce. *The Heart of Dogmatics: Christology and Christocentricism in Herman Bavinck*. Göttingen: Vandenhoek & Ruprecht, 2020.
Pedersen, Daniel. *Schleiermacher's Theology of Sin and Nature: Agency, Value, and Modern Theology*. New York: Routledge, 2022.
Peels, Rik. 'Sin and Human Cognition of God'. *Scottish Journal of Theology* 64 (2011): 395–6.
Peels, Rik, Hans Van Eyghen, and Gijsbert van den Brink. 'Cognitive Science of Religion and the Cognitive Consequences of Sin'. In *New Developments in the Cognitive Science of Religion: The Rationality of Religious Belief*, 199–214. Springer, 2018.

Peppiatt, Lucy. *The Imago Dei: Humanity Made in the Image of God*. Eugene: Cascade, 2022.
Perkins, Harrison. '*Meritum Ex Pacto* in the Reformed Tradition: Covenantal Merit in Theological Polemics'. *Mid-America Journal of Theology* 31 (2020): 57–87.
Plantinga, Alvin. *Warranted Christian Belief*. Oxford: Oxford University Press, 2000.
Polyander, Johannes, Andreas Rivetus, Antonius Walaeus, and Anthonius Thysius. *Synopsis puroris theologie*. Edited by Herman Bavinck. Leiden: D. Donner, 1881.
Polyander, Johannes, Andreas Rivetus, Antonius Walaeus, and Anthonius Thysius. *Synopsis of a Purer Theology: Latin Text and English Translation*. Volume 1: Disputations, 1–23. Edited by Dolf te Velde. Translated by Dolf te Velde and Riemer A. Faber. Leiden: Brill, 2014.
Powery, Luke A. *Becoming Human: The Holy Spirit and the Rhetoric of Race*. Louisville: Westminster John Knox, 2022.
Ralston, Joshua. 'Islam as Christian Trope: The Place and Function of Islam in Reformed Dogmatic Theology'. *Muslim World* 107 (2017): 754–76.
Rasmussen, Joel D. S. 'The Transformation of Metaphysics'. In *The Oxford Handbook of Nineteenth-Century Christian Thought*, 11–34. Edited by Joel D. S. Rasmussen, Judith Wolfe, and Johannes Zachhuber. Oxford: Oxford University Press, 2017.
Riccucci, Norma M. *Critical Race Theory: Exploring Its Application to Public Administration*. Cambridge: Cambridge University Press, 2022.
Schaefer, Donovan O. *Religious Affects: Animality, Evolution, and Power*. Durham: Duke University Press, 2015.
Schaefer, Donovan O. *The Evolution of Affect Theory: The Humanities, the Sciences, and the Study of Power*. Cambridge: Cambridge University Press, 2019.
Schilder, Klaas. *The Klaas Schilder Reader*. Edited by George Harinck, Richard Mouw, and Marinus De Jong. Bellingham: Lexham Press, 2022.
Schleiermacher, Friedrich. *Christian Faith: A New Translation and Critical Edition*. Edited by Catherine L. Kelsey and Terrence N. Tice. Translated by Terrence N. Tice, Catherine L. Kelsey, and Edwina Lawler. Louisville: Westminster John Knox, 2016.
Schleiermacher, Friedrich. *On Religion: Speeches to Its Cultured Despisers*. 3rd Edition. Translated by John Oman. London: Paul, Trench, Trubner, 1893.
Smith, James K. A. *Desiring the Kingdom: Worship, Worldviews, and Cultural Formation*. Grand Rapids: Baker Academic, 2009.
Smith, James K. A. *Imagining the Kingdom: How Worship Works*. Grand Rapids: Baker Academic, 2013.
Sonderegger, Katherine. 'The Doctrine of God'. In *The Oxford Handbook of Reformed Theology*, 389–403. Edited by Michael Allen and Scott Swain. Oxford: Oxford University Press, 2021.
Strange, Daniel. *Their Rock Is Not Like Our Rock: A Theology of Religions*. Grand Rapids: Zondervan, 2015.
Sung, Elizabeth. '"Racial Realism" in Biblical Interpretation and Theological Anthropology: A Systematic-Theological Evaluation of Recent Accounts'. *Ex Auditu* 31 (2015): 3–21.
Sutanto, Nathaniel Gray. 'Christian Worldview: Context, Classical Contours, and Significance'. *Reformed Faith and Practice* 5 (2020): 28–39.
Sutanto, Nathaniel Gray. 'Confessional, International, and Cosmopolitan: Herman Bavinck's Neo-Calvinistic and Protestant Vision of the Catholicity of the Church'. *Journal of Reformed Theology* 12 (2018): 22–39.
Sutanto, Nathaniel Gray. 'Consummation Anyway: A Reformed Proposal'. *Journal of Analytic Theology* 9 (2021): 223–37.

Sutanto, Nathaniel Gray. 'Divine Providence's *Wetenschappelijke* Benefits: A Bavinckian Model'. In *Action and Providence: Explorations in Constructive Dogmatics*, 96–114. Edited by Fred Sanders and Oliver Crisp. Grand Rapids: Zondervan, 2019.

Sutanto, Nathaniel Gray. 'Egocentricity, Metaphysics, and Organism: Sin and Renewal in Bavinck's *Ethics*'. *Studies in Christian Ethics* 34 (2021): 223–40.

Sutanto, Nathaniel Gray. '*Gevoel* and Illumination: Bavinck, Augustine, and Bonaventure on Awareness of God'. *Pro Ecclesia* 30 (2021): 265–78.

Sutanto, Nathaniel Gray. *God and Knowledge: Herman Bavinck's Theological Epistemology*. London: Bloomsbury T&T Clark, 2020.

Sutanto, Nathaniel Gray. 'Herman Bavinck and Thomas Reid on Perception and Knowing God'. *Harvard Theological Review* 111 (2018): 115–34.

Sutanto, Nathaniel Gray. 'Herman Bavinck on the Image of God and Original Sin'. *International Journal of Systematic Theology* 18 (2016): 174–90.

Sutanto, Nathaniel Gray. 'Neocalvinism and General Revelation: A Dogmatic Sketch'. *International Journal of Systematic Theology* 20 (2018): 494–516.

Sutanto, Nathaniel Gray. 'Questioning Bonaventure's Augustinianism?: On the Noetic Effects of Sin'. *New Blackfriars* 102 (2021): 401–17.

Sutanto, Nathaniel Gray and Cory Brock, Editors. *T&T Clark Handbook of Neo-Calvinism*. London: Bloomsbury T&T Clark, 2024.

Swain, Scott. 'Covenant of Redemption'. In *Christian Dogmatics: Reformed Theology for the Church Catholic*, 112–30. Edited by Michael Allen and Scott Swain. Grand Rapids: Baker Academic, 2016.

Sytsma, David. 'The Logic of the Heart: Analyzing the Affections in Early Reformed Orthodoxy'. In *Church and School in Early Modern Protestantism: Studies in Honor of Richard A. Muller on the Maturation of a Theological Tradition*, 471–88. Edited by Jordan Ballor, David Systma, and Jason Zuidema. Leiden: Brill, 2013.

Tiele, C. P. *Inleiding tot de godsdienstwetenschap*. 2 Volumes. 2nd Edition. Amsterdam: P. N. Van Kampen & Zoon, 1900.

Tisby, Jemar. *How to Fight Racism: Courageous Christianity and the Journey toward Racial Justice*. Grand Rapids: Zondervan, 2021.

Tran, Jonathan. *Asian Americans and the Spirit of Racial Capitalism*. Oxford: Oxford University Press, 2021.

Troeltsch, Ernst. 'Die Christliche Religion: Mit einschluss der Israelitsch-Jüdischen Religion'. In *Die Kultur der Gegenwart* I. VI. Leipzig: Teubner, 1905.

Turner, James T. 'Perfect Obedience, Perfect Love, and the (So-Called) Problem of Heavenly Freedom'. In *Love, Divine and Human: Contemporary Essays in Systematic and Philosophical Theology*, 239–57. Edited by Oliver Crisp, James M. Arcadi, and Jordan Wessseling. London: Bloomsbury; T&T Clark, 2019.

Turretin, Francis. *Institutes of Elenctic Theology*. 3 Volumes. Edited by James T. Dennison. Translated by George M. Giger. Philipsburg: P&R, 1997.

Vanden Born, Jack, Nelson Kloosterman, and John Bolt. 'Translator's Introduction'. In 'Foundations of Psychology'. Translated by Jack Vanden Born, Nelson Kloosterman, and John Bolt. *The Bavinck Review* 9 (2018): 1–270.

Van den Brink, Gijsbert. *Reformed Theology and Evolutionary Theory*. Grand Rapids: Eerdmans, 2020.

Van Dixhoorn, Chad. *Confessing the Faith: A Reader's Guide to the Westminster Confession of Faith*. Banner of Truth, 2014.

Van Driel, Edwin Chr. *Incarnation Anyway: Arguments for Supralapsarian Christology*. Oxford: University Press, 2008.

Van Eyghen, Hans, Rik Peels, and Gijsbert van den Brink. 'The Cognitive Science of Religion, Philosophy, and Theology: A Survey of the Issues'. In *New Developments in the Cognitive Science of Religion: The Rationality of Religious Belief*, 1–15. Edited by Hans Van Eyghen, Rik Peels, and Gijsbert van den Brink. Cham: Springer, 2018.

Vanhoozer, Kevin. *Biblical Authority after Babel: Retrieving the Solas in the Spirit of Mere Protestant Christianity*. Grand Rapids: Brazos, 2016.

Van Huyssteen, J. Wentzel. *Alone in the World? Human Uniqueness in Science and Theology*. Grand Rapids: Eerdmans, 2006.

Van Keulen, Dirk. 'Herman Bavinck's *Reformed Ethics*: Some Remarks about Unpublished Manuscripts in the Libraries of Amsterdam and Kampen'. *The Bavinck Review* 1 (2010): 25–56.

Van Mastricht, Petrus. *Theoretical-Practical Theology*. 4 Volumes. Edited by Joel Beeke. Translated by Todd Rester. Grand Rapids: Reformation Heritage Books, 2022.

Vilmar, A. *Theologische Moral: Akademische Vorlesungen*. Gütersloh: Bertelsmann, 1871.

Visala, Aku. 'Human Cognition and the Image of God'. In *The Christian Doctrine of Humanity: Explorations in Constructive Dogmatics*, 91–110. Edited by Fred Sanders and Oliver Crisp. Grand Rapids: Zondervan, 2018.

Vorster, Nico. 'African Decolonization and Reformed Theology'. In *Reformed Public Theology: A Global Vision for Life in the World*, 47–69. Edited by Matthew Kaemingk. Grand Rapids: Baker Academic, 2021.

Vos, Geerhardus. 'The Eschatological Aspect of the Pauline Conception of the Spirit.' In *Redemptive History and Biblical Interpretation: The Shorter Writings of Geerardus Vos*, 91–125. Edited by Richard B. Gaffin. Phillipsburg: Presbyterian & Reformed Publishing, 1980.

Vos, Pieter. 'Calvinists among the Virtues: Reformed Theological Contributions to Contemporary Virtue Ethics'. *Studies in Christian Ethics* 28 (2015): 201–12.

Ward, Graham. *How the Light Gets In: Ethical Life I*. Oxford: Oxford University Press, 2016.

Webster, John. *Confessing God*. London: Bloomsbury T&T Clark, 2005.

White, Clair. 'What Does Cognitive Science of Religion Explain?'. In *New Developments in the Cognitive Science of Religion: The Rationality of Religious Belief*, 35–49. Edited by Hans Van Eyghen, Rik Peels, and Gijsbert van den Brink. Cham: Springer, 2018.

Williams, Rowan. *On Augustine*. London: Bloomsbury, 2016.

Wilson, Stephen A. *Virtue Reformed: Rereading Jonathan Edwards's Ethics*. Leiden: Brill, 2005.

Wolfe, Judith. *Heidegger's Eschatology: Theological Horizon's in Martin Heidegger's Early Work*. Oxford: Oxford University Press, 2013.

Wood, William. *Analytic Theology and The Academic Study of Religion*. Oxford: Oxford University Press, 2021.

Wrathall, Mark. 'Introduction'. In *Skillful Coping: Essays on the Phenomenology of Everyday Perception and Action*, 1–22. Edited by Mark Wrathall. Oxford: Oxford University Press, 2014.

Yadav, Sameer. 'Religious Racial Formation Theory and Its Metaphysics: A Research Program in the Philosophy of Religion'. In *The Lost Sheep in Philosophy of Religion: New Perspectives on Disability, Gender, Race, and Animals*, 365–90. Edited by Blake Hereth and Kevin Timpe. New York: Routledge, 2020.

Zachhuber, Johannes. 'The Historical Turn'. In *The Oxford Handbook of Nineteenth-Century Christian Thought*, 53–71. Edited by Joel D. S. Rasmussen, Judith Wolfe, and Johannes Zachhuber. Oxford: Oxford University Press, 2017.

Zahl, Simeon. 'On the Affective Salience of Doctrine'. *Modern Theology* 31 (2015): 428–44.

Zahl, Simeon. *The Holy Spirit and Christian Experience*. Oxford: Oxford University Press, 2021.

Ziegler, Philip. '"Those He Also Glorified"': Some Reformed Perspectives on Human Nature and Destiny'. *Studies in Christian Ethics* 32 (2019): 165–76.

INDEX

Adam
   Christ as second 158, 174–6, 179, 182–3
   and consummation 177–9, 184
   covenant with God (*see* covenant, of works)
   as federal head 1, 9, 13, 15, 104–8, 174, 202
   sin of 1, 15, 160
Adams, Marilyn McCord 170 n.3, 171
affect theory 8–9, 18, 42–4, 48, 51–2, 55, 58–9, 62–7, 69–71, 73–5, 80, 91–3, 95–6, 99–100, 166, 201
affective
   dimension of revelation 49, 52, 73, 83, 154
   knowledge 70, 79–81, 202
agency-detecting device 67, 69–70, 76, 100
Allen, Michael 7, 116 n.52, 185 n.1
Allison, Henry 133 n.44
apartheid 125, 127–8
Aquinas, Thomas 89, 99, 181, 194
Aristotle 20, 94
Aryanism 130–1, 134–6, 138, 141, 202
asceticism 116, 118
atomism 112
Augustine 14, 29, 39, 85, 120
   inner sense of the self 34–5, 49–50
Ayres, Lewis 8 n.16, 14 n.44

Bacote, Vincent 123 n.1, 126 n.12, 127–8, 135
Barret, Justin 64, 65 n.84
Barth, Karl 121, 202
Bauckham, Richard 164 n.75
Bavinck, Johan Herman 97 n.80, 98, 156 n.40, 160 n.58
beatific vision 1–2, 5, 8–9, 167, 174, 184–92, 194, 196–9, 200, 203
Biddiss, Michael 134 n.52, 135, 138
Bildung tradition 104, 120–1, 167, 202

body–soul relation 1–2, 5–6, 8, 10–13, 17–20, 22, 28, 30, 39, 41, 201
Boersma, Hans 185 n.1, 188, 191, 194, 196
Boesak, Allan 125, 126 n.8
Bonaventure 92 n.65, 181, 194
Botman, H. Russell 127
Bowleg, Lisa 125 n.5
Bratt, James 97 n.80, 127 n.13, 140
Brock, Cory 3, 4 n.5, 34 n.76, 45–7, 48 n.18, 49, 50 n.26, 82, 163 n.72, 185, 193 n.35, 197–8

Calvin, John 5, 86, 91, 97, 154
   sensus divinitatis 45, 47, 76–7, 88–9
Carter, J. Kameron 132 n.37, 134–6
catholicity 156–8, 162, 164, 203
Chalcedon 186, 196–7
Chamberlain, Houston S. 134–5, 137, 141, 143
Clark, Kelly James 65–7, 69
Cochran, Elizabeth Agnew 119, 120 n.65
cognitive faculties 25, 65, 76–9, 84–5, 88–9, 91. *See also* faculty, of knowing
cognitive science of religion 6, 8–9, 18, 42, 44, 55, 63–71, 75–6, 81, 84–6, 88–92, 99, 201–2
cognitively natural theism 73, 79, 81, 89
colonialism 147–8, 150, 166–7
common grace 48–9, 97–9, 124, 126, 155–6
compulsion 55, 57–8
consummated new nature 176–7
consummation anyway 169–71, 174–80, 183–4, 203
Cortez, Marc 99, 170–1, 174–6, 184, 203
covenant
   of grace 104, 106, 172, 181, 183, 193, 195
   theology 8–9, 14, 107, 158, 172, 175, 183, 199, 203
   of works 104, 106, 129, 172, 174–8, 183–5, 190, 193, 203

Creator-creature distinction 81–2, 130–1, 169, 187, 192, 199
Crenshaw, Kimberlé 125 n.5
Crisp, Oliver 119–20, 170 n.3, 171
critical race theory 125
CSR. *See* cognitive science of religion
culture
    leavened by Christianity 162
    multiformity of 123, 143–4, 150–1, 163, 165–6

decolonization theology 126
De Cruz, Helen and Johan De Smedt 76, 77 n.10, 80, 90 n.60, 125 n.5
Dennett, Daniel 64 n.82
Diller, Kevin 88 n.52
Dreyfus, Hubert 47, 52–3, 55, 73, 75, 86–7, 92–5, 99
Duby, Steven 46 n.9, 48 n.19, 50 n.25, 120 n.64, 181 n.40

Edwards, Jonathan 104, 107, 202
    moral theology of 119–20
Eglinton, James 4, 7, 22 n.23, 105 n.6, 127 n.17, 129, 156 n.40, 162 n.68, 164 n.75, 166 n.83, 167 n.88, 185 n.1
egocentricity 9, 103, 111–13, 202
Engelke, Matthew 138 n.69, 140 n.78, 150, 166 n.84
entrainment 55–7
eugenics 137, 139–41
Euro-centrism 9, 122–3, 141, 166
Everhart, D. T. 159 n.53
evolutionary theory
    and religious phenomena 54, 62, 64, 76–8, 154
    social 109, 123, 133, 137–9, 142, 145, 147–52, 156

Fabian, Johannes 151
faculty
    of desiring 12, 17, 21, 23–4, 28–30, 41
    God 69–70
    of knowing 13, 17, 21, 23, 25–30, 41, 61, 95 (*see also* cognitive faculties)
    psychology 5, 18, 26, 41
Farris, Joshua Ryan 99 n.91
federalism 1–2, 103, 107, 120, 202. *See also* Adam, as federal head

feeling
    of absolute dependence 3, 45–6, 48–51, 70, 83, 87, 90
    as an activity of the soul 12, 22–4, 28, 31, 33, 35, 37, 39, 46, 52, 58, 61–2
Feser, Edward 100 n.95
Fesko, John V. 175 n.22

God
    communion with 9, 77–9, 99, 169, 186, 189–99
    transcendence of 14, 81–2, 156
Gospel 90, 161
    affective experience of 74–5, 98
    as a leavening agent 104, 118
Gould, Paul and James Dew 49 n.23
grace 73, 75, 104, 121, 202–3
    and consummation 171–5, 184
    super-added 192
grace restores nature 157–8, 193–4
Green, Adam 57 n.56, 65 n.84
guilt 2, 59, 74, 110, 175, 179
    Adam's 1, 15, 107
    communal 108, 159–60

Haeckel, Ernst 33, 39 n.96
Harinck, George 127 n.16, 128, 129 n.25, 163
Harris, Harriet 100
Haslanger, Sally 59 n.64, 130
Hegel, Georg W. F. 137, 153, 154 n.31
Heidegger, Martin 94
    phenomenology of 43–4, 47, 51–5, 60, 75, 86–7, 99, 201
Helm, Paul 5 n.7, 17 n.1, 18 n.3, 20 n.13, 21
Herdt, Jennifer 104, 115, 117 n.54, 120–1, 165, 202
historicism 32, 133, 136, 141–2, 148. *See also* evolutionary theory, social
history 1, 22, 62, 156, 181–2, 185
    and diversity of humanity 141–5, 151–2, 158
    and ethics 133–8, 167, 202
    of psychology 17–20
    redemptive 98, 148
Holy Spirit 113, 177, 179, 197
    illumination by 91
    transformed by 38, 74, 104, 162
    unity through 15, 113–16, 119, 121, 143, 164

humanity
    as an organism 4, 7, 15, 103–5, 109, 112–17, 121, 124, 142, 156, 158, 161, 185, 190, 202
    redemption of 8, 104, 112–13, 128, 142, 144, 156, 160, 180–3, 185
Hunter, Justus 176 n.24, 178 n.27, 180–1

idolatry 78–9, 89–92, 142, 192, 202
illumination 3, 49–50, 91
image of God 10–11, 51, 62, 130, 141, 189, 193, 197
    as corporate 2, 6–7, 9, 103–9, 115, 129, 156, 158, 166, 202
    embodied 5–6, 11–12, 22
    and sin 97–8, 103, 112, 124, 159
    structural account of 13, 74, 99–101
implicit beliefs 81, 84–90, 95–6
impossibility thesis 176. *See also* consummation anyway
inaugurated new nature 176–7
incarnation anyway 169–71, 178, 180–1, 183
Ince, Irwin 7 n.12
individualism 109, 112, 138
infralapsarianism 182–4
Inkpin, Andrew 47, 48 n.16, 95 n.77
inner sense of the self. *See under* Augustine
intransigence 38, 51, 58–9, 61, 65, 73–5, 92, 96, 101

Jaarsma, Cornelius 17 n.1, 41, 42 n.110
Jennings, Willie James 123, 128 n.18, 132 n.37, 134–5, 147–8, 155, 162–3
Jesus Christ 42, 74–5, 99
    as federal head 9, 13, 15, 103–7, 158
    imitation of 115, 118, 174
    incarnation of 171, 174, 176, 180–1, 185–9
    as mediator between God and humanity 83, 180, 182–3, 190–2, 194–200
    restoring unity-in-diversity of humanity 113–14, 135–6, 143–4, 157, 161, 164
Jochemsen, Henk and Garrit Glas 121 n.69
John of Damascus 188
Johnson, Dru 56 n.54 58

Johnson, Mark 57–8
Jones, Paul Dafydd 52 n.35
Jong, Jonathan, Christopher Kavanagh, and Aku Visala 85, 89
Joustra, Jessica 5–6, 129 n.27

Kaemingk, Matthew 155 n.38
Kant, Immanuel 34–5, 46, 55, 87, 106, 121
    and moral law 131–3
Kevles, Daniel J. 139 n.75
Kilby, Karen 14 n.45
kingdom of God
    and the church 161
    and personality 38, 115–16
    as telos 169, 198
    unity-in-diversity of 15, 119, 121, 123, 157–8, 162–3, 165, 202
knowledge
    conceptual 23, 46–7, 86, 93–5
    pre-theoretical 7, 23, 28, 53, 61, 91–2
knowledge of God 133, 153
    natural 73, 75–6, 79–80, 84–6
    pre-cognitive 81, 83, 87–90, 94, 96–7
    universal 147, 157
Kuiper, D. Th. 137 n.64
Kuyper, Abraham 7, 9, 123–9, 144–5, 203

Lapine, Matthew 20 n.13
Launonen, Lari and Ryan T. Mullins 81, 84–6, 89–90
Leiden Synopsis 22, 43, 163, 199
Leidenhag, Joanna 80 n.22
Levering, Matthew 99, 101 n.98
Lewinsky, Monica and Max Joseph 57
linguistic fallacy 51, 53–4, 59, 93
Liou, Jeff 124, 125, 128, 129, 136, 164 n.75
Lubbock, John 149
Lutheranism 74–5, 186, 188–9, 196

MacDonald, Scott 50 n.26
MacIntyre, Alasdair 120 n.64, 121 n.69
materialism 1, 18, 20–1, 32, 35, 38, 53, 62–3
Mattson, Brian 4–5, 6 n.9, 172 n.10, 174–5, 193 n.35
McCall, Thomas 14 n.43, 107
McDonald, Suzanne 190–1
McDowell, John 86–7, 93
McFarland, Ian 81–3, 107, 188 n.13

McNabb, Tyler 65 n.83, 69, 86 n.41
Methodism 116–18
missions 118, 147, 150
Molendijk, Arie 148 n.5, 149 n.9, 150, 153
monism 137–8, 142–4, 151
Mouw, Richard 127–8, 155 n.36
Mullins, Ryan T. 81, 84–6, 89–90
multiformity 144, 151, 162. *See also* unity-in-diversity
mystical union 34, 186–8, 196–9
mysticism 116, 186–7, 197

nationalism 9, 131, 134, 137, 144
    German 6, 119, 121–2, 130, 135–6, 141
natural religion 85, 90, 192
natural theology 48–9, 82
nature-grace relation 11, 185, 192–4
Nelson, Derek 160 n.55

Ong, Andrew 167 n.86
onto-phenomenology 51, 53–4, 58–60, 92, 96
organic motif 10, 185
Orr, James 151 n.15
Oviedo, Lluis 63 n.79, 67
Owen, John 186, 190–2, 196

para-cognition 51, 55–9, 63, 71, 92, 96, 101
Pass, Bruce 3, 192 n.28
Patterson, Jennifer 193 n.35
Pedersen, Daniel 90 n.60
Peels, Rik 76–80
Peppiatt, Lucy 42 n.110, 99 n.91
Perkins, Harrison 173 n.15, 193 n.35
personality
    and the body 12, 39–40, 42
    definition of 17–18
    free 115–16, 121
    of God 70
    and revelation 45, 60–2, 71, 80
    and sin 13, 92, 159
    and the unconscious 22–7, 29–30, 32–4, 36–8, 41, 100, 201
phenomenology 3, 6, 8, 19, 42, 58–9, 62–3, 74–5, 80, 91–3, 132, 201 (*see also* Heidegger, Martin, phenomenology of)
Pietism 116–17

Plantinga, Alvin 66 n.85, 77 n.10, 88 n.50
Plato 11, 20, 29, 35, 93
Powery, Luke A. 140
protestant principle 184, 186, 193–4, 196, 199
psychology 12, 17–21, 30, 34, 39. *See also* faculty, psychology
    empirical 31–3, 61–3
    religious 69, 97

racism 7, 9, 130–1, 166–7. *See also* Euro-centricism
    origins of 123, 133–4, 136, 145, 156, 165, 202
Ralston, Joshua 154–5
Rasmussen, Joel D. S. 132 n.37
realism 1, 2, 107, 202
redemption
    Christ's work of 170, 176, 178, 180–3
    corporate 104, 112–13, 142–4, 160
relativism 32, 136, 163, 166
religion. *See also* cognitive science of religion
    origins of 147–56
revelation 14, 30–3, 61, 96, 99, 122, 135, 139, 141–4, 167
    general 8–9, 43, 45–50, 52, 60, 62, 65, 69–71, 73–6, 78–81, 83–92, 153–5, 165
    incarnation as 180–1, 183, 185
Riccucci, Norma 127
Roman Catholicism
    anthropology 11, 110, 192–3
    on beatific vision 187–9, 191–2, 195–6
    on sin 112

sanctification 38, 59, 74–5, 118
Schaefer, Donovan O. 43–4, 51–9, 62
Schilder, Klass 167 n.85
Schleiermacher, Friedrich 3, 46, 108, 154, 160
Scholasticism 14, 20, 25–6, 47–8, 85, 188
Seals, Zachary 197 n.50
self-consciousness 22–32, 45–6, 49–50, 53–5, 60, 153
sin 162, 193
    collective 14, 159–60
    and culture 140, 151
    and egocentricity (*see* egocentricity)

psychical effects of 8–9, 13, 18, 73–5, 78, 87, 92, 96–7
systemic 124–5
transmission of 1–2, 105–10
skillful coping 73, 75, 86–7, 92–6, 101
Smith, James K. A. 47 n.12, 96 n.79
social trinitarianism 14
Sonderegger, Katherine 89 n.53
soul
and body (*see* body–soul relation)
and personality 17–18, 24–5, 36, 38–41
and revelation 30–3, 70
and the unconscious 24–30, 33–5, 37, 61–3, 94
unity of 20–1
Strange, Daniel 156 n.40
Sung, Elizabeth 124 n.1
supersessionism 134, 141
suppression 75–6, 78–80, 92, 95–6, 98–9
supralapsarianism 182–4
Swain, Scott 181 n.40
Sytsma, David 20 n.14

theism 14, 69, 84–6, 89
theism-tracking 84–6, 89
theory of mind 67–70, 76, 100
Tiele, Cornelis P. 149, 152–3
Tisby, Jemar 7 n.12
Tran, Jonathan 125 n.5
Trinity 7, 9, 13, 107, 202
Troeltsch, Ernst 152 n.23
Turner, James T. 169, 176–7
Turretin, Francis 5 n.7, 17 n.1, 154, 173, 174 n.18, 193 n.35, 199 n.58

unity-in-diversity
of body and soul 12, 42, 32
of God 10
humanity as 8–9, 13–14, 104–5, 107, 113, 129, 143, 158, 167

Van den Brink, Gijsbert 64 n.80, 65 n.83, 76–80, 142 n.87
Van Dixhoorn, Chad 173 n.14
Van Driel, Edwin Chr. 170 n.3, 171
Van Eyghen, Hans 65 n.83, 77 n.11
Vanhoozer, Kevin 187 n.7
Van Huyssteen, J. Wentzel 100 n.97
Van Keulen, Dirk 119 n.62
Van Mastricht, Petrus 5 n.7, 12 n.29, 173 n.13
Vilmar, August 110 n.24
Visala, Aku 68, 85, 89 n.54, 99–100, 101 n.98
Vorster, Nico 126
Vos, Pieter 120 n.64, 121

Ward, Graham 56–7
Webster, John 7, 8 n.16
White, Clair 67, 68 n.93, 69 n.96
Williams, Rowan 50–1, 100 n.96
Wolfe, Judith 48 n.16, 132 n.37
Wood, William 56 n.54
Wrathall, Mark 47 n.14, 52 n.31

Yadav, Sameer 130 n.34, 166 n.84

Zachhuber, Johannes 132 n.37
Zahl, Simeon 43 n.2, 59, 73–5
Ziegler, Philip 5–6, 104 n.1, 114 n.43

www.ingramcontent.com/pod-product-compliance
Lightning Source LLC
Chambersburg PA
CBHW052108300426
44116CB00010B/1579